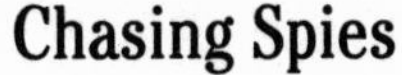

Chasing Spies

ATHAN THEOHARIS

Chasing Spies

How the FBI Failed in Counterintelligence But Promoted the Politics of McCarthyism in the Cold War Years

Ivan R. Dee
CHICAGO 2002

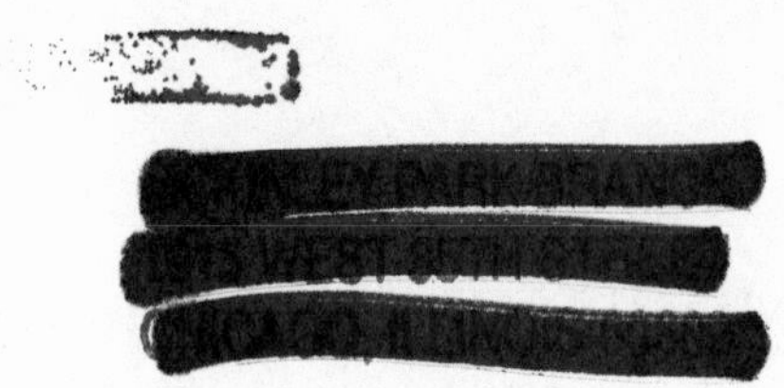

 For information, address: Ivan R. Dee, Publisher, 1332 North Halsted Street, Chicago 60622. Manufactured in the United States of America and printed on acid-free paper.

Library of Congress Cataloging-in-Publication Data:
Theoharis, Athan G.

Chasing spies : how the FBI failed in counterintelligence but promoted the politics of McCarthyism in the Cold War years / Athan Theoharis.

p. cm.

Includes bibliographical references and index.

ISBN 1-56663-420-2 (alk. paper)

1. Intelligence service—United States. 2. United States. Federal Bureau of Investigation—History—20th century. 3. Espionage, Soviet—United States. 4. Cold War. 5. United States—Politics and government—1945–1989. I. Title.

UB251.U5 T44 2002
327.1273047'09'045—dc21 2001047399

To Nancy,

for whom Micah 6:8 has always been a calling

Acknowledgments

I HAVE ACCRUED a number of debts in researching and writing this book. I am greatly indebted to the Field Foundation, the Warsh-Mott Funds, the C. S. Fund, and the Fund for Investigative Journalism for funding my numerous Freedom of Information Act requests; and the Roosevelt Institute and the Truman Institute for funding my research at the Roosevelt and Truman presidential libraries. The staff of the FBI's Freedom of Information Act section, particularly Robert Watson and Linda Kloss Colton, efficiently processed my various FOIA requests while the staff at the Roosevelt and Truman presidential libraries provided invaluable assistance and direction. John Donovan, Patrick Jung, Cathleen Thom, Christopher Gerard, and Seth Rosenfeld provided invaluable research assistance. Excerpts from Chapter Six have been published in *Rhetoric & Public Affairs* (Vol. 2, No. 3, 1999). Steven Avella and Deborah Koller of Marquette University provided crucial instruction and encouragement, enabling me to acquire rudimentary competence in the use of a word processor. Finally, I am once again indebted to Ivan Dee, whose thoughtful and demanding editing immeasurably refined and sharpened the narrative.

A. T.

Milwaukee, Wisconsin
January 2002

Contents

	Acknowledgments	vii
	Preface: The Hazards of Research into Soviet and American Secrets	3
1	The Soviet Espionage Threat	15
2	The Failure of U.S. Counterintelligence	34
3	The Comintern Apparatus Investigation	62
4	The Counterintelligence Dilemma: Containment or Law Enforcement?	79
5	Politicizing Justice: The Hiss and Remington Indictments	110
6	The Politics of Counterintelligence	139
7	The Politics of Morality	170
8	The Perils of Partisanship	198
9	The Lessons of History	235
	Notes	251
	Index	295

Chasing Spies

Preface: The Hazards of Research into Soviet and American Secrets

THE END of the cold war, with the collapse of Communist governments in Eastern Europe and the former Soviet Union, suggested an end to restrictions on research into Soviet espionage activities in the United States and the American response. The new Russian leadership had no vested interest in safeguarding the secrets of Soviet espionage activities; in Washington, national security considerations no longer barred the release of information about FBI counterintelligence operations directed at Soviet agents and their American recruits. Theoretically the post–cold war era would bring about unprecedented access to formerly secret records. The reality, however, proved to be less promising. Archival materials became relatively more open, but restrictions ensured an incomplete, possibly distorted understanding of Soviet intelligence and U.S. counterintelligence activities.

Ironically, researchers temporarily found easier access to Soviet than to U.S. secrets. During the early 1990s, American scholars were able to peruse the records of the Soviet Union's secretive intelligence agency (the KGB and its predecessors); the Comintern; and the national headquarters of the American Communist party (deposited in Moscow).

The most promising research opportunity proved at the same time to be the most problematic: the temporary if restricted opening of KGB records. In 1993, Albert Vitale, president of Random House publishers, entered into a unique agreement with Russia's Foreign Intelligence Service (SVR). Under this contract, in return for "payments" to the Association of Retired Intelligence (KGB) Officers reportedly totalling half a million dollars, SVR officials granted former KGB agent Alexander Vassiliev, who was a researcher for the American scholar Allen Weinstein, "substantial and exclusive access to Stalin-era operational files of the KGB and its predecessor agencies." Until 1995, Vassiliev was allowed to "review archived documents and to make summaries or verbatim transcriptions from the files." His notes were then submitted to a panel of the SVR's "leading officials for review and eventual release." After 1995, however, SVR officials became "less cooperative about providing timely release," then in 1996 they ended all such assistance. In addition, Weinstein and Vassiliev claimed, "a great deal of additional and unreviewed KGB material reached us informally from other, non-KGB sources."[1]

Vassiliev's—and thus Weinstein's—privileged access to KGB records raises a series of questions apart from the fact that their access was purchased. In the book they produced from their research, the two authors fail to disclose the criteria that determined which of the KGB's massive records were archived and thus could be reviewed. This agency, after all, was responsible for criminal investigations and internal security within the Soviet Union and even more extensive foreign intelligence—not only in the United States but in Europe, Asia, Africa, and South America. Thus there arise a series of questions: Which KGB records were not archived? Was Vassiliev allowed to review archived records because he was a former KGB agent and thus would not compromise sensitive programs and procedures? Or had he been granted unlimited and unhindered access to all KGB records, subject only to limitations of time (he made twelve research trips)? Did SVR officials allow Vassiliev to review indices or finding aids to identify the most valuable files? Or did SVR officials simply provide files on individuals named by Weinstein? Were Vassiliev's notes censored, and if so, what information was withheld? Was the SVR's "informal" assistance random or in response to specific record requests?

Vassiliev's privileged access poses a second problem. Because other interested scholars cannot review the KGB records he researched, the accuracy of his paraphrased and quoted notes cannot be verified. This is no incidental matter, for questions of accuracy and comprehensiveness are at the heart of historians' conflicting interpretations of Soviet espionage and the American response. For example, Vassiliev's translations of these documents might convey too sinister a feeling, considering that the KGB agents writing these reports had a bureaucratic and career interest in exaggerating both their successes in recruiting sources and the uniqueness of the information they were reporting. There is the additional matter of the mind-set and experiences of KGB agents. The openness of the American political system, and the willingness of American bureaucrats (in addition to White House aides and congressional staff) to share "secrets" with reporters and political associates, would make it easier for a KGB agent to obtain information about U.S. policy and priorities that in the United States would not be considered espionage.

A comparable situation of open, then shut policy also shaped research into Comintern and American Communist party records. These were held in Moscow at the Russian Center for the Preservation and Study of Documents of Recent History. Unlike Weinstein and Vassiliev, the American scholars John Haynes and Harvey Klehr did not purchase access to these records, nor were they required to clear their research notes with archival officials. After the failed coup against Mikhail Gorbachev in 1991, the Russian government under Boris Yeltsin seized the records of the Soviet Communist party, including those relating to the Comintern and the American Communist party headquarters, and temporarily opened them to scholarly research. Traveling to Moscow in 1992, 1993, and 1994, Haynes and Klehr were able to review "virtually all" these records, subject only to their time limitations. In follow-up research trips in 1995 and 1996, however, Haynes discovered that some of the Comintern files he had consulted earlier "had been closed," and that records pertaining to the American Communist party's "contacts" with Moscow "were open to research, [but] some had been closed for security reasons." By this time Haynes and Klehr had also learned that the records of the American Communist party deposited in Moscow "end with material from 1944." They were unable to determine whether American Communist party headquarters records after that date were not sent to Moscow or "were placed in a repository that remains closed."[2]

The research findings of Weinstein, Klehr, and Haynes clearly enrich our understanding of Soviet espionage activities in the United States during the 1930s and early 1940s. Still, until restrictions are lifted and other scholars are given uncensored access to all relevant records, including those not archived or separately maintained, the scope and significance of Soviet espionage operations cannot be fully reconstructed. Why this is so will be demonstrated throughout this book.

The 1990s produced another important source documenting Soviet espionage activities: U.S. military intelligence's highly secret, code-named Venona Project. Its records were released in July 1995, when Russian officials were first limiting and then curbing research into KGB records.

The Venona Project began after the outbreak of World War II in September 1939, with the German invasion of Poland. A month earlier the Soviet Union had concluded a mutual nonaggression pact with Germany, under which the Soviets acquired free rein to annex the Baltic states and parts of Poland, Finland, and Romania.

This treaty lasted until the German invasion of the Soviet Union in June 1941. The United States, the Soviet Union, and Great Britain did not become military allies against the Axis powers until December 1941. But while the United States was still formally neutral, military intelligence officers in the Army Security Agency (later renamed the National Security Agency, NSA) began in 1940 to intercept both German and Soviet consular messages, and specifically those of the Soviet consulate in New York City and the Soviet embassy in Washington, D.C. This interception program was later authorized by the War Powers Act of 1941. Under Executive Order 8895, President Franklin D. Roosevelt created an Office of Censorship to monitor "mail, cable, radio and other means of transmission passing between the United States and any foreign country." Even after the U.S.-Soviet alliance, military intelligence continued to screen "all international message traffic," including Soviet consular messages, by effecting an arrangement with the three international telegraph companies—RCA Global, ITT World Communications, and Western Union International—an arrangement that began in 1940 and continued until 1948.

Because the intercepted Soviet messages were sent in code, a special unit within the Military Intelligence Division was created in 1943 to attempt to decipher these messages. The first breakthrough in this effort came in 1946. Over the next thirty-four years, military intelligence analysts eventually deciphered 2,900 of these intercepted messages. In the process they discovered that Soviet agents operating out of Soviet consular offices in New York City and Washington had engaged in espionage and had successfully recruited sources in various federal agencies and departments, some of whom were American Communist party members. But the names of the Soviet agents and their sources were disguised under special code names.

Seeking to identify the code-named individuals, military intelligence operatives asked for help from the FBI in 1948 and then from the CIA in 1952. Together with these agencies, military intelligence eventually identified the real names of most of the Soviet agents and approximately half of their American sources. NSA officials released the first batch—numbering 49 messages—of the deciphered 2,900 messages in July 1995 and the remainder over the next two years.[3]

The released Venona messages constitute a potentially invaluable source for the understanding of Soviet espionage activities and the U.S. counterintelligence response. Yet, just as Russian officials restricted research into Soviet records, CIA and NSA officials have released only the deciphered texts of the intercepted Soviet consular messages, and no other relevant records. Those withheld include the internal correspondence of NSA analysts, documenting how they first translated the messages and then identified the disguised code-named Soviet agents, and, just as important, the FBI reports upon which these identifications were made.* Both these materials would advance our understanding of Soviet espionage and the American response.

Release of the Russian language text is essential. How specific phrasings were translated can help resolve whether a Soviet agent's relationship with a source was an espionage or political intelligence operation, and further whether the reports of Soviet agents exaggerated their achievements and source contacts.† The withheld re-

*When processing my FOIA request for the minutes of the FBI Executive Conference in 2001, the FBI withheld all records pertaining to FBI participation in the Venona project. Withheld six years after NSA and CIA officials publicly released the deciphered Soviet consular messages, these records include at least eight memos from the FBI Executive Conference to the FBI Director: April 20, 1950, FBI 66-2554-7683; April 21, 1950, FBI 66-2554-7679; April 21, 1950, FBI 66-2554-7885; June 12, 1950, FBI 66-2554-7853; September 20, 1950, FBI 66-2554-8098; January 9, 1952, FBI 66-2554-9337; March 6, 1952, FBI 66-2554-9462; March 18, 1952, FBI 66-2554-9522.

†An FBI analyst made this same point in May 1950 in the context of emphasizing the difficulty of identifying individuals who had been disguised

ports would also document how NSA analysts were able to identify the names of the Soviet agents and their American sources disguised through code names. The FBI reports upon which these identifications were based have a further research value: they comprise a contemporary record of FBI surveillance activities during the 1930s and 1940s. These records would provide insights into the FBI's counterintelligence failure—why FBI officials, despite the intensity of FBI monitoring of Soviet and Communist activities during the 1930s and 1940s, failed to uncover Soviet agents and their American contacts, or develop admissible evidence for their prosecution.

Despite having successfully deciphered the Venona messages, military intelligence officials never briefed President Harry Truman on this major breakthrough.[4] During an October 1949 meeting with General Carter Clarke, chief of the then-named Armed Forces Security Agency, FBI agent Howard Fletcher learned that Clarke had decided not to brief the president about the Venona Project, believing that "the only people entitled to know anything about this source were [deleted] and the FBI." Clarke's purpose in informing Fletcher of this decision was to ensure that "the Bureau does not handle the material in such a way that [CIA director Roscoe] Hillenkoetter or anyone else outside the Army Security Agency, [deleted], and the Bureau are aware of the contents" of the Venona messages. Clarke added that the chairman of the Joint Chiefs of Staff, General Omar Bradley, had assumed "responsibility of advising the president or anyone else in authority of the con-

through code names: "The fragmentary nature of the messages themselves, the assumptions made by the cryptographers, in breaking the messages themselves, and the questionable interpretations and translations involved, plus the extensive use of cover names for persons and places, make the problem of positive identification difficult." This May 13, 1950, memorandum is quoted by Morton Sobell in a letter to the editor published in *The Nation,* 272, no. 13 (April 2, 2001), p. 2.

tents of any of the material so demanded." FBI memoranda of October 1950 and February 1951 further suggest that the question of briefing Truman was again raised, but that it was decided to give him Venona-related material "in carefully paraphrased form." Again the stated purpose was to minimize the risk that this intelligence breakthrough might be leaked.[5] No released record directly confirms that President Truman was ever briefed on the Venona Project—a fact of crucial importance to understanding the relationship between the presidency and the intelligence community, and about Truman's attitude toward Soviet espionage—another key factor that will reappear throughout this book.

Military officials' failure to brief the president suggests an unwillingness to accept his authority to make national security policy, including the declassification of information. Did they and others in the intelligence community assume they had the right to question the president's judgment regarding the release of such information? After all, Truman held elective office. Had he damaged legitimate security interests, he would have been subject to impeachment or repudiation by the electorate.

That Soviet agents spied on the United States is unsurprising. Nation states have conducted espionage from time immemorial, directed at allies as well as adversaries—as illustrated most recently by the Jonathan Pollard, Harold Nicholson, Aldrich Ames, Earl Pitts, and Robert Hanssen cases of the 1980s and 1990s. Soviet espionage activities differed only because of the nature of an American Communist movement that adhered closely to direction from Moscow. Dating from the Bolshevik Revolution of 1917, presidential policy had consistently been based on the assumption that the Soviet Union, and American Communists, posed an internal security threat—leading to FBI monitoring of Communist activities in the United States throughout the 1920s. Following the normalization of relations with U.S. diplomatic recognition of the Soviet

Union in 1933, U.S. counterintelligence policy continued to be predicated on the promise that American Communists were subject to the influence, if not the control, of the Soviet Union.

Presidents Roosevelt and Truman and their attorneys general shared and endorsed these concerns. Both during the wartime U.S.-Soviet alliance between 1941 and 1945, and when the two nations were adversaries before and after that period, Roosevelt and Truman not only feared that Soviet agents and American Communists might steal classified diplomatic and military information. In addition, FBI officials sought to limit Soviet (and American Communist) influence in American politics and the popular culture and in an emerging and more powerful labor union movement.

This conception of the Soviet threat—and a companion concern about Nazi Germany's influence over American fascist movements—led President Roosevelt to issue a series of secret executive directives that expanded FBI investigative authority and responsibilities. FBI director Hoover responded to this presidential mandate by issuing, secretly and on his own authority, a series of orders further expanding the FBI's investigative role. Thus in May 1940, Roosevelt and his wartime attorneys general authorized FBI wiretapping; in August 1936, FBI "intelligence," that is, noncriminal investigations of "fascist and communist" activities, and in September 1939 of "subversive activities"; and in 1939–1940, investigations to purge "disloyal" federal employees and identify alien residents and radical citizens for preventive detention. But Hoover, acting on his own, formally authorized FBI bugging and break-in operations in 1942, and in 1940 approved a series of eight mail-opening programs targeting suspected "subversives" and espionage agents.[6]

Roosevelt (and later Truman) also successfully lobbied for a substantial increase in FBI appropriations. From 1936 through 1952, FBI appropriations increased by more than 1,800 percent, from $5,000,000 to $90,665,000, with the greatest percentage increase occurring during World War II. Appropriations were still only $6,578,076 in 1939, but in 1942 they exploded to $24,965,000 and in 1945 to $44,197,146. With the end of World War II and the dissolution in 1947 of the FBI's foreign intelligence role in South America, FBI appropriations declined slightly to $43,900,000 in 1948 before more than doubling in 1952 to $90,665,000. At the same time the FBI's personnel and thus its capacity to conduct counterintelligence investigations similarly exploded from 609 agents and 971 support staff in 1936, and 713 agents and 1,199 support staff in 1939, to 2,987 agents and 5,000 support staff in 1942, 4,370 agents and 7,442 support staff in 1945, and 6,451 agents and 8,206 support staff in 1952.[7]

Considering this unprecedented authorization and expansion, why was the FBI, dating from 1936, unable to uncover Soviet espionage activities and develop evidence to prosecute Soviet agents and their recruited American sources? Much as the restrictions on access to relevant KGB documents limit our understanding of Soviet espionage operations, similar restrictions on relevant FBI documents make it difficult to understand this counterintelligence failure. FBI records released under the Freedom of Information Act (FOIA) are more heavily censored than those released by the SVR to Vassiliev. Indeed, FBI records pertaining to its investigations of the Communist party and Soviet intelligence activities within the United States are so heavily redacted as to make it almost impossible to understand the scope and results of FBI counterintelligence operations. Two released FBI policy files—the minutes of the FBI Executives' Conference and SAC (Special Agent in Charge) Letters—illustrate how these restrictions undermine research.

The FBI Executives' Conference was composed of senior FBI officials at FBI headquarters in Washington. It met regularly to review and recommend changes in current programs and procedures. The minutes of these conferences record the subject of these discussions, the participants' recommendations, and the FBI director's controlling decision. The subjects ranged from the mundane—whether to invite certain local police officers to attend the FBI National Academy—to changes in FBI records policy, reassessment of important investigations and cases, and proposed changes in how "national security" investigations were to be conducted. The released minutes of the Executives' Conference discussions and decisions about counterintelligence for the period 1939–1952 have been totally redacted on "national security" grounds.[8]

The FBI's SAC Letters file, in contrast, consists of directives that the FBI director regularly sent to the heads of FBI field offices. These directives specified changes in FBI policy and procedure, and, as in the case of FBI Executives' Conference minutes, cover a wide range of subjects. Yet whenever SAC Letters record policy and procedures relating to investigations of Communist and Soviet agent activities, those sections have been entirely redacted.[9]

Despite these obstacles, FBI counterintelligence investigations can sometimes be partially reconstructed from otherwise accessible FBI records. Director Hoover's regular reports to Presidents Roosevelt and Truman between 1939 and 1952 are accessible at presidential libraries and are not redacted. These reports, however, do not disclose how the reported information was developed or what follow-up action was taken. A second source of information about FBI procedures and discoveries involves those occasions when an FBI investigation produced an indictment and trial. Court records and, just as important, the recently released grand jury minutes involving the perjury indictments of Alger Hiss and William Remington, offer invaluable insights into FBI practices and procedures. A third source involves FBI records, released in response to FOIA requests, from an FBI investigation that spilled over into protected First Amendment or political activities. These records have not been redacted, as the information does not meet the FOIA's exemptive standards to sustain a "national security" or "sources and methods" claim.

In sum, currently accessible FBI, KGB, and Venona Project records constitute only a partial record of Soviet espionage and U.S. counterintelligence activities. Any conclusions based on these records must be considered suggestive, not definitive. These records have expanded our understanding of the scope and nature of Soviet espionage and the American response, yet they may offer a distorted version of a more complex reality.

CHAPTER ONE

• • •

The Soviet Espionage Threat

THE VENONA PROJECT messages provide invaluable insights into Soviet intelligence activities in the United States and the covert relationship between KGB agents and American Communists. They provide conclusive evidence of Soviet espionage operations and the willingness of American Communists to spy on behalf of the Soviet Union or to persuade sensitively positioned federal employees to steal classified documents or provide information about U.S. government decisions. These espionage activities gave Soviet officials invaluable intelligence about the wartime Manhattan (atomic bomb) Project and other technological breakthroughs; about U.S. and British negotiating strategies and plans for postwar Europe, including the texts of President Roosevelt's communications with British Prime Minister Churchill; about those Office of Strategic Services (OSS) employees who were suspected Soviet agents or sympathizers; and, as early as 1948, about Washington's successful breaking of Soviet coded consular messages under the Venona Project.

The deciphered Soviet consular messages also provide fascinating insights into the parochialism and paranoia that shaped Moscow's intelligence activities. The KGB's obsessive secrecy and monolithic intolerance led it to monitor the activities of American Trotskyites, emigré Russian monarchists and Social Democrats, and ethnic Americans who sharply criticized Soviet leaders and their domestic and foreign policies. These reports about the Soviet Union's ideological enemies had little effect on American security interests. American Trotskyites and Russian monarchists enjoyed minuscule followings within the United States. Their lack of influence on U.S. policy or on developments within the Soviet Union make the KGB's spying on these individuals' activities at best silly. KGB agents' reports on the plans and objectives of the Democratic National Committee, or of Republican presidential nominee Thomas Dewey, or of American congressional committees, or of the commentary of syndicated columnist Walter Lippmann only serve to document the mind-set of individuals operating in a closed society. Much of what the KGB reported to Moscow as sensitive information was available to any astute reader of the American press.

But the Venona messages do tell us much about the motivation of American Communists and about other sources whom KGB agents recruited, whether or not they were employed in sensitive federal agencies. For example, much of the statistical information about wartime U.S. industrial production and troop levels reported by the so-called Silvermaster spy ring—federal employees recruited by Nathan Gregory Silvermaster to pilfer classified documents and information—did not seriously damage U.S. security interests or necessarily advance Soviet interests at U.S. expense. The essence of this information was officially conveyed to the Soviet Union under the wartime lend-lease assistance program, or in response to specific requests of the Soviet Government Purchasing

Commission, the liaison Soviet agency stationed in the United States to promote delivery of military-related materials under lend-lease. Since the United States and the Soviet Union were wartime allies, the reported information confirmed U.S. capabilities to wage war effectively against the Axis powers. In contrast to the advance intelligence that the British Communist Donald Maclean reported about the policy priorities of President Roosevelt and Prime Minister Churchill at wartime summit conferences, or the scientific data about the Manhattan Project provided by the British Communist Klaus Fuchs, the information about U.S. industrial productivity and military strength provided by the Silvermaster group—the numbers being overwhelming—might have deterred Soviet officials from pursuing an aggressive negotiating strategy. American spies may have aimed to further Soviet interests and betray their own nation, but the effect of their actions compromised neither long-term nor immediate U.S. security interests—only the secrecy that American intelligence officials and the White House valued in formulating national security policy.[1]

The deciphered Soviet consular messages also proved to be crucial for U.S. counterintelligence operations. When individuals with code names were identified, in some cases as early as 1948–1949, the FBI (and the NSA) was able to determine that Donald Maclean, Morris Cohen, Klaus Fuchs, Harry Gold, Julius Rosenberg, David Greenglass, Theodore Hall, Judith Coplon, Joseph York, and William Weisband were KGB recruits. Yet this intelligence breakthrough, which compromised a series of Soviet espionage operations, did not necessarily produce convictions. Hall was never indicted, and Maclean and Cohen escaped arrest and conviction, having been forewarned by another KGB agent, Harold "Kim" Philby, that they were the subjects of an inquiry. The FBI did arrest Gold, Rosenberg, Greenglass, and Coplon—aborting Coplon's ongoing espionage activities and ensuring the conviction of Gold, Rosenberg, and Greenglass for their wartime atomic espionage activities.* The identification of York enabled FBI officials to pressure him, first, into admitting espionage, and then to identifying Weisband as a co-participant. U.S. intelligence officials exploited this information to suspend Weisband from his position in the Armed Forces Security Agency, where he was reporting to the Soviets on the progress of the Venona Project. But Weisband denied having committed espionage and was indicted and convicted in 1950 only for contempt (refusing to testify before a federal grand jury) and not for espionage.[2]

As useful as they are, the deciphered Venona messages constitute an incomplete record of Soviet espionage operations in the United States. NSA analysts successfully deciphered only a "tiny fraction" of the intercepted messages.[3] And not all reports of Soviet agents were relayed by cable through the Soviet consulates. Other reports were conveyed by couriers, through diplomatic mail, through the regular mail disguised in microdots, or by Soviet officials traveling to the Soviet Union. Furthermore, some of the code names of sources and supervisors cannot be conclusively identified, or the NSA identifications are not reliable.

Allen Weinstein, Alexander Vassiliev, John Haynes, and Harvey Klehr claim to have uncovered additional evidence of Soviet espionage activities dating from the 1930s and extending through the early cold war years—Weinstein and Vassiliev through their privileged access to the closed KGB records deposited in Moscow, Haynes and Klehr through their research into congressional, presidential, and FBI records which they claim enable them to flush out the tantalizing disclosures of the deciphered Venona messages.

*FBI officials also alerted their British counterparts to Klaus Fuchs's wartime atomic espionage activities. Working with British intelligence, FBI agents succeeded in breaking Fuchs, getting him to admit his guilt and to identify Harry Gold as the courier to whom he gave his reports for transmission to the Soviet Union.

The promise of Weinstein and Vassiliev's research derives from their access to KGB records relating to some of the most hotly contested cold war internal security cases. Much of their documentation, however, does not record Soviet espionage activities directed at the U.S. government. Many of their research discoveries also border on the banal—recounting Martha Dodd's actions as a courtesan, Boris Morros's successful scamming of the wealthy American Communist Alfred Stern to invest $130,000 in a money-losing music production business,* and Congressman Samuel Dickstein's offer to Soviet agents to provide sensitive information in return for a monthly stipend of $2,500 (the Soviets agreed to pay $1,250 and never received the promised information).[4] With two exceptions, Weinstein and Vassiliev's documentation of Soviet espionage activities merely supplements the Venona revelations, adding detail but no new examples of Soviet espionage operations and recruited sources. The two exceptions involve evidence about Alger Hiss's recruitment as a Soviet agent in the 1930s, and about a Soviet espionage operation aimed at the State Department in the mid-1930s.

To recapitulate the story briefly: In December 1948, ex-Communist Whittaker Chambers abruptly changed his public testimony of August that year to charge that Alger Hiss had during the 1930s provided him with classified State Department documents. This espionage relationship, Chambers said, continued at least until April 1938, when Chambers defected from the Communist party. Because Chambers had earlier accused Hiss only of being a member of a Communist cell whose purpose was to promote Communist infiltration of the New Deal, not espionage, and

*The FBI, however, had learned of the Morros-Stern financial relationship as early as October 1944, having broken into Stern's New York office to photocopy his records. Report, name-redacted agent, October 27, 1944, FBI 100-203581-3392.

because Chambers had dated his own break from the Communist party to 1937, his changed testimony raised questions about the reliability of his account. In grand jury testimony, and during his two trials in 1949 and thereafter, Hiss affirmed his own innocence, but he was indicted for and convicted of perjury. In their book, supposedly based on new evidence from KGB files, Weinstein and Vassiliev reconstruct the history of the Hiss-Chambers case, confirming Hiss's guilt and the veracity of Chambers's account of his espionage relationship with Hiss during the 1930s. But the authors' sole source for their treatment of the Hiss-Chambers case is not the KGB records but Weinstein's 1978 book *Perjury*.[5] In a footnote, Weinstein and Vassiliev briefly note their failure to uncover any KGB records documenting their long narrative on the Hiss-Chambers case: "Since [Soviet] military intelligence (GRU) archives were not available for this or any other book, we have been able to further clarify Alger Hiss's role as a Soviet agent only through his occasional appearances in NKVD/NKGB archives* cited in [their book's] Chapters 1, 4, and 12."[6]

Will closed GRU records confirm the Hiss-Chambers espionage relationship and the contention that Chambers was a recruited GRU agent? Will these records confirm that Chambers recruited Hiss as a GRU source during the 1930s, receiving from him classified State Department documents? Will they further confirm that Chambers defected in April 1938? In fact, we do not know—nor do Weinstein and Vassiliev—what the closed GRU

*The "occasional appearances" turn out to be based on a series of questionable speculative conclusions. These are that KGB agents assigned Hiss and Harry Dexter White the same code name (Lawyer), that KGB agents either "forgot" or "did not know" Hiss's code name when citing him by name in their reports (which would seem to confirm that Hiss was not a recruited agent but a valued or helpful source), and that Ales was Hiss's assigned code name in 1945. Weinstein and Vassiliev, *The Haunted Wood,* pp. xxiii, xxiv, 5, 7, 43, 79n, 80, 157, 165, 165n, 267–268.

records may or may not confirm. It is dishonest for Weinstein and Vassiliev to imply, first, that their reconstruction of the Hiss-Chambers case is based on new evidence from KGB files, and, second, that when accessible, GRU records will confirm this as fact.

While the accessible KGB records do not confirm Hiss's espionage activities, they do record a previously unsuspected and potentially significant Soviet espionage operation. In 1934 the KGB successfully recruited a sensitive State Department source, code named Willie/Daniel/Albert. This source provided the KGB with seemingly invaluable intelligence that included "numerous ambassadorial, consular, and military attaché reports from Europe and the Far East" and, more important, "transcripts of recorded conversations Secretary of State Cordell Hull and his assistants had with foreign ambassadors."[7]

Weinstein and Vassiliev, however, do not even summarily describe the contents of these various transmissions, and thus we are left in the dark as to whether U.S. foreign policy interests and the conduct of difficult negotiations with the Soviet Union were thereby compromised. Just as surprisingly, the authors seem indifferent either to the length of Willie/Daniel/Albert's service as a KGB source in the State Department or how Willie/Daniel/Albert could deliver to his KGB handler "transcripts of recorded conversations." Had he bugged the office of the secretary of state? Or listened in on and transcribed the secretary's and assistant secretaries' conversations with foreign ambassadors from an adjoining office?* How long did he serve as a KGB source, and were his espi-

*The KGB reports seemingly confirm an account of Ludwig Lore, an FBI informer, who told the FBI in 1941 that Whittaker Chambers headed a KGB operation of approximately seventy recruits, including "two girls who were private secretaries to Assistant Secretaries of State" and who had provided "copies" of President Roosevelt's correspondence. The FBI reports on Lore are reprinted in Edith Tiger, ed., *In Re Alger Hiss Volume II* (New York, 1980), pp. 208–209.

onage activities coordinated with other KGB sources recruited later in the 1930s?

Despite having discovered the Willie/Daniel/Albert espionage operation through their research in KGB records, Weinstein and Vassiliev show little interest in its scope and its relationship to other Soviet intelligence operations aimed at the State Department. This is puzzling, particularly since the authors quote a KGB report characterizing as "precious" the information that Willie/Daniel/Albert provided. Owing to the quality of his information, the KGB station chief concluded "we consider inexpedient any further penetration into the State Department either by legal or illegal operations. The task is to develop the agents we already have." Willie's annual retainer of $15,000 (approximately $190,000 in 2000 dollars) offers further evidence of how much the KGB valued his importance, as do the KGB's monthly stipends to "two other" recruited State Department sources working with Willie: $500 to Daniel and $400 to Albert. (Combining the two monthly stipends and annualizing them would be approximately $140,000 in 2000 dollars.) KGB officials, however, later discovered that their contact with Willie/Daniel/Albert, a "free lance journalist" code-named Leo, had falsely claimed to have received information from Daniel and Albert, then pocketed the monthly stipends. Leo's sole source, KGB agents established, was actually Willie. Nonetheless, even after discovering Leo's scam, KGB officials simply discontinued the monthly stipends and continued to "rely on 'Leo' for several more years as a paid agent handling the genuine 'Willie,' though it did not inform him about others at State subsequently recruited."[8]

Another KGB report confirms Willie's importance. In this report Willie advised his KGB handlers that U.S. ambassador to Moscow William Bullitt had complained that "the contents of his reports" to Washington were known to Moscow officials. In response, an assistant to Secretary of State Cordell Hull questioned

Willie "about the possible leak of these reports," then charged Willie "with checking the employees and investigating the department"—seemingly confirming Willie's high-level position in the State Department at the time. Surprisingly, Weinstein and Vassiliev do not pursue this matter. Consistent with their downplaying of the Willie espionage operation, they do not even list Willie and Leo in their "Cast of Characters" recruited by the KGB as "American Agents and Sources."[9]

Yet the Willie-Leo operation (as sketchily described by Weinstein and Vassiliev) offers invaluable insights into Soviet espionage operations. On the one hand, Willie's annual stipend and Leo's dishonesty in pocketing the monthly stipends to Daniel and Albert confirm that Soviet espionage operations depended on mercenaries—contradicting Weinstein and Vassiliev's unqualified assertion that Soviet agents "normally paid" individuals employed in defense industries for information, but that this was "not a practice followed with Moscow's more ideologically driven Washington sources of political or governmental data." Continuing, Weinstein and Vassiliev contend that "Paid [Soviet] informants worked mainly for U.S. defense-related industries, while many of the [ideologically motivated] 'believers' rose steadily through the ranks of the Roosevelt administration's bureaucracy. Ideological reliability and access to top-secret scientific information, however, converged at times, most notably during the Second World War."[10] The Willie and Leo cases, like those of Boris Morros, Congressman Dickstein, and even Nathan Silvermaster,* challenge this distinction between mercenaries and "believers."

Because other scholars cannot research the KGB records made accessible to Weinstein and Vassiliev, the significance of the Willie-Leo operation cannot be fully understood. Nor do John Haynes

*Silvermaster not only received "expense" stipends but requested and was paid $6,000 ($60,000 in 2000 dollars) to purchase a farm.

and Harvey Klehr extend our understanding of Soviet espionage activities. Their research into congressional, presidential, and FBI records does not add substantially to what can be learned from simply reading the deciphered Venona messages, reprinted in Robert Benson and Michael Warner's *Venona* or accessible on the Internet. As in the case of Weinstein and Vassiliev, Haynes and Klehr's "new" information often turns out to be nothing more than a priori speculations about the contents of deciphered and undeciphered Venona messages.

For example, they report Elizabeth Bentley's statements to the FBI—in the month following her November 1945 defection—that in 1944, Roosevelt White House aide Lauchlin Currie had warned Soviet intelligence agents that the United States was on the verge of breaking the Soviet code. Haynes and Klehr speculate that Currie "may well have heard an overly optimistic report sent to the White House about the early Venona effort." The Soviets, Haynes and Klehr continue, "appear to have learned of the existence of the Venona Project within a year and a half of its origin."[11]

Haynes and Klehr's speculations are unsubstantiated, and in fact are contradicted by recently released military intelligence records. In February 1943, Colonel Carter Clarke unilaterally created a special Russian section within the Signal Intelligence Service (the predecessor to the National Security Agency) to decipher the intercepted Soviet consular messages. Clarke did so without consulting the White House or the State Department and adopted strict safeguards to ensure that the activities of this section could not become known, even to other units within the Signal Intelligence Service itself. Because this section did not successfully decipher any of the intercepted Soviet consular messages, no reports were sent to the White House (as was done, for example, in the case of deciphered Japanese messages).[12] Currie could hardly have alerted the Soviets to this code-breaking operation.

Haynes and Klehr further contend that Currie's statement

about the Venona breakthrough was immediately forwarded to Soviet officials. But this is not confirmed by their source: Benson and Warner's citation of an October 31, 1943, Venona message. The referenced message merely reports that KGB officers had recently received a new codebook to replace the Petsamo code documents. Benson and Warner attribute this Soviet decision to change the code not to information obtained from American sources but to "a Soviet agent in Berlin," who at the end of 1941 "reported that the Germans were trying to exploit a Russian codebook [Petsamo] acquired through their Finnish allies."[13]

Haynes and Klehr continue, "There is also evidence, although it is not conclusive, that Currie attempted to kill the Venona project before it revealed the contents of Soviet cable traffic." Their source is an uncorroborated assertion of two military intelligence officials, Colonels Harold Hayes and Frank Rowlett, offered in an interview during the 1990s. They claimed that their superior, Colonel Clarke, had "told them he received instructions from the White House to cease work on Soviet ciphers." They were then instructed by Clarke to ignore this order and "continue the Venona Project." While conceding that "No written record exists of these [White House] instructions," and that the two military officers referred generically to the White House "and not to anyone in particular," Haynes and Klehr claim that Currie's usual practice was to intercede verbally, confirmed by his intervention to foreclose a security investigation into the Communist orientation of Silvermaster—though in the Silvermaster case a written record had been created by the persons whom Currie had contacted.[14]

This account poses a number of problems. At the most basic, Haynes and Klehr cannot corroborate that Currie's verbal intercession on behalf of Silvermaster constituted his usual practice, thereby explaining the absence of any War Department record of his attempt to kill Venona. Currie had acted as a character reference in the Silvermaster case; to the extent that his intercession carried weight, it stemmed from his status as a trusted White House aide. But Currie had no authority to speak for the White House on a substantive policy matter such as killing Venona—a decision that would have required the direct authority of the president relayed through the secretaries of state or war. Had Currie issued such a verbal order, he would have had to know that Colonel Clarke had established this code-breaking unit. In any event, the thrust of the Hayes and Rowlett recollection pertained to a quite different matter—the acquisition in 1944 by the Office of Strategic Services (OSS), from emigré Finnish cryptanalysts, of a partially burned KGB codebook. Over OSS chief William Donovan's objections, Secretary of State Edward Stettinius urged President Roosevelt to return the codebook to the Soviet embassy, and the president so ordered. Despite the order, some have contended that OSS officials retained a copy of this partially burned codebook,* returning the original to the Soviets. This codebook, in any case, did not enable military analysts to break the Soviet code. Instead they benefited from their successful deciphering of Japanese consular messages. One of these deciphered messages relayed information that Japanese military attachés had learned from the Finns about Finnish code-breakers' knowledge of Soviet codes and enciphering procedures.[15]

Haynes and Klehr further speculate about the contents of undeciphered Venona messages. After conceding that three individuals named by Bentley as Soviet spies—Michael Greenberg, Joseph Gregg, and Robert Miller—"are not identified in those KGB cables that were deciphered in the Venona Project," they contend that "Given, however, the high degree of corroboration of Elizabeth Bentley's testimony, her statements about these persons must be regarded as having great credibility. There are, moreover, nu-

*For example, Robert Lamphere, the FBI's liaison to military intelligence, claims that cryptanalyst Meredith Gardner had a copy of this codebook.

merous cover names in Venona that one or more of these persons might hide behind." The authors repeat this tactic in the case of the radical journalist I. F. Stone. "There is no evidence in Venona," they concede, "that Stone ever was recruited by the KGB, but [Soviet KGB official Oleg] Kalugin's comments in the 1990s that he 're-established' contact leave open the possibility that Stone may have met with KGB agents on some basis after the [innocuous 1944] meeting documented in Venona." Haynes and Klehr also speculate about the contents of undeciphered Venona messages, lamenting that "Some of the GRU's known activities in the United States during World War II are not mentioned in the decrypted Venona cables. Undoubtedly, these are among the thousands of cables that were never deciphered." They specifically cite the case of Arthur Adams* whom they note "was not identi-

*Adams became the subject of the FBI's COMRAP program (see Chapter Three). While Adams's activities were closely monitored (including wiretaps and break-ins), FBI agents were never able to confirm his involvement in espionage. Having monitored his contacts with three employees of the Manhattan Project in Chicago, who were described as having "Communist and pro-Soviet backgrounds," FBI agents suspected that these three were the source for the microfilmed documents they found in Adams's possession through a break-in to his hotel room in New York. The FBI was unable to establish that Adams or the three had been involved in espionage, and eventually lost contact with Adams, reporting in January 1946 that he had "disappeared." Nonetheless, in this as in other cases, Haynes's and Klehr's clairvoyance—assuming that Adams's reports must have been transmitted by Soviet consular officials—misses a different reality. Adams was an "illegal," entering the United States through Canada and not officially assigned to a Soviet consular post or to an agency such as the Soviet Government Purchasing Commission. FBI agents suspected that Adams's activities were funded through the Electronic Corporation of America, and that he used the company as a cover for his espionage activities. Through the break-in to Adams's hotel room, moreover, FBI agents learned that the microfilm documents contained chemicals "used in connection with microscope dots." Confidential Letter, Conroy to FBI Director, November 15, 1944, FBI 100-203581-3425; Teletype, Conroy to FBI Director, November 14, 1944, FBI 100-203581-3428.

fied in Venona messages, nor were several of his closest collaborators. Either they are among the cover names that have never been identified or else the messages dealing with them were never decrypted."[16]

Do the deciphered Venona messages, then, document the essence of Soviet espionage operations? Will other unreleased Soviet records reveal a more extensive and successful espionage threat or simply confirm that our present knowledge is substantially accurate? The speculations of Weinstein, Vassiliev, Haynes, and Klehr do not advance our understanding of this question. We cannot know the contents of withheld or inaccessible documents. But our current knowledge leaves open the possibility that the deciphered Venona messages and accessible KGB records represent either a mosaic or an iceberg. A mosaic in the sense that the accessible records describe the general picture, with the likelihood that future disclosures will add detail but not alter the essence of known Soviet espionage operations. An iceberg in the sense that what we now know is only a small part of the scope and significance of Soviet espionage in the United States. The resolution of these differing appraisals awaits the full release of all records of Soviet espionage operations conducted during World War II and the cold war.

The accessible Venona messages also raise a quite different question relating to U.S. counterintelligence operations. They confirm that Soviet agents recruited a number of Americans, some employed in sensitive government agencies, including members of the American Communist party. This contrasts sharply with the record of espionage prosecutions during World War II and the cold war eras, a record that also underscores a series of paradoxical disparities. In some cases, individuals whom the Venona messages confirm as Soviet spies were indicted and convicted; in other cases, individuals who were *not* identified in the Venona messages as Soviet recruits were indicted and convicted (but for perjury, not espionage); in still other cases, individuals whose espionage activities were confirmed by the Venona messages were never indicted and thus not convicted.

For example, after her defection in November 1945, Elizabeth Bentley described to FBI agents her role as a courier for two Soviet espionage rings headed by Nathan Silvermaster and Victor Perlo. She named more than 150 federal employees whom she claimed delivered government secrets to her that she then transmitted to her KGB handler for transmission to the Soviet Union. She further claimed that some of the 150 named individuals were aware they were involved in Soviet espionage, but others believed the information was to be given to officials of the American Communist party. Bentley identified William Remington as one of the latter group, claiming that he paid her Communist party dues, personally gave her "scraps of information" and oral reports, and was not a member of either the Silvermaster or Perlo rings. The Venona messages confirm Bentley's account of Silvermaster's and Perlo's roles, and of the activities of those whom she described as members of these two espionage rings. No Venona message documents Remington as providing written or oral reports to Bentley which she then delivered to her KGB contact. Nonetheless, none of those whom Bentley identified—and whom the Venona messages confirm—as members of the Silvermaster-Perlo espionage rings were indicted—but Remington was indicted and convicted (but for perjury, not espionage).

This same disparity recurs in the case of Alger Hiss. Convicted in 1950 for perjurious testimony—denying before a federal grand jury that he gave classified information to a known Communist—Hiss's alleged espionage activities are not confirmed by the Venona records. Hiss is cited by name, however, in one of the intercepted Soviet consular messages, of September 28, 1943. This report of the GRU's New York station chief observes that Hiss was mentioned in a KGB report about the State Department. The remainder of this GRU report, however, could not be deciphered by U.S. code-breakers.[17] Does the fact that Hiss was cited by name in this GRU report (and that his identity was not disguised by a code name) indirectly confirm that he was not a recruited Soviet agent? We cannot know from the deciphered Venona messages.

Another Venona message, dated March 30, 1945, led NSA analysts to conclude that in 1945 Hiss had been assigned the code name Ales. The concluding paragraph of this deciphered message reads: "After the Yalta Conference, when he had gone to Moscow, a Soviet personage in a very responsible position (ALES gave it to understand that it was Comrade VYSHINSKIJ) allegedly got in touch with ALES and at the behest of the Military NEIGHBORS [GRU] passed on to him their gratitude and so on."[18] Hiss attended the Yalta Conference as a member of the U.S. delegation, then traveled to Moscow with Secretary of State Edward Stettinius and three other members of the U.S. delegation. Does this awkwardly worded translation confirm that Ales had gone to Moscow after the Yalta Conference, or instead that Ales had been briefed by this "Soviet personage"? The preceding paragraphs of this Soviet consular message, moreover, suggest that Ales might not be Hiss. These passages describe Ales as having worked with the GRU "continuously since 1935" and "obtaining military information only. Materials in the 'Bank' [State Department] allegedly interest the NEIGHBORS [GRU] very little and he does not produce them regularly." Hiss was employed in the Justice Department's Solicitor General office in 1935, however, and did not transfer to the State Department until 1936. While the writer of this 1945 message might have erred on the date of Ales's recruitment, the unqualified assertion that this GRU recruit provided only military information is inconsistent with Hiss's State Department responsibilities, which involved trade and diplomatic matters. The State Department documents that Chambers turned over in 1948, which he claimed to have received from Hiss in 1938, reported information about trade and diplomatic matters.*

The Venona messages highlight even more puzzling disparities in espionage prosecutions. They confirm that Julius Rosenberg and Theodore Hall had been witting participants in atomic espionage. The Venona intercepts document that Rosenberg had recruited his brother-in-law, David Greenglass, a military draftee assigned to Los Alamos, and that Hall had approached a KGB agent in New York to volunteer sensitive information he had learned about the atomic bomb project as a current employee at

*Weinstein and Vassiliev claim that an April 2, 1945, KGB report corroborates that Ales was Hiss's code name. Their conclusion is not borne out by this report. Contrary to their implication that Ales's report to a KGB recruit alerted the KGB to FBI monitoring of a Soviet espionage operation, the referenced FBI investigation involved the leaking of classified documents to a radical journal of Far Eastern affairs, *Amerasia* (this case will be discussed in detail in Chapter Four). Weinstein and Vassiliev base their conclusion that Ales was Hiss's code name on a reference in this report to Secretary of State Stettinius having been told that FBI agents had identified Ales as one of "only three people" who had access to the leaked documents and that Stettinius had then confronted Ales, stating, "I hope it is not you" who leaked the documents. Because the leaked documents pertained to Far Eastern policy and involved an individual who would have had access to documents relating to that policy over the preceding eighteen months, the suspected Ales more logically would be either John Carter Vincent, who headed the Far Eastern desk at State, or Assistant Secretary of the Treasury Harry Dexter White, given his role in drafting the Treasury Department's position on a proposed gold loan to the Chinese Nationalist government. An FBI wiretap installed during the *Amerasia* investigation lends further credence to the White identification, in addition to the fact that the KGB's source for this report, Harold Glasser, was a Treasury Department employee. The intercepted conversation records the claim of one of the suspects that an associate could obtain "a lot of stuff on Far Eastern things that the other guys don't get" through weekly meetings with White, as White "will tell you a lot of stuff." Harvey Klehr and Ronald Radosh, *The Amerasia Spy Case: Prelude to McCarthyism* (Chapel Hill, 1996), pp. 52–53.

Los Alamos. FBI and Justice Department officials learned about Rosenberg's and Hall's espionage activities almost at the same time in 1950. Rosenberg was indicted and convicted for atomic espionage, as was his wife Ethel, despite the fact that the Venona messages record that while she knew of her husband's activities, she was not a co-conspirator. Hall was never indicted.

The deciphered Venona messages also led to the FBI's discovery that the KGB had recruited a junior Justice Department employee, Judith Coplon, who would be in a position to obtain information about FBI surveillance activities. An intensive FBI investigation and sting operation was launched leading to Coplon's indictment and conviction. Nonetheless Coplon's conviction was reversed on appeal, but she was never retried. Justice Department officials delayed until 1967 before formally dropping the case.

The most perplexing disparity in FBI and Justice Department decisions on prosecution, however, relate to the leadership of the American Communist party. The Venona messages confirm that the wartime head of the party, Earl Browder, was aware of and encouraged Soviet efforts to recruit American Communists to steal industrial and governmental secrets. No Venona message, however, documents that other senior party officials—notably Eugene Dennis, William Foster, John Williamson, Henry Winston, Jack Stachel, Benjamin Davis, Carl Winter, John Gates, Irving Potash, Robert Thompson, Gil Green, and Gus Hall—either knew or encouraged such espionage activities. Yet Browder was never indicted for violating either the Foreign Agents Registration or the Espionage acts while all the other party officials named above were indicted in 1948 and subsequently convicted for conspiring to overthrow the U.S. government by force or violence.

In light of what the deciphered Venona messages tell us, does this confusing record of prosecution and nonprosecution indirectly support the charges of "softness toward communism" leveled against the Roosevelt and Truman administrations by Senator

Joseph McCarthy and his followers in the 1950s? Did President Roosevelt's indifference make possible Soviet espionage, and did President Truman's partisanship or indifference foreclose FBI investigations of Soviet espionage activities that could have ensured the prosecution of guilty spies? The answers to these questions are closely tied to the performance of the FBI.

CHAPTER TWO

• • •

The Failure of U.S. Counterintelligence

WHY DID the FBI, the federal agency principally responsible for domestic counterintelligence, fail to apprehend Soviet spies and their American informers? Why, between 1934–1945, were Soviet agents able to recruit sources employed in sensitive federal agencies to steal classified government information, particularly individuals who were Communist party members, Communist sympathizers, or members of alleged Communist front organizations? After all, FBI agents had intensively monitored the Communist movement since 1917, and through wiretaps, bugs, break-ins, and mail openings had become privy to membership and contribution lists and the covert plans and strategies of Communist activists.

This question about the FBI's counterintelligence failure is raised starkly by the Venona messages. Even if they are an incomplete record, they confirm that Soviet intelligence successes marked an important breakdown in the government's control over classified information. Through their recruited sources, Soviet officials were alerted to some of the nation's military secrets, to some of President Roosevelt's negotiating strategies and foreign policy priorities, and to statistics on the nation's industrial production and military capabilities.

During the cold war era, the question whether Soviet espionage successes confirmed the FBI's counterintelligence failure never emerged as a major political issue. The sole charge, raised by the McCarthyites, was that the Roosevelt and Truman administrations' "softness toward communism" produced greater Soviet influence and the onset of international tensions. By tolerating Communist employment in sensitive government positions, the McCarthyites alleged, these Democratic administrations had enabled Communists to "shape" foreign policy decisions—at the Yalta Conference, for example—in ways that benefited Soviet interests. In a February 9, 1950, speech that catapulted him to national prominence, Senator Joseph McCarthy contended that the State Department "is thoroughly infested with Communists" and that "card carrying [Communist party] members or certainly loyal to the Communist Party . . . are still shaping our foreign policy." The solution to this problem and victory over communism, McCarthy continued, required a "moral uprising" that would bring about a "new birth of national honesty and decency in Government."[1] McCarthy and his followers never suggested that the FBI might bear responsibility for Communist subversion, having failed to uncover the Soviet espionage threat. Their exclusive focus on Roosevelt's and Truman's alleged indifference continues to underlie the writing of some recent historians such as Richard Gid Powers, John Haynes, and Harvey Klehr.

In his biography of former FBI director Hoover, Powers reaffirms this view of President Roosevelt's responsibility. His analysis rests on a single episode: Assistant Secretary of State Adolf Berle's response to a meeting in September 1939 with the Communist defector Whittaker Chambers. At this meeting, Chambers claimed that eighteen current federal employees, whom he named, were members of a Communist underground. Berle did not pursue the matter, Powers observes, but two years later he belatedly checked into it and forwarded his notes to the FBI in 1942. This was not Berle's personal failure, Powers contends, as "the Roosevelt Administration was not at all eager to unleash the unpredictable and probably uncontrollable passions of a hunt for Red spies." He adds that this inaction extended to the FBI director, who did not "press energetically for action when he received the same reports from Chambers a few years later, or when he came across evidence that the Soviets were using American Communists for espionage." The Roosevelt administration, however, had not restrained Hoover, for he and the president, Powers writes, "were in general agreement about the nature of the threat to domestic security. While Germany and Japan were the enemies [1941–1945], German and Japanese spies and their sympathizers were their main worry. . . . That changed after the war, when the Soviet Union succeeded Germany as the enemy."[2]

In fact, FBI surveillance of American Communists and Soviet agents continued after the German invasion of Poland in 1939 and even when the United States and the Soviet Union became military allies in 1941. German and Japanese agents and their sympathizers were *never* the FBI's main worry. After 1941, FBI surveillance of Soviet officials and Communist activists actually intensified.

Powers's contention that the Roosevelt administration downplayed Chambers's 1939 revelations, fearing an uncontrollable Red Scare, is pure speculation. Berle never briefed the president about Chambers's allegations chiefly because the assistant secretary did not understand that Chambers's "underground" group reference suggested a Soviet espionage operation. In striking contrast to Elizabeth Bentley's later testimony, Chambers had not described his own role as a courier for spies. Chambers's apologists have argued that by this cryptic reference he intended to forewarn the administration, and that he had expected a follow-up investigation. Given the context (1939) and the public position of the individual who arranged this meeting (Isaac Don Levine), Berle not unreasonably interpreted Chambers's underground reference as a rehash of charges that conservatives had leveled throughout the late 1930s, namely that Communists had infiltrated New Deal agencies and used their positions to shape domestic policy. Only in December 1948 did Chambers provide documentary evidence and specific testimony about Communist espionage—though having had earlier opportunities to do so.

The first such opportunity came in May–August 1941. In two interviews, Ludwig Lore, an FBI informer, claimed to know an individual who had direct knowledge of a Communist espionage operation in the United States. In the first interview, Lore did not name this Soviet espionage agent, whom he claimed was "afraid to reveal the true story of his OGPU [Soviet intelligence] activities in the United States, believing he will encounter serious trouble." This agent, Lore maintained, had been "in contact with two girls who were private secretaries to Assistant Secretaries of State and was also in touch with a girl who was employed in a secretarial capacity with one of the high officials of the Department of Commerce." The Commerce Department secretary had provided "all necessary statistical data" and the State Department secretaries "two extra copies" of Roosevelt administration correspondence which they had typed. According to Lore, the individual in question supervised approximately seventy OGPU agents and had recently identified to a U.S. government official federal employees "who were Communists or possessed pro-Russian political sympathies." But, said Lore, nothing had been done with this information, even though an intermediary had brought the matter to FBI director Hoover's attention earlier that year.

Responding to this briefing, Hoover ordered a follow-up interview with Lore. In this second interview, Lore "in strictest confidence" identified Chambers as the Soviet agent, reaffirming that Chambers had "handled arrangements for placing agents in the OGPU; that he definitely handled arrangements for placing agents in the Government service at Washington or for making contacts through which the OGPU agents could obtain information at Washington."[3]

Essentially contradicting Lore's account, in his FBI interviews Chambers never admitted to supervising an espionage operation—one that the administration might have decided to investigate. Instead he vaguely described the purpose of the Communist "underground" group as influencing government policy, and named twenty individuals as members—two more than during the Berle interview, but no private secretaries. In another March 1946 FBI interview, Chambers was again nonspecific, even though in this case FBI officials had taken the initiative to reinterview him.[4]

The event triggering this 1946 interview was the defection in 1945 of Igor Gouzenko, a Soviet consular official in Ottawa, Canada. Interrogated by Canadian security officials, Gouzenko described extensive Soviet espionage activities in Canada during World War II, which had depended on the assistance of Canadian Communist party members, including Canadian scientist Dr. Allan May, who was assigned to the Manhattan Project. One of his Soviet supervisors, Gouzenko added, had told him that the Soviets had "more agents in the United States," and that one of them was "an assistant to [Secretary of State Edward] Stettinius."

This "assistant" reference, FBI director Hoover immediately surmised, was Alger Hiss. Conceding that "there was no direct evidence to sustain this suspicion," Hoover based his hunch on Chambers's FBI interviews of 1942 and 1945, and on Elizabeth Bentley's vague remark that one of her sources had mentioned Hiss's name and that she had learned that Hiss was "an adviser to [Assistant Secretary of State] Dean Acheson."

An intensive FBI investigation of Hiss was launched to confirm this suspicion. In this investigation, Hiss's office and home phones were tapped; his telephone toll call records for 1943 and 1944 were obtained from Washington, D.C., telephone companies; his mail was intercepted and opened; and telegrams to him were intercepted. This FBI investigation uncovered no evidence that Hiss was involved in espionage. Nonetheless Hoover urged Secretary of State James Byrnes, Stettinius's successor, to "move Hiss to an innocuous position where he would understand the situation and resign." Byrnes, however, proposed that a security dismissal hearing be convened, as required under Civil Service regulations. The FBI director rejected this course, stressing that the FBI's "material against Hiss was confidential and if it were not used there would not be enough evidence against him." Hoover urged Byrnes to leak the unsubstantiated allegations of Hiss's disloyalty to congressional leaders "like [Senator] Thomas Connally, [Senator] Arthur Vandenburg [sic], [Congressman] John McCormack or [House Speaker] Sam Rayburn." At the time Byrnes was preparing for a United Nations Security Council meeting and had no time to "contact anyone on the hill as the Director suggested." He decided to question Hiss directly about whether "he was ever a member of any organization with subversive tendencies." Hiss denied any such membership, agreed to repeat this denial to the FBI, arranged for such an interview, and did so.[5]

In the wake of Byrnes's action, the only available option to removing Hiss was to convene the required security dismissal hearing. Since the FBI had been unable to corroborate the hearsay allegations of Chambers, Bentley, and Gouzenko, it would have to establish Hiss's Communist party membership. Under the 1939 Hatch Act, such confirmation would be grounds for Hiss's dismissal—thus the decision to reinterview Chambers in March 1946.

During this interview, FBI agent Thomas Spencer pressed Chambers about his earlier statement that Hiss, as an employee of the Agricultural Adjustment Administration (AAA) during the mid-1930s, had been a member of a Communist "underground organization," and that after the AAA he had served on the staff of the so-called Nye Committee, where "he was segregated from the group and had no more official contact with them, but would meet socially with a lot of them." In response, Chambers stated that "his actual knowledge of HISS' activities concerned the period shortly preceding 1937 and he was unable to elaborate" on Hiss's connections with the Communist party or Communist front organizations beyond what he had told the FBI in 1942 and 1945. He had "absolutely no information that could conclusively prove that HISS held a membership card in the Communist Party," Chambers advised Spencer, or that Hiss "was an actual dues paying member of the Communist Party even when he [Chambers] was active prior to 1937." Gratuitously adding that Hiss "was favorably impressed with the Communist movement," Chambers admitted to having "no documentary or other proof" to substantiate this belief. Pressed again for "documentary evidence or any independent recollection that HISS was a dues paying member of the Communist Party," Chambers again denied that he had any such information, "and that if he did have this information he would be more than glad to supply it to this Bureau."

When Spencer asked whether the FBI could use him as a source in a security dismissal hearing, Chambers demurred, preferring not to be identified or called to testify. He assured Spencer that in his previous FBI interviews he "had never purposefully held out any information and had always been forthright in relaying any information that he had in which the Bureau had shown an interest."[6] Chambers at no time disabused Spencer of the agent's impression that his sole knowledge of Hiss's Communist activities involved the time when Hiss was an AAA employee. In sum, there is no evidence that the Roosevelt administration or the FBI director purposefully sought to avoid an exposé of Soviet espionage activities.

Then, did the Truman administration constrain FBI investigations? Summarizing a view advanced by the McCarthyites during the 1950s, John Haynes and Harvey Klehr contend:

> In late 1945 and in 1946, the [Truman] White House had reacted with a mixture of indifference and skepticism to FBI reports indicating significant Soviet espionage activity in the United States. Truman administration officials even whitewashed evidence pointing to the theft of American classified documents in the 1945 *Amerasia* case . . . because they did not wish to put at risk the continuance of the wartime Soviet-American alliance and wanted to avoid the political embarrassment of a security scandal.

By early 1947, however, this indifference ended."[7]

Haynes and Klehr's charges of "indifference and skepticism" distort the complex history of the period and the problems posed by FBI investigative procedures. The charges relate to President Truman's response to a series of reports that Hoover sent to the White House (and to Secretary of State James Byrnes, Attorney General Tom Clark, Secretary of the Navy James Forrestal, Secretary of the Treasury Fred Vinson, Assistant Secretary of State Spruille Braden, White House aide William Leahy, Lieutenant General Hoyt Vandenberg, and Special Assistant to the Attorney General A. Devitt Vanech) in late 1945 and early 1946. These reports were based on Elizabeth Bentley's uncorroborated allegations growing out of her service as a courier for two Soviet espionage rings in wartime Washington. As one of 150 sources, she identified Harry Dexter White. When he first submitted these reports, the FBI director intended to brief the president and senior cabinet officials about Bentley's various allegations. Hoover's purpose soon expanded, as he sought to convince President Truman to withdraw his nomination of White as executive director of the International Monetary Fund.

Truman and other senior administration officials did not blindly follow Hoover's recommendations. After all, Hoover reported only the unsupported allegations of a recent Communist defector, not identified by name in these reports. Moreover, although an intensive FBI investigation was immediately launched to verify Bentley's charges,* FBI agents could not corroborate them. The skepticism of the president and senior administration officials was thus hardly irresponsible. To the contrary, administration officials would have acted irresponsibly had they acted on such allegations against White, given his unblemished record of loyalty and his recognized expertise in monetary policy. Although he was unwilling to withdraw White's nomination, Truman did seriously weigh the charges against him. Indeed, Bentley's allegations, as White House aide George Allen advised Ralph Roach, Hoover's White House liaison, led the president later in 1946 "to disapprove numerous appointments that come up to the President for a decision." One such involved blocking William Remington's† appointment to the staff of Assistant to the President John Steelman in December 1946.[8]

With the knowledge of the attorney general, FBI director Hoover assigned more than two hundred agents, in a special squad headed by FBI Supervisor Thomas Donegan, to investigate Bentley's charges. During this investigation at least twenty of those named by Bentley were wiretapped,[9] at least fifteen had their mail

*The FBI wiretapped at least twenty of those named by Bentley, seeking and obtaining Attorney General Tom Clark's authorization—in itself confirming that the administration was neither indifferent nor engaged in a whitewash.

†Remington was one of the government employees named by Bentley as one of her sources for classified information. The Remington matter is discussed further in Chapter Five.

intercepted and opened,[10] and FBI agents conducted at least three break-ins.[11]

Despite this intrusive investigation, by October 1946 FBI agents had failed to corroborate Bentley's allegations. A report on this investigation, a copy of which was sent to the Truman White House, in effect merely recapitulated Bentley's earlier allegations. In a lame effort to rationalize the paucity of the FBI's investigative findings, the FBI agent who wrote this report emphasized the "time element." The alleged espionage dated "back several years," the writer observed, and became known only in November 1945. "Consequently the reader must consider the difficulty of actually proving these activities by investigation at this later date." He continued, "The facts are strong in many instances and circumstantial in others primarily because of the disparity in time between the date of these activities and the actual report of these activities to the authorities. A determined effort has been made to prove or disprove the basic charges."[12] In fact the FBI investigation independently corroborated *none* of Bentley's charges. Its corroboration was at best circumstantial—discovering that the individuals named by Bentley knew one another personally and professionally and were in frequent contact through political meetings, correspondence, social engagements, or as house guests during visits to the Washington area.

Rather than showing indifference or skepticism, the Truman administration had given FBI officials a long leash to corroborate Bentley—and FBI agents had failed to do so. Indeed, FBI agent E. P. Morgan counseled Hoover in January 1947 against recommending that the Justice Department seek indictments: "We have no evidence from which 'intent or reason to believe' can be proved or reasonably inferred" against any of those named by Bentley. "At this point," Morgan unqualifiedly admitted, "the evidence very definitely is insufficient to sustain a successful prosecution under the espionage statutes."[13]

Although they recognized the weakness of the evidence, Justice officials chose to convene a grand jury in September 1947. Their strategy—risky and ultimately counterproductive—was based on the premise that, under threat of a grand jury indictment for perjury, one or more of the suspects, a possible "weak sister," would "crack" and corroborate Bentley. This tactic failed, with one exception. When called before the grand jury, all the suspects either denied Bentley's charges or took the Fifth Amendment. The exception, William Remington, was sufficiently frightened to cooperate, even volunteering to act as an informer. But he had no direct knowledge of the operation of the alleged wartime spy ring. Remington's relationship with Bentley had been personal and episodic.[14]

The matter did not die, however, when the grand jury returned no indictments. Instead Bentley repeated her charges publicly in 1948—first in a five-part series headlined "Blonde Spy Queen," published in the *New York World-Telegram*, then in dramatic public testimony before two congressional committees.[15]

Bentley's now public charges received a mixed response that reflected the deep partisan divisions of the time. Her account was enthusiastically endorsed by American conservatives and denounced or viewed skeptically by American liberals. These reactions reflected differences, dating from the mid-1930s, over whether the New Deal had been infiltrated by Communists. Nonetheless, independent of how the Bentley charges played out politically, especially during a presidential election, the actions of the Truman administration rested on the quality of the FBI's evidence. Neither in 1947 nor thereafter were FBI agents able to corroborate Bentley. In a 1970 memorandum, an FBI official admitted that, despite having analyzed the case "over and over again," agents were never able "to obtain information to substantiate and corroborate the allegations of BENTLEY." In 1954, FBI officials had even attempted to exploit new legislation by granting immunity to

Edward Fitzgerald, one of those named by Bentley. Fitzgerald was then required to testify before a grand jury but "refused to talk" and was sentenced for contempt, serving a five-month prison term.[16]

Then in November–December 1948, Whittaker Chambers produced notes (in Alger Hiss's handwriting) and typed and microfilm copies of State Department documents, which he claimed Hiss had given him in 1938 at the time of Chambers's defection from the Communist party. That same year, continuing for more than three decades, military intelligence agents deciphered more of the Venona messages—in 1947–1949 learning that Judith Coplon had in 1944 been a KGB source and that Julius Rosenberg, also in 1944, had recruited his brother-in-law to steal information relating to the atomic bomb project.

The Chambers and Venona developments raise questions about the effectiveness of FBI counterintelligence operations: good fortune, more than the skills and diligence of FBI agents, proved crucial. Chambers might have misled FBI agents between 1942 and 1946 about his knowledge of Soviet espionage operations, and in the process he might have withheld crucial information that would have led to the earlier unmasking of Soviet spies. His production of these documents in 1948, resulting in Hiss's perjury conviction, could scarcely have been anticipated by FBI officials.

Luck also provided the break that uncovered the Rosenberg atomic espionage ring. U.S. analysts were able to decipher intercepted Soviet consular messages because in 1942 the KGB cryptographic center in Moscow had assembled duplicate copies of more than 35,000 pages of what were intended to be unique encoding pads for onetime use. Soviet code clerks inadvertently used these duplicates in coding messages for transmission. Spotting the duplicate usage, American cryptanalysts were able by 1946 to begin to break the coded messages. This error, subverting the security of onetime pads, proved to be crucial to the American military's counterintelligence success, or at least expedited the breakthrough.[17]

Because Soviet agents believed their encoded messages to be secure, they often neglected to disguise their sources through code names. This overconfidence helped the FBI identify the KGB's American sources—for example, Judith Coplon and Julius Rosenberg, whose identities were disguised through code names (Sima, in Coplon's case; Antenna, then Liberal, in Rosenberg's case).

The Venona messages reveal that in July 1944 Sima was considered for recruitment as a potential KGB source and at the time was employed in the Economic Section of the Justice Department's Military Department. Messages of October and December 1944 and January 1945 record Sima was in fact recruited and that the FBI might have monitored her recent meeting with another KGB source, an Office of War Information employee. A December 1944 Venona message further reports that Sima was employed in the Justice Department's Foreign Agents Registration branch in New York. Finally, a June 1945 Venona message reports Sima's transfer to Washington, D.C., and a March 1945 message identifies her supervisor in the Justice Department's Military Department as Woolworth (in fact, Robert Wohlforth, who headed the Justice Department's Economic Warfare Department). The information about Sima's employment history—the specific dates of her employment, transfer, and FBI surveillance pertaining to her security clearance; her gender; and the name of her Justice Department supervisor enabled FBI agents in 1948 to identify Sima as Judith Coplon.[18]

Julius Rosenberg's identity was disguised in the Soviet consular reports under the code name Antenna, later changed to Liberal. A September 1944 Venona message, which refers to him by code name, nonetheless records the recruitment of the "wife of his wife's brother, Ruth Greenglass." It further cites Ruth Green-

"to refrain from removing documents until she was quite sure that she was trusted."[21]

KGB officers in Moscow also knew (or anticipated) that FBI agents closely monitored the American Communist party and had recruited informers to infiltrate the party. The KGB thus mandated strict conditions whenever Communist party contacts were involved "in intelligence matters." KGB agents were to meet "only with special reliable undercover contacts" of the party "who are not suspected" of involvement in intelligence work, and were to obtain advance approval before each meeting.[22] Consular staff were also ordered not to use "real surnames of recruits" but code names, to destroy all notes when sending coded messages, and to limit their knowledge of intelligence work on a need-to-know basis.[23]

KGB officials in New York responded to these directives by regularly assuring Moscow of their intention to ensure the "maximum degree of security" and by instituting safeguards. For example, to counter possible wiretapping or bugging of the New York consulate, all consular personnel were specifically ordered to be careful what they said and not to "talk loudly." In special cases, KGB agents used automobiles to arrange secret meetings and to shake FBI surveillance. KGB agents also discontinued all meetings or suspended the transfer of a recruit whenever they suspected that their actions were being monitored by the FBI.[24]

These precautions, however, were not always sufficient. FBI counterintelligence activities were intense. An FBI wiretap of Communist party headquarters in New York alerted officials to a planned March 29, 1943, meeting between party activist Steve Nelson and Joseph Weinberg, a physicist employed at the University of California's Berkeley Radiation Laboratory. FBI officials bugged Nelson's residence and discovered that Weinberg had delivered "highly secret information regarding experiments being conducted at the Radiation Laboratory, Berkeley, pertaining to the atomic bomb." Continuing to monitor Nelson, they suspected that he had delivered this classified information to Soviet consular officer Ivan Ivanov for transmittal to the Soviet Union. The FBI's bug of Nelson's residence produced an even more dramatic discovery on April 10, 1943, recording his conversation with KGB officer Vassili Zubilin, third secretary at the Soviet embassy in Washington but in fact the senior KGB resident officer in the United States.* The FBI bug confirmed that Zubilin had "paid a sum of money" to Nelson "for the purpose of placing Communist Party members and Comintern agents in industries engaged in secret war production for the United States Government so that the information could be obtained for transmittal to the Soviet Union." FBI director Hoover acted quickly to forestall this espionage operation by instituting a special code-named COMRAP program to "identify all members of the Communist International (Comintern) apparatus with which Steve Nelson and Vassili Zubilin are connected as well as the agents of this apparatus in various war industries."[25]

KGB officials at the time were unaware of this FBI windfall. Within a year, however, they were scurrying to counteract a potentially disabling exposé resulting from the April 1944 defection of Victor Kravchenko, a member of the Soviet Government Purchasing Commission stationed in New York. David Dallin, a Soviet

*At the time FBI officials did not know that Zubilin (whose real name was Vassili Zarubin) was Nelson's visitor. They later established that Zubilin held the rank of general in the KGB and "engaged in the movement of Soviet agents into and out of the United States" and "organizes secret radio stations, prepares counterfeit documents, obtains industrial and military information for transmittal to the Soviet Union." Zubilin was a sophisticated if ruthless operative who had risen quickly in Soviet intelligence. Benson and Warner, *Venona,* pp. xvii, 57, 108; Benjamin Fischer, "The Katyn Controversy: Stalin's Killing Field," *Studies in Intelligence* (Winter 1999–2000), p. 61.

emigré and ardent anti-Communist with close ties to the Trotskyite political community, was instrumental in engineering Kravchenko's defection.

From sources they had recruited among American Trotskyites, KGB officials sought information about Kravchenko's plans and specifically whether and what he intended to tell U.S. officials. They were also keenly interested in his writing plans, having learned of his intention to write articles and a book. KGB agents unsuccessfully sought to arrange a personal meeting with Kravchenko—perhaps to persuade him to redefect or else to kill him—and were particularly interested in reports that he feared he might be killed and had hired two bodyguards, and that Roosevelt administration officials might succumb to pressure and turn him over to the Soviets.[26]

KGB officials had good reason for their concern about Kravchenko's defection. As early as February 1944, Dallin had approached former U.S. Ambassador to the Soviet Union William Bullitt about an unnamed employee of the Soviet Government Purchasing Commission who was interested in asylum. Bullitt relayed this information to Attorney General Francis Biddle, who in turn directed Hoover to interview Dallin. At first Dallin declined to identify the Soviet employee, but three days later Biddle obtained President Roosevelt's approval for "whatever arrangements" Hoover might make for "the use of the Russian." Contacted on March 3, Dallin identified Kravchenko as the defector and arranged a series of FBI meetings with him. Kravchenko told his FBI interviewers about the Soviet Government Purchasing Commission, where he was employed, and, more generally, about "Soviet activities inimical to the United States." Denying that he was an intelligence agent, he named "certain" KGB officers "attached to the [Soviet Government Purchasing] Commission and the [Soviet] Embassy."

During these discussions, Kravchenko specified the terms of his defection. He insisted on a number of guarantees: an opportunity to learn English, physical protection, a permit to carry firearms, a change of identity, a place to live and work, and "no monetary worries for about a year and a half," though he did not "mention any sum of money in exchange for information." In return, Kravchenko offered to "furnish" information about Soviet "espionage activity" in the United States; "illegal conspiracies between American firms and the Soviet Government"; KGB activities in the United States; and information about the "organization" of the KGB in the Soviet Union. Even though President Roosevelt had already given Hoover complete freedom to enter negotiations with Kravchenko, the FBI director recontacted Biddle to seek the president's approval to "go forward in this situation" in view of Kravchenko's "conditions."

Biddle thereupon discussed the matter of Kravchenko's defection with Secretary of State Cordell Hull, who at first was "very much against our doing anything, being nervous about the effect it might have on Russia." Assured that the attorney general would "take no criminal action against any Russian connected with the Russian Government without first obtaining [the Secretary of State's] approval," Hull agreed to defer to Biddle. The attorney general promised to handle the matter "discreetly," adding that no one except himself and Hoover knew of the proposed plan. Ordered to proceed, Hoover promised Biddle to "carry through immediately."

Kravchenko defected publicly on April 3, 1944, and was immediately interviewed by FBI agents on April 4, 5, 6, and 17. During these interviews he "continued to supply information" along the lines he had promised earlier in the March meetings. But "when no promises of assistance [from the U.S. government] were forthcoming, he urgently requested that the interviews be stopped so that he could look to his own affairs." Kravchenko eventually published his memoir, *I Chose Freedom,* and in 1949 acquired U.S. citizenship through special legislation introduced by Senator Karl Mundt.[27]

What Kravchenko told FBI agents in March and April 1944 remains unknown.* The Kravchenko folder in Hoover's secret office file and Biddle's one-page blind memo reveal Kravchenko's offer to name names and describe KGB operations, but they do not recount what Kravchenko specifically reported. Biddle and Hoover, in any event, did protect Kravchenko from being returned to the Soviet Union. A December 26, 1944, memorandum describes how they finessed a State Department plan to pressure Kravchenko to return to the Soviet Union—an agent in the FBI's New York office, acting on Biddle's advance instructions, was to tip off Kravchenko anonymously so that he could "flee and carefully hide himself."[28]

Kravchenko's defection, combined with the results of the FBI's COMRAP investigation, appear to have triggered Zubilin's departure from the United States in August 1944. In any event, when Zubilin left, KGB officials reassessed their security procedures to prevent Soviet espionage operations from being compromised—specifically the so-called Silvermaster spy ring.

Nathan Gregory Silvermaster headed a highly centralized operation. A government economist, he recruited individuals employed in wartime agencies and departments, maintained contact with them, and then filmed the documents they provided, sometimes storing them for weeks in the basement of his residence. This operation posed serious risks should Silvermaster's role as a Soviet operative become known to the FBI. As early as September 1943, KGB officers recognized this problem, having recently learned that the FBI was trying to determine whether Silvermaster was a member of the Communist party. This concern led Silver-

*I requested Kravchenko's FBI file more than three years ago, but my request has as yet not been processed.

master's KGB supervisor in August 1944 to propose decentralizing the operation. Silvermaster resisted his supervisor's recommendation, even though he conceded that "this is the only thing to do." The proposed splitting of the Silvermaster organization "into smaller units" to ensure "greater secrecy and more effective organization of the work" was renewed in October 1944 and then again in January 1945. By then, the concerns of KGB officials had heightened. The FBI's investigation suggested that Silvermaster might be dismissed from his government position, thereby destroying the KGB's sources of information. Unwilling to defer to Silvermaster's protest that bypassing him could alienate his recruited sources, KGB officers in April 1945 instituted a new arrangement. Information developed by the former Silvermaster ring would now be conveyed to New York "only in film and in several batches," with several couriers—not to include Silvermaster or Bentley—taking "turns in making the trip to Washington for Silvermaster materials."[29]

Having just resolved the Silvermaster problem, KGB officials six months later learned of the intensity of FBI surveillance practices. In October 1945, Judith Coplon provided her KGB handlers a series of FBI reports. Although none of these reports related to current KGB espionage operations, their contents convinced KGB officers of the need to reassess their view of FBI surveillance limitations. One of the reports that Coplon delivered recorded the FBI's wiretapping of J. Robert Oppenheimer and the interception of a letter from the estranged wife of Victor Perlo (another KGB recruit employed in wartime Washington) to President Roosevelt. KGB officials were impressed by "how thoroughly the smallest facts from conversations, correspondence, and telephone talks held by our organizations, individual representatives, and workers in this country are recorded [by the FBI]. We observed how numerous is the [FBI's] cadre involved in the described."[30]

Before KGB officials could institute further safeguards, they suffered a crippling blow to one of their ongoing operations: Elizabeth Bentley's November 1945 defection. Learning of her desertion through another KGB recruit, Harold "Kim" Philby, KGB officials took immediate action in light of Bentley's involvement in numerous Soviet espionage operations dating from 1936. The heads of the KGB's New York and Washington offices were ordered to "cease immediately their connection with all persons known to Bentley in our work [and further] to warn the agents about Bentley's betrayal." At minimum, those advised included Joseph Katz, Charles Kramer, Harold Glasser, Eva Getsov, Nathan Silvermaster, Bernard Schuster, Alexander Koral, and (undeciphered code name) Art. They were instructed that if they were interrogated by the FBI, they "should deny their secret connections with [Bentley], stating that her testimony was a lie" but "shouldn't deny simply being acquainted with her"—because FBI agents might have monitored their recent meetings with her. These agents were also to "cease all connections with their subsources." Many of these subsources had been led to believe that the information they provided was being given to the American Communist party, not the Soviet Union, so to allay any concern the agents were to attribute this cessation to "intensified" FBI "counterintelligence activity against Communists and progressive elements in the U.S." In the event the agents had violated orders and were keeping pilfered "documents and notes which could compromise agents and their subsources" in their homes, these records "should be destroyed immediately." The heads of the KGB's New York and Washington offices were recalled to the Soviet Union, but only after they had reviewed "all the files and notes" maintained in their offices and personally destroyed "all unnecessary ones."[31]

This crippling of a Soviet espionage network, however, was not the result of FBI counterintelligence investigations so much as the fortuitous defections of Bentley and Kravchenko. Does this mean that FBI counterintelligence, though intense, was ineffective? Because relevant FBI records are either closed or massively redacted upon release, this question cannot be answered definitively. But a tentative answer can be offered as to whether the FBI failed to uncover Soviet espionage operations, or whether there were none other than the Willie, Chambers, Bentley, and Rosenberg spy rings that we now know. A tentative assessment is based on the incomplete if tantalizing FBI records released since the mid-1970s, either by the so-called Church Committee or in response to Freedom of Information Act requests (and often heavily redacted), and the accessible copies of FBI records deposited at the Roosevelt presidential library. These undeniably incomplete records of FBI investigative activities confirm the intensity of FBI monitoring of American Communists throughout the World War II era, an intensity that should have uncovered the Soviet recruitment of American Communists.

For example, from a wiretap of American Communist party headquarters, FBI officials learned in late 1942 that party activist Steve Nelson had been recruited by a "man from Moscow," and that this action was known to party head Earl Browder. Bugging Nelson's residence in Oakland, California, FBI agents first learned in March 1943 that Nelson had successfully recruited Joseph Weinberg, a physicist engaged in classified research for the atomic bomb project, and then the next month had met with Vassili Zubilin, the head of KGB operations in the United States, to discuss the further recruitment of American Communists for Soviet espionage operations.[32]

In addition, FBI agents had, at least from September 1940, wiretapped the Soviet embassy in Washington and in December 1942 had twice broken into a New York City warehouse rented by the Soviet Government Purchasing Commission.[33] FBI agents also bugged meetings of Communist party officials, though the number and specific targets of such bugging operations remain unknown. Accessible FBI records at the Roosevelt presidential library confirm at least two such installations. In the first, FBI director Hoover learned that the party's national leadership had instructed its Illinois branch of a decision to fortify the party's "secret apparatus" by forming a special "underground" organization to be headed by Soviet agent Joszef Peters. From the second bug, Hoover learned that Communist party officials in Butte, Montana, had established a secret branch within the Congress of Industrial Organizations (CIO) union in plants producing munitions and war materials.[34] The scope of FBI surveillance and its discovery of some of the most sensitive activities of the American Communist party is further documented by records confirming that, dating from the late 1930s, FBI officials knew that the Soviet Union was funding the party, the activities of some Communist activists, and underground or other activities "detrimental to the national defense of the United States with regard to espionage, sabotage, propaganda activities and otherwise."[35]

FBI counterintelligence operations—and the use of illegal investigative techniques such as break-ins, wiretaps, bugs, and mail openings—were not confined to Soviet agents and Communist party officials. Given their own political definition of espionage, FBI officials were just as interested in learning of Communist efforts to influence domestic politics. One such politically motivated investigation targeted German emigré writers, refugees who had fled Nazi Germany and had settled primarily in New York and Los Angeles, some of them employed in the film industry or as playwrights. As these refugees were neither government employees nor employed in defense work, FBI investigations uncovered only their efforts to influence public opinion about the postwar governance and economy of Germany after the defeat of the Nazis. Specifically the FBI was interested in their role in organizing and promoting the Free Germany Committee and the Council for a Democratic Germany. FBI agents also monitored and recorded their personal habits. Unwilling to rely on less intrusive physical surveillance, FBI agents used illegal investigative techniques. They wiretapped Bertolt Brecht, Thomas Mann, Heinrich Mann, Helene Weigel, Berthold Viertel, Anna Seghers, and Bode and Alma Uhse.[36] They broke into residences to photocopy the papers of Brecht, Ruth Berlau, Leonhard Frank, Erwin Picator, Ludwig Renn, and Anna Seghers,[37] and bugged the residences of Brecht, Berlau, Hanns Eisler, and Billy Wilder. They also recorded the illicit sexual affair of Brecht and Berlau through a bug installed in the Chalet Motor Hotel.[38] FBI agents monitored the domestic mail and, through the wartime censorship program, the international mail of Seghers, Renn, Brecht, Berlau, Viertel, Heinrich Mann, Lion Feuchtwanger, Thomas Mann, Klaus Mann, Osker Graf, Egon Kirch, and the Free Germany Committee.[39]

Consistent with their concern about Communist "propaganda" activities, FBI officials in 1942 looked into Communist influence in the motion picture industry in a massive investigation code-named COMPIC. Again, the targets of this investigation were not employed in the government or in defense industries. FBI officials concluded that Communists had indeed influenced the production of "propaganda," even though the suspected films that prompted this concern had promoted anti-fascist themes or had favorably depicted a wartime ally.* This investigation continued until 1956, by which time FBI officials concluded that Communist influence in Hollywood was "practically nonexistent at the present time."

By 1947–1948, the Hollywood investigations had produced a further objective: convict those Hollywood Communists indicted in 1947 for contempt of Congress—for refusing on First Amendment grounds to answer questions about their Communist affilia-

*Discussed more fully in Chapter Six.

tions posed by the House Committee on Un-American Activities. As in the case of the German emigré writers, FBI agents again used illegal investigative techniques extensively. Through a series of break-ins between 1943 and 1947, FBI agents had photocopied the membership records of the Los Angeles branch of the Communist party, then identified those party members employed in the film industry and the specific films on which they had worked as producers, directors, writers, actors, stagehands, and other laborers.[40] The FBI wiretapped Communist activist Elizabeth Leach; the Los Angeles Workers School; Marguerite Anderson of the CIO's Maritime Committee; Progressive party activist C. B. Baldwin; screenwriters John Lawson, Waldo Salt, and Hubert Biberman, and screen reader David Robison; and Bartley Crum, Martin Popper, David Wahl, attorneys of the indicted Hollywood producers, writers, and directors. A February 1948 wiretap authorization request of Richard Hood, the head of the FBI's Los Angeles field office, confirms the political purpose that shaped FBI investigations. Hood requested approval to wiretap Benjamin Margolis, whom he described as an attorney for the recently indicted Hollywood screenwriters and directors and a prominent Communist. This wiretap, Hood claimed, would resolve one of the Los Angeles field office's problems: the strict security precautions that Communist activists and their supporters had recently instituted to foreclose discovery of what Hood believed to be invaluable information about Communist cultural groups—which were "potentially the most dangerous from the standpoint of their propaganda and financial value to the [Communist] Party." Endorsing Hood's request, the supervising assistant director at FBI headquarters emphasized that the wiretap would provide crucial information "regarding meetings, conferences, and legal maneuverings of the Communist elements as they pertain to the Communist Party cultural groups generally and specifically for Motion Picture Industry."[41]

The COMPIC and German emigré investigations confirm an underlying purpose of FBI counterintelligence—to determine Communist influence on American culture. But the scope of such politically motivated investigations cannot be fully understood because the FBI's massive files on the American Communist party have not yet been released. The size of the FBI's file on the Communist party, which FBI personnel "conservatively" estimate at 1,275,000 pages,[42] underscores how intensively FBI agents monitored American Communists. Did their focus on political, trade union, and propaganda activities distract them from the discovery of Soviet espionage?

Isolated FBI memoranda, accessible at the Roosevelt presidential library, document the confident belief of senior FBI officials that they had successfully contained Soviet espionage activities in the World War II era. FBI "espionage and counter-espionage operations," Hoover assured the Roosevelt White House in October 1940, were fully conversant with the plans and actions of fascist and Communist agents. Through "constant observation and surveillance a number of known and suspected Agents of the German, Russian, French and Italian Secret Services," the FBI director reported, FBI agents were able to "maintain a careful check upon the channels of communication, the sources of information, the methods of finance and other data relative to these agents." Hoover concluded by counseling against arresting any of these agents "except in extraordinary cases because counter espionage methods and observation and surveillance result in a constantly growing reservoir of information concerning not only known but also new agents of these governments."[43]

In May 1941, Hoover again unqualifiedly advised the Roosevelt White House that the FBI's

> active and intensive [counterespionage] operations are carried on in keeping under observation and constant study the operations of

> the German, Italian, Soviet and Japanese Agents. . . . The identities of all major representatives of the Governments specified are known and their activities are under constant scrutiny.[44]

The Roosevelt library contains no further reports from the FBI director about FBI counterintelligence operations after 1941—unless such reports remain classified. Hoover's 1940 and 1941 reports were sent to allay any of President Roosevelt's concerns about FBI counterintelligence activities and their effectiveness. As it happened, during the cold war era Hoover's confident assurances that the FBI had "checked" any and all Soviet agents did not come back to haunt him or the FBI. Questions about Soviet espionage successes instead became politicized as McCarthyites in Congress and the media contended that the Roosevelt administration's "softness toward Communism" had hamstrung FBI operations. The FBI's ineffectiveness in counterintelligence never became an issue.

The Roosevelt White House and Attorneys General Robert Jackson and Francis Biddle had in fact willingly deferred to Hoover, granting the FBI director free range in monitoring Soviet agents and American Communists. This deference is further confirmed by a massive FBI investigation launched in April–May 1943 to monitor what officials concluded was a Comintern espionage operation involving Soviet and American Communists.

CHAPTER THREE

• • •

The Comintern Apparatus Investigation

IN MARCH 1943, senior FBI officials learned that Joseph Weinberg, a physicist engaged in classified research on the atomic bomb project at the Berkeley Radiation Laboratory of the University of California, had delivered "highly secret information" to Communist party activist Steve Nelson. Then, in April 1943, senior FBI officials further learned that Vassili Zubilin, the senior KGB official in the United States, had given Nelson a large "sum of money" for the "purpose of placing Communist Party members and agents in industries engaged in secret war production in the United States so that information could be obtained for transmittal to the Soviet Union." This arrangement, FBI director Hoover advised the Roosevelt White House, had been approved by American Communist party chairman Earl Browder. Hoover also noted that Nelson and Zubilin "will meet in the near future with other leaders of the Communist International (Comintern) apparatus active in the United States."[1]

Hoover immediately launched two code-named programs to

stymie this planned Soviet espionage operation: CINRAD (Communist Infiltration of the University of California Radiation Laboratory) and COMRAP (Comintern Apparatus). Under CINRAD, FBI agents sought to "identify" any "members of the Comintern apparatus" employed in the Radiation Lab at Berkeley or at the separate atomic bomb research project at Los Alamos, New Mexico, who had been recruited to obtain sensitive classified information "for transmittal to U.S.S.R." FBI officials shared the results of this investigation with officials of the Military Intelligence Division, the agency that had principal security responsibility for the atomic bomb project. The FBI's COMRAP investigation, in contrast, was "broader" in scope and was "conducted without any jurisdictional limitation imposed" (as in the case of CINRAD) by military intelligence. Under the COMRAP program, FBI agents sought to "identify the members of the Apparatus and to obtain complete data regarding the various activities in which the Apparatus is interested." The premise of this intensive investigation was that current and future suspects "are very probably experienced revolutionaries who have been well-schooled in Moscow."[2]

Almost concurrent with the discovery of the Zubilin-Nelson initiative, Hoover received an anonymous letter written in Russian and dated August 7, 1943. This letter, apparently written by a Soviet official stationed in the United States (it bore a Washington, D.C., postmark), claimed that Vassili Zubilin and his wife Elizabeta had personally placed "agents into and out of the U.S.A.," some of whom were employed in "almost all [U.S.] ministries including the State Department." The author of this letter identified by name the Soviet officials stationed in the United States who comprised a larger network of Soviet espionage agents operating under Zubilin's control. Those named were consular officials Pavel Klarin (New York) and Gregory Kheifets (San Francisco); Amtorg (the Soviet trading company) employees Semen Semenov and Leonid Kvasnikov; Soviet embassy officials Vassili Dolgov and Vassili Mironov; Soviet Government Purchasing Commission (the Soviet agency that coordinated the delivery of lend-lease materials with American officials and industries) employees Andrei Schevchenko and Serghei Lukianov; and an American Communist involved in the music and film industry, Boris Morros.[3]

The COMRAP investigation lasted from 1943 through early 1945. (Although the COMRAP file contains documents dated 1947–1948, these essentially summarize the findings of the 1943–1945 investigations.) The catalyst to this intensive investigation (confirmed by the size of the file—approximately ten thousand pages) stemmed from the FBI's discovery of Zubilin's plans through the bugging of Nelson's residence and the anonymous letter. In response, Hoover ordered FBI agents in all field offices—but primarily San Francisco, New York, Los Angeles, and Washington, D.C.—to track Nelson and the identified Soviet agents through physical surveillance, wiretaps, mail covers and intercepts, bugs, and break-ins. Agents were then to investigate those individuals with whom they came in contact. The ensuing investigation expanded in concentric circles as each new suspect's contacts were then investigated.

The key question for our purposes is, how successful was this investigation? Did it uncover evidence that Soviet agents had recruited American Communists and Communist sympathizers to steal classified or politically sensitive information? Massive redactions in the released COMRAP file preclude a definitive answer. Some reports in the file have been withheld entirely; others have been heavily redacted; and the names of the subjects and other identifying information, and the information developed by FBI agents has sometimes been redacted from otherwise uncensored reports. Still, the general contours of this FBI investigation can be discerned—either by combining a close reading of the unredacted sections with the contents of an unredacted CIA memorandum of February 1948, or by integrating released information in the COMRAP file that summarizes the results of the investigation.

Not a single report, paragraph, or sentence in the released sections of the COMRAP file confirms that FBI agents monitored any Soviet official except Schevchenko, or that they uncovered information that any Soviet official had engaged in espionage. But this is because all references that pertain to Soviet officials were redacted on "national security" grounds. That FBI agents in fact closely monitored the activities and contacts of Vassili and Elizabeta Zubilin, Semenov, Klarin, Lukianov, Schevchenko, Dolgov, Mironov, and Kheifets is confirmed by a 1948 CIA memorandum and a partially redacted FBI summary memorandum of December 1944.

The December 1944 memorandum summarizes the results of the COMRAP investigation to date. Its contents include paragraphs on Semenov, Klarin, Lukianov, Schevchenko, Dolgov, and Mironov—but, surprisingly, none on the Zubilins. After an initial sentence referring to the named Soviet official, the remainder of the paragraph is redacted, thus rendering it impossible to determine what information the FBI developed on this individual. The exception is a cryptic sentence noting, "There are indications pointing to a number of Soviet officials in the Washington area who may be cooperating with the Comintern Apparatus." The remainder of that paragraph and a succeeding paragraph, however, are again redacted.[4]

In addition, though unredacted sections of the COMRAP file refer episodically to the August 1943 anonymous letter, the released sections confirm only that this letter triggered an FBI investigation which included a companion effort to identify the letter writer. Again, because of massive redactions it is impossible to determine what this FBI investigation uncovered—except that FBI agents suspected that the letter writer "was an employee of the USSR Embassy, Washington, D.C."[5]

While all information pertaining to these Soviet officials (excepting Schevchenko, to be discussed later) in the released COM-

RAP file was redacted, a CIA "memorandum for the file" of February 1948 confirms that FBI agents had in fact investigated all the suspected Soviet spies and could not confirm that they had engaged in espionage or recruited American Communists to do so. The writer of this CIA memorandum described its contents as based on "a brief summary" of the FBI's "extensive operational Soviet espionage case [COMRAP] within the U.S." which Zubilin controlled until August 28, 1944 (when he left the United States), and that this espionage operation "possibly subsequently" continued under the direction of his unknown successor. The CIA analyst who prepared this summary then described the subjects of the COMRAP investigation as personnel "who, prior to 1943, had been long active in the illegal conspiratorial and quasi-intelligence operations of the Comintern Apparatus."

After citing the April 1943 Nelson-Zubilin meeting and the August 1943 anonymous letter as confirming Zubilin's leadership of the suspected Comintern Apparatus, the CIA memorandum reports no specific example of either of the Zubilins' espionage activities after Vassili Zubilin's April 10, 1943, meeting with Nelson. The memorandum does report that Kheifets had been "active in operational Soviet espionage" in the San Francisco area but cites no specific action, and further that Kheifets's "personal papers" (photocopied during an FBI break-in) revealed that "he maintained a tremendously large number of contacts on the West Coast and that he undoubtedly was responsible for other extensive intelligence operations which were never completely identified."

The FBI's COMRAP investigation also failed to document that the other Soviet agents—Mironov, Lukianov, Semenov, Dolgov—were involved in espionage. Thus the CIA writer reports that "independent investigation failed to substantiate the allegations concerning [Mironov's] espionage operations"; "it was impossible to substantiate the allegations of [Lukianov's] espionage activities in the U.S."; it was "impossible to substantiate the allegations concerning SEMENOV"; and it was "not possible to substantiate the [espionage] allegations [concerning Dolgov] through independent investigation." The CIA summary of the FBI's COMRAP investigation recounts only one such case of espionage, Klarin's "operation of an extensive espionage net in the New York area." The alleged espionage activities of this net, however, did not involve the pilfering of U.S. military or diplomatic secrets but pertained to Klarin's role in the so-called Altschuler case. This was a mail-drop operation centered in Mexico and involved secret communications intended to pressure the Mexican government to release the imprisoned Soviet agent convicted of assassinating Leon Trotsky in 1940.[6]

Perhaps because it might have been the sole FBI success, the released reports in the COMRAP file itself inexplicably describe FBI tactics and the results of their investigation only of Schevchenko. These unredacted reports confirm that Schevchenko's movements and contacts were closely monitored, and that FBI agents wiretapped his residence and initiated a mail cover—that is, recording the names and addresses of individuals with whom he corresponded. Agents confirmed that Schevchenko, under the guise of his official relationship with the Bell Aircraft Corporation in Buffalo as a representative of the Soviet Government Purchasing Commission, obtained "restricted information" from individuals employed in defense work. One of these individuals was eventually recruited as a "Bureau informant," who then entrapped Schevchenko into providing him "with expensive cameras to photograph for [Schevchenko] restricted data on aircraft research" and "jet propulsion experiments." As a consequence, in January 1946, Schevchenko was expelled from the United States.[7]

If the CIA summary memorandum accurately describes the FBI's failure to document Soviet espionage, does this mean that Zubilin failed to obtain the "secret war production" information he wanted? Or had FBI agents failed to uncover a successful Soviet espionage operation—thus illustrating the limitations of FBI counterintelligence operations? And what did FBI agents learn about the suspected espionage activities of American Communists, the primary targets of the COMRAP program?

Because it is heavily redacted, the released COMRAP file precludes definitive answers. It does show that FBI agents extensively used intrusive investigative techniques, which would seem to suggest that they would have uncovered any espionage activities.

For example, FBI agents employed a great many wiretaps during the course of this investigation. But the names of and identifying information about many targets of these wiretaps have been redacted in the released COMRAP file.[8] In those cases where names were released, they confirm that Attorney General Biddle gave the FBI broad latitude in conducting this investigation, approving all of Hoover's wiretap authorization requests, which the FBI director justified in order to determine "the extent of [each identified subject's] activities in the Comintern Apparatus and for the additional purpose of determining the identities of other espionage agents."* Those wiretapped whose names were not redacted included Alexander Bittelman, a leading Communist party official described as "a member of it not actually the leader of the Apparatus, which as you have been advised, contains Soviet agents in its membership";[9] Boris Morros, a Hollywood film and music producer described as "a member of the Communist International (Comintern) operation in the United States";[10] Jean Tatlock, a

*Biddle in fact approved all of Hoover's wiretap authorization requests under COMRAP. His approval effectively refutes the McCarthyites' contentions that the Roosevelt administration's "softness toward communism" hamstrung FBI investigations. In 1970, moreover, as part of a general effort to sanitize FBI wiretap records in order to preclude any future assessment of the scope and targets of FBI wiretap practices, the head of the FBI's Washington, D.C., field office solicited Hoover's approval to destroy all logs of the wiretaps installed during the course of the COMRAP investigation. Memo, SAC Washington to FBI Director, April 24, 1970, FBI 100-203581-5548.

psychiatrist and personal friend of J. Robert Oppenheimer, described as Oppenheimer's "paramour"—and on another occasion as a woman of "loose morality"—who accordingly was in a "position to solicit secret information from men with whom she associates, but is also in a position to pass the information on to espionage agents within the Apparatus";[11] Haakon Chevalier, a friend of Oppenheimer's whom FBI agents discovered "has solicited secret information regarding United States military matters [the atomic bomb program] for transmittal to the Soviet Union";[12] the Russian American Club in Los Angeles, described as "a gathering place for a number of the prominent subjects under investigation as possible espionage agents";[13] William Dieterle, an employee in the film industry in Hollywood;[14] Arthur Adams, described as "a Soviet agent believed to be illegally in the United States" and whose espionage activities were reportedly funded through the Electronic Corporation of America;[15] Joris Ivens, a Dutch alien suspected of having "international Comintern contacts";[16] the Joint Anti-Fascist Refugee Committee;[17] the Maritime Book Shop, a Communist hangout; Electrical Communications, a business firm; and James Miller and three other radical activists.[18]

Under the COMRAP program FBI agents also conducted numerous break-ins to photocopy records;[19] monitored Communist party headquarters in New York to identify those who entered and left;[20] rented a room in a building across the street from the site of a Communist party plenum scheduled for June 12–13, 1943, to monitor and photograph those attending the plenum;[21] instituted mail covers and mail intercepts (opening and photocopying the letters) in, for example, the Seattle, Baltimore, New York City, San Francisco, Washington, D.C., Pittsburgh, Los Angeles, Cincinnati, Buffalo, Chicago, and New Haven field offices;[22] submitted names for inclusion on the Office of Censorship's watch list of those whose international communications (letters, cables, telephone conversations) were to be intercepted;[23] rented a house in New York City near the residence of a targeted suspect in order to follow this individual's activities "more closely";[24] had an FBI agent register at the Hotel Albert in New York City, one block from Communist party headquarters, as the hotel "has strong patronage from Communist Party leaders and sympathizers";[25] had San Francisco and other field offices submit "copies of photographs of all individuals who have been or are now under physical, technical [wiretap] or microphone surveillance" "as well as any other person related to Comintern Apparatus";[26] and installed numerous microphones (bugs) to intercept conversations at known meetings.[27]

The FBI's extensive use of illegal investigative techniques effectively foreclosed prosecution of any of the suspected Comintern Apparatus recruits. Any acquired evidence could not be used for prosecution. Nonetheless the question arises: Did FBI agents uncover evidence that American Communists, or Communist sympathizers, had committed espionage? Owing to their intrusiveness, these investigations should have uncovered such activities. Again, that question cannot be definitely answered owing to the heavily redacted nature of the released COMRAP file. But unredacted sections of two FBI reports of 1944 and 1945, summarizing the results of this intensive investigation, offer a tentative answer.

In November 1944, Hoover directed the FBI's San Francisco field office to compile a report summarizing the results of the COMRAP investigation. To ensure that the report would be comprehensive, he ordered all FBI field offices that had participated in this investigation to forward their findings to the San Francisco office. The FBI director specifically identified the information to be forwarded to bring "up to date the known activities of the Soviet agents and subjects in the United States along the following lines: (1) military espionage, (2) industrial espionage, (3) propaganda and (4) political activity." The SACs, heads of these field offices, however, were not to be "too specific in your statement regarding

Soviet controls. Actually the Bureau does not know, nor is it aware, that any intelligence agency outside the Soviet Union knows the exact chain of control." SACs were also to keep in mind that various "official and unofficial" Soviet agencies in the United States—such as the Soviet Government Purchasing Commission, Soviet consulates, and the Soviet embassy—"exist not merely as a cover for Apparatus activity, but because the organization itself, as such, has a definite function to perform."[28]

The summary report based on these submissions began by highlighting the key findings of the intensive COMRAP investigation. The analyst concluded that the investigation confirmed the existence of "a vast illegal and conspirative Russian-controlled and dominated International Communist Organization, 'Comintern Apparatus.'" This apparatus, the analyst continued, has "as its several objectives":

> Military and Industrial Espionage
>
> Influencing the people and Government of the United States toward acceptance of Soviet foreign policy through highly political language groups.
>
> Distribution of pro-Russian propaganda through the media of books, pamphlets, screen and radio, and "Front group" technique.
>
> Operation of an illegal courier system, based on American Communist seamen, which facilitates the aforementioned objectives.
>
> The Apparatus operates for the ultimate advantage, protection, and security of the USSR and for Soviet Russia's goal of world domination, to the detriment of the United States and other countries in which the Apparatus exists. . . .
>
> Russian espionage and propaganda activities in the United States appear to be channelized through commissariats of the Soviet Government maintaining offices and performing official func-

> tions in this country. It is known that these activities are performed with the cooperation of members of the Communist Party. The individuals of primary importance in the transmission of Russian propaganda and transmission of espionage information are, for the purpose of this investigation, considered in a coordinated association referred to as the Communist Apparatus.

No example was cited in the introduction to this summary report of actual espionage. Instead the analyst focused on the efforts of Soviet agents and Communist activists to promote Soviet foreign policy interests or Communist ideology. Nor did the analyst cite a single instance of industrial, military, or diplomatic espionage in the remaining unredacted 624 pages of his detailed report. This does not mean that FBI agents uncovered no instance of actual espionage. Whole sections, paragraphs, and lines are redacted in the released COMRAP file—particularly sections where the analyst was summarizing the results of the FBI investigation of Soviet officials Semenov, Klarin, and Lukianov. As noted earlier, however, the 1948 CIA summary seems to confirm that the FBI's "independent" investigation failed to find evidence of espionage by these Soviet officials. An unredacted section in this summary report seems to capture the underlying view of Soviet espionage that drove this investigation—namely, that the targeted suspects had been found to be "(1) collecting political information of value to the USSR; (2) infiltrating foreign racial or minority groups for political pressure purposes; (3) infiltrat[ing] U.S. Government bodies or agencies by Communist Party members." Elaborating on this Communist infiltration effort, the FBI analyst described the purpose as "to influence foreign policy" and to "secure information of value for the [Communist] Party. In addition, through their official duties and acquaintances, they are contacted by Party functionaries for the employment of other Communists in Government work."[29]

In January 1945, Hoover ordered FBI analysts to prepare a series of detailed "narratives" on the forty-six* individuals whom FBI agents had concluded were participants in the Comintern Apparatus. The prepared sketches document the intensity of this investigation. Each sketch lists background personal information (date of birth, education, profession, marital status); information on the individual's financial status, bank accounts, income tax payments, and all sources of income; draft status and arrest record or alleged criminal activities; and political sympathies and organizational affiliations. More important, each sketch contains a section called "Activities of an Espionage Nature Pertinent to This Investigation," a subsection of which reports "Types of Information He Is Securing and Its Source." Even when this subsection is redacted in the released COMRAP file, we can see whether FBI agents conducting this investigation had uncovered evidence of what they characterized as "activities of an espionage nature."

Only twelve of the forty-six biographical sketches even include a listing under this subsection. Of these twelve, the information listed includes: Marcia Hiskey's services as a mail drop; Felix Kusman's organizational work for the Joint Anti-Fascist Refugee Committee; Steve Nelson's pre-COMRAP contact with Joseph Weinberg; Boris Morros for "general information" activities; and Philip Levy for "types of information being secured unknown." A listing of a name-redacted seaman reports that he contacted Communist party headquarters whenever visiting a foreign country.

*In releasing the COMRAP file, the FBI redacted the names of nineteen of these forty-six. The named individuals are: Arthur Adams, Jacob Aronoff, Samuel Becker, Eric Bernay, Alexander Bittleman, Ralph Bowman, Louise Bransten, Earl Browder, Eveline Carsman, Haakon Chevalier, Albert Edwards, Gerhart Eisler, Joseph Freeman, Shuji Fujii, Grace Granich, Max Granich, Lement Harris, Julius Heiman, Marcia Hiskey, Getzel Hochberg, Felix Kusman, Philip Levy, Boris Morros, Steve Nelson, Andrei Schevchenko, Edward Smith, and Victoria Stone.

The names of four of the six other individuals, and the subsection, are both redacted. Of the other two, information about Samuel Becker's activities in the Manhattan Project in Chicago is partially redacted, and Andrei Schevchenko's activities are described as having contacted two employees at the Bell Aircraft Corporation who had "access to highly classified information" and a couple, Mr. and Mrs. Joseph Franey, to "get information concerning the Carborundum Company."[30]

Overall, the FBI's intensive COMRAP investigation appears to have documented that American Communists were Communists, not Soviet spies.* Rather than confirming the existence of a Comintern Apparatus, FBI agents confirmed that American Communists, both publicly and covertly, sought to promote a Communist agenda of radical economic and political change, in part by capitalizing on the sympathetic political climate resulting from the wartime U.S.-Soviet alliance. FBI agents' apparent failure to document that American Communists spied for the Soviets is further confirmed by their reports on Steve Nelson and Boris Morros.

The 1944 and 1945 summaries of the COMRAP investigation of Nelson are the most revealing, especially since the catalyst to Hoover's decision to launch the COMRAP program was the FBI's discovery (from the bugging of Nelson's residence) that Zubilin had paid Nelson a large "sum of money" for the "purpose of placing Communist Party members and agents in industries engaged

*The sketch on Earl Browder, for example, reports that he "receives communications and directions from Moscow through other individuals," was in contact with "practically all subjects in this case," allegedly (according to ex-Communist Benjamin Gitlow) "probably worked with [KGB] agents," and "was used to transmit money from Soviet Government to the Pan-Pacific Trade Union Secretariat." In addition, FBI agents discovered that Browder was in "constant contact with all important figures in the Communist Political Association" as well as "in contact with officials of CP [Communist party] fron [sic] organizations." Narrative, January 30, 1945, FBI 100-203581-3914.

in secret war production . . . so that information could be obtained for transmittal to the Soviet Union." According to Hoover's report to the White House, the bug had also confirmed that Zubilin and Nelson planned to meet "in the near future with other leaders of the Communist International (Comintern) apparatus active in the United States." FBI agents thereafter closely followed Nelson's activities in Oakland, California, where he lived, and in his travels around the country. The intensity of this surveillance is reflected in their discovery that, on returning home from a cross-country trip, Nelson had baby clothes in his suitcase and had then frequently visited his hospitalized wife who had given birth to their baby. Yet in December 1944 the FBI analyst who summarized the results of the COMRAP inquiry simply reported that Nelson's "local and national importance in the several parallels of the Comintern Apparatus is attested to by the character of his associates as well as his varied activities within the Apparatus over a period of years. He is shown as engaging in military and industrial espionage [the sole examples cited were his meetings in March with Weinberg and in April with Zubilin]; to be active in political and Governmental aspects of the Apparatus; and is further shown as active in the gathering and dissemination of propaganda favorable to the Soviet Union." A follow-up report covering the period October 1, 1944, through January 31, 1945, describes Nelson as having been "principally engaged in directing the activities of the Communist Political Association [the renamed Communist party]. His daily contacts have been almost solely with persons identified in the Communist movement and with labor leaders allied to the Communist cause."[31]

In contrast, Boris Morros first came to the attention of FBI agents in May 1943 upon their discovery of his contact with Nelson. Interest in Morros intensified as a result of a one-sentence reference to him in the anonymous letter that Hoover received in August 1943. According to this letter, Vassili Zubilin's wife, Elizabeta, sent "false information" (which she obtained from "a vast network of agents in almost all ministries [of the U.S. Government] including the State Department") to the KGB "and everything of value passes on to the Germans through a certain Boris MOROZ (HOLLYWOOD)."

These allegations were intentionally misleading, designed to ensure that the FBI would investigate Vassili Zubilin as a German spy. FBI officials did not suspect that Zubilin was a double agent for Germany. Released KGB files confirm that since 1934 Morros had provided cover for Soviet intelligence operations in Germany through a Paramount Studio film distribution office in Berlin.[32]

Like Nelson, Morros was intensively investigated under the COMRAP program (including wiretapping his phone and monitoring his various contacts). Again, as in Nelson's case, this FBI investigation uncovered "no evidence" of Morros's "participation and membership" in the suspected Comintern Apparatus beyond his contacts with Zubilin and with other American Communists. Nor did FBI agents suspect that his work in the music and film industries served as a cover for Soviet intelligence operations outside the United States. The section of the January 1945 sketch on Morros's espionage activities vaguely describes them as "General Information." And a February 1947 memorandum further summarizes the results of the FBI's intensive investigation of Morros: "with the aid of physical and technical [wiretap] surveillance but which failed to produce any information that he might have engaged in espionage work." In 1946 FBI officials ordered agents to reopen an investigation of Morros "with the thought in mind of ultimately interviewing MORROS, not only for information he may be able to furnish concerning Soviet espionage operations and his contacts with ZUBILIN but also with the possibility in mind of utilizing MORROS' services as a confidential informant or double agent."[33] In time FBI agents did turn Morros into a double agent, but after the completion of the COMRAP program.

FBI priorities appear to have been to document the efforts of American Communist party officials to promote Communist interests, and their ideological sympathy for the Soviet Union. These priorities might explain why FBI agents failed to uncover, as early as December 1944, Nathan Silvermaster's and Charles Flato's roles as participants in a wartime Soviet espionage ring for which Elizabeth Bentley served as a courier. Through their surveillance of Louise Bransten, a suspected member of the Comintern Apparatus, FBI agents uncovered her contacts with Silvermaster and Flato. The section of the FBI report pertaining to this discovery has been redacted, but a preceding section, titled "Infiltration into the United States Government," reports only that "there is an unusual number of Communist Party members or fellow travelers who are presently in the employ of the United States Government and who have cooperated with or have indicated their willingness to cooperate with present suspects in [the COMRAP] case." The purpose of this infiltration, the FBI analyst concluded, was to "obtain information relative to foreign Governments," to "secure information of value for the [Communist] Party," and "through their official duties and acquaintances, they are contacted by Party functionaries for the employment of other Communists in Government work."[34]

Although FBI agents had been alerted to the possibility that Silvermaster and Flato might have been recruited as members of a Comintern Apparatus, they never uncovered Silvermaster's role in coordinating a wartime espionage ring, or Flato's role in stealing government secrets. Nor, despite their discovery in 1939 that the national leadership of the Communist party had established a "secret" "underground" group headed by Joszef Peter, and that Earl Browder, the party head, had urged Nelson to cooperate with Zubilin, had FBI agents uncovered the full scope of Soviet-Communist espionage operations. This failure could mean that the later disclosures by Bentley and Chambers; the Venona confirmation that Judith Coplon, Julius Rosenberg, and Thedore Hall had been recruited as Soviet agents; and the KGB records pertaining to Willie's espionage activities comprise the totality of Soviet espionage operations. If not, the meager results of the FBI's COMRAP investigation would appear to indicate an abysmal waste of resources and a failure of the public trust. There is, however, another possibility: that the needs of counterintelligence made espionage prosecutions inadvisable, and thus that the full record of FBI counterintelligence operations remains a closely held secret.

CHAPTER FOUR

• • •

The Counterintelligence Dilemma: Containment or Law Enforcement?

WHY DID the FBI fail to develop evidence to ensure the indictment and conviction of Soviet agents and their American recruits for violating the nation's espionage laws? The bureau's intensive monitoring of Communist activists, dating from the 1930s and continuing through the cold war era, in fact uncovered Soviet financing of Communist activities within the United States and the participation of leading Communist officials in espionage activities. Yet Communist party leaders were indicted and convicted only in the late 1940s and early 1950s—not for violating the Espionage Act or the Foreign Agents Registration Act but the Smith Act—conspiring to overthrow the government by force or violence.

It was not simply a matter of FBI competence. Had FBI and Justice Department officials attempted to indict Communist party officials for violating the Espionage Act, or for failing to register as agents of the Soviet government under the Foreign Agents Registration Act, they would have been placed in an awkward position. They would have had to disclose that their sources were sensitive investigative techniques (access to bank records or the deciphered Venona messages) or illegal investigative techniques (break-ins, wiretaps, bugs, mail openings). The less risky course was to seek indictments under the Smith Act, then rely on FBI informers who had infiltrated the Communist party to testify about Communist revolutionary plans, and question the indicted Communist officials and FBI informers about the texts of Communist publications. The Smith Act's ideological tenets allowed prosecutors to portray the American Communist party as an "illegal" organization and to show that "the patriotism of Communists is not directed toward the United States but towards the Soviet Union and world Communism."[1]

This strategy of avoiding espionage prosecutions was not confined to suspects in the American Communist party. No indictments were returned against any of those named by Communist defector Elizabeth Bentley as members of a wartime Soviet espionage ring. Only William Remington was indicted—and Bentley had named him as a peripheral figure and not a member of the Silvermaster or Perlo spy rings. Remington, moreover, was convicted of perjury, not espionage. The government's failure to indict any of the persons named as spies by Bentley was not due to FBI officials' unwillingness to compromise the Venona Project. At the time the grand jury was convened in 1947, the Soviet consular messages confirming Bentley's courier activities had not yet been deciphered. But federal prosecutors could not introduce the FBI's circumstantial evidence—developed in 1945–1946—that those named by Bentley were close associates, or that Silvermaster could film pilfered documents in his basement, because the FBI's confirmation had been acquired through illegal wiretaps, mail openings, and break-ins.[2]

FBI officials were also unwilling to disclose the Venona Project breakthrough when, after 1950, they considered retrying Judith Coplon. That year an appeals court reversed Coplon's conviction on grounds of illegal wiretapping and the failure of arresting FBI agents to obtain a warrant. To retry her would have required disclosing in open court that the FBI first learned of Coplon's recruitment as a Soviet spy from the Venona messages, not from wiretaps of her office and residence.

The deciphered Venona messages confirmed that Julius Rosenberg had recruited his brother-in-law, David Greenglass, for atomic espionage, and had made arrangements for Greenglass to turn over to Harry Gold his handwritten notes and sketches of a high-explosive lens mold experiment for transmittal to the Soviet Union. The Venona messages, however, also confirmed that another physicist employed at Los Alamos, Theodore Hall, had also delivered sensitive information relating to the Manhattan Project to a Soviet agent. Yet while Julius Rosenberg and his wife Ethel, and David Greenglass and Harry Gold were indicted and convicted, Hall was not.

The contrast between the Rosenbergs' indictment and the inaction in Hall's case had nothing to do with the Rosenbergs' actions being more damaging to the nation's security interests than Hall's. Julius Rosenberg's role in this Soviet-directed atomic conspiracy, confirmed by the Venona messages, was indirect,* limited to recruiting Greenglass, who was in a position to transmit classified information to Soviet courier Harry Gold. The Venona messages also confirm that Ethel Rosenberg played no role in her

*The Venona messages further confirm that Julius Rosenberg recruited others to engage in industrial espionage and solicited information from an individual employed in the Bureau of Standards. See, for example, New York to Moscow, No. 1053, July 26, 1944; New York to Moscow, No. 1314, September 14, 1944; New York to Moscow, No. 1600, November 14, 1944; Venona messages.

husband's recruitment of her brother or in arranging for the transmission of secret reports to the Soviets. The KGB supervisor reporting on this operation described her role as "knows about her husband's work and the role of METR [the code name for either Joel Barr or Alfred Salant] and NIL [an unidentified code name]. In view of delicate health does not work."[3]

In contrast, the Venona messages reveal the direct participation in atomic espionage of two scientists employed at Los Alamos: Theodore Hall and PERS. Never able to identify PERS, FBI agents had no difficulty identifying Hall, who was cited by name in the Venona messages. The intercepted Soviet consular messages describe Hall as a nineteen-year-old physicist who had majored in physics at Harvard and who in 1944 was employed at Los Alamos doing research on the thermodynamic process of nuclear implosion. A deciphered Venona message reports that Hall "handed over" a report about the Los Alamos project to KGB agent Sergej Kurnakov, in which he identified the "key personnel" who were conducting research on the atomic bomb. Hall's report disclosed that "All the outstanding physicists of the U.S., England, Italy and Germany (immigrants) were working" on the atomic bomb project, detailed the billions of dollars being spent, and reported that the scientists relied on four cyclotrons. Hall further summarized for Kurnakov the principles of the research project and supplemented this with a written detailed report. Another partially deciphered Venona message records the "great interest" of Soviet officials in Moscow in this report.[4]

Without minimizing the importance of Rosenberg's recruitment of Greenglass, his culpability—even more so his wife's—appears to have been less than Hall's. Hall's brilliance and educational background (he was a Harvard student while Greenglass had only a high school education) would seem to have made him a more promising recruit. Furthermore, FBI officials learned of Hall's recruitment in May 1950, almost at the same time as

Rosenberg's actions. They immediately launched an "intensive investigation" in which they confirmed Hall's Marxist views and membership in the John Reed Society while a student at Harvard. Nonetheless, although Julius and Ethel Rosenberg were indicted in 1950 following their interview with the FBI, Hall was not indicted following his 1951 FBI interview.[5] Why these differing responses?

Reflecting the problems inherent in FBI counterintelligence investigations, FBI officials did not need to disclose the Venona messages in order to indict and convict the Rosenbergs. They had successfully broken Harry Gold, David Greenglass, and Max Elitcher, who admitted their own espionage roles and testified against the Rosenbergs. The independent evidence developed by the FBI and introduced during the trial was circumstantial, corroborating the testimony of David and Ruth Greenglass and Harry Gold against the Rosenbergs. This included evidence of the Rosenbergs' purchase of an expensive console table in 1944 or 1945 (used to film stolen documents); evidence documenting Gold's overnight stay in a Hilton Hotel in Albuquerque in June 1945 (to retrieve information from Greenglass); evidence that Ruth Greenglass had deposited $400 in a banking account she opened in Albuquerque in June 1945 (confirming the Gold visit and the payoff); and evidence that the Rosenbergs had passport photos taken in June 1950 (when they were preparing to flee the country).[6] But Hall escaped prosecution because FBI agents could neither break him nor produce other witnesses who could testify to his espionage role. The indictment of Hall would have required disclosure of the Venona messages. At the time, in 1951, neither FBI nor military intelligence officials were willing to compromise the Venona Project.

The Hall and Rosenberg examples do not suggest FBI incompetence. They illustrate the counterintelligence dilemma: the difficulty of learning about inherently secret and closely safeguarded espionage operations without resorting to intrusive investigative techniques. This difficulty determined how FBI officials responded to Elizabeth Bentley's defection and Judith Coplon's exposure. In both cases their primary objective was to determine whether those named by Bentley and Coplon were continuing to steal government secrets; they also wanted to identify and apprehend Bentley's and Coplon's Soviet contacts. These objectives could not be achieved through physical surveillance, though it might produce admissible evidence. Only intrusive—but illegal—investigative techniques, such as wiretaps, bugs, break-ins, and mail openings, could uncover such contacts and continuing activities. The consequence was to forestall prosecution.

This counterintelligence dilemma is underscored by the uniqueness of our knowledge of Coplon's espionage activities and the failure to ensure her conviction. The ultimately risky decision of Justice Department officials first to arrest her and then to proceed with the case, led to the inadvertent public disclosure of FBI wiretapping practices. They were discovered through the FBI documents that Coplon intended to deliver to her Soviet contact.

Here is what happened. In December 1948, military intelligence analysts, with FBI help, identified code-named Sima (a recruited Soviet agent employed in the Justice Department's Foreign Agent Registration section) as Judith Coplon. Based on this intelligence breakthrough, FBI officials obtained Attorney General Tom Clark's authorization to wiretap Coplon's office and home phones and closely monitor her movements, hoping thereby to identify her Soviet contacts and determine whether she was collaborating with other recruited federal employees. From their physical surveillance, in January 1949 FBI agents uncovered Coplon's furtive meeting in New York with an individual whom they later identified as Valentin Gubitchev, a Soviet employee on the United Nations staff. Attorney General Clark and FBI director Hoover decided not to initiate loyalty dismissal proceedings under the Federal Employee Loyalty Program, even though they would not have had to reveal wiretaps and the Venona Project. They decided instead to set a trap by creating a memorandum "that contained enough truth to make it seem important and enough false information to make it imperative for Coplon to grab it and quickly deliver it to her Soviet contact."

The strategy worked. In February 1949, Coplon pilfered the memorandum. But FBI agents who followed her on her trip to New York were unsure whether she had attempted to transfer the memorandum to Gubitchev, and thus they made no arrest. After another attempt to bait Coplon, FBI agents arrested her and Gubitchev, discovering in her handbag twenty-eight FBI memoranda. Coplon was thereupon indicted and tried, first in Washington, D.C., on a charge of unauthorized possession of classified documents, then in New York on a charge of intent to deliver classified information to an agent of a foreign power.[7]

It remains unclear whether Coplon acquired information about FBI counterintelligence activities directed at Soviet agents. The contents of the documents found in her handbag at the time of her arrest in March 1949 record only that FBI agents had intensively monitored liberal New Dealers Edward Condon and David Niles, Hollywood actors Frederick March and Edward G. Robinson, supporters of Henry Wallace's 1948 Progressive party presidential campaign, critics of the House Committee on Un-American Activities, and the author of a master's thesis on the New Deal in New Zealand. Another memorandum summarized Coplon's failure to "get the top secret report . . . on Soviet and Communist activities in the U.S." Coplon had learned of this report from her superior in the Foreign Agent Registration section. Her summary, which she intended to hand over to Gubitchev, explained that, having "rapidly perused this report," she remembered "very little"—namely, that "Soviet 'intelligence' activities, including [Ludwig] Martens, [Ludwig] Lore, [Juliette] Poynts

[sic], [Lydia] Alschuler [sic], [Nathan] Silvermaster [all Soviet or Communist agents who had operated either in the 1920s or early 1940s] et al. It had a heading on Soviet U.N. delegation, but that was all I remember. The rest of the report I think was on Polish, Yugo, etc. activities and possibly some info on the C.P. [Communist party], U.S.A."[8]

A recently accessible KGB report apparently confirms that Coplon had been unable to obtain information about current FBI counterintelligence activities. This October 1945 memorandum, which Weinstein and Vassiliev found in the KGB archives,* merely disclosed that FBI agents had wiretapped J. Robert Oppenheimer in 1943, concluding that Oppenheimer and his friend Haakon Chevalier "have a reputation as extremely liberal or belonging to the Communist Party"; that Victor Perlo's estranged wife had sent a letter to President Roosevelt in 1944 denouncing her husband and others as "members of an illegal Communist Party group"; and that Soviet agent I. V. Volodarsky had informed the FBI in 1941 about meetings between Soviet agents Jacob Golos and Gaik Ovakimyan and had identified Elizabeth Bentley as Golos's courier.[9]

Whether or not Coplon had compromised U.S. security interests, her trial proved embarrassing to FBI officials. Judge Albert Reeves ruled that in order to convict her on the charge of unauthorized possession of classified documents, government prosecutors must produce in open court the originals of the FBI summaries found in Coplon's handbag at the time of her arrest. Producing these memoranda did not compromise sensitive national secrets, for some had been made available to Coplon for the

*Because Weinstein and Vassiliev have not clarified the conditions governing their access to extant KGB records, it remains unclear whether this report constituted Coplon's sole successful transmission of FBI information to her KGB handlers.

express purpose of trapping her. But their public release confirmed that FBI agents intensively monitored political activities and wiretapped extensively—with the subjects of their interest ranging from New Deal liberals to critics of the House Committee on Un-American Activities, and with information in fifteen of the twenty-eight reports coming from wiretaps. And because Coplon's own phone had been wiretapped, her conviction was later reversed on appeal. The appeals judge concluded that FBI wiretapping had possibly tainted Coplon's indictment, under the Supreme Court's 1937 and 1939 rulings in *Nardone v. U.S.*, requiring the dismissal of any case based on illegal wiretaps.

Anticipating this problem but fundamentally opposed to the public release of information relating to FBI operations, Hoover sharply criticized Attorney General Clark's decision to comply with Judge Reeves's disclosure order rather than drop the case. Producing the documents in open court, Hoover protested, posed the "broader issue of the future of the Bureau." It would risk identifying FBI double agents and thereby compromise national security investigations. The FBI director further contended that the public release of the memoranda, by revealing the subjects of FBI investigative interest, would also ensure "an unprecedented outburst of criticism" of the FBI, the Justice Department, and the attorney general. Hoover preferred to "see the Coplon case go by default if other legal steps are not available for the protection of the security of our files and the rights of individuals [identified in FBI reports] not yet formally charged with any crime."

Not content to lodge his protest with the attorney general, Hoover ordered Ralph Roach, his liaison to the White House, to show a copy of it to White House aide John Steelman (but not to leave the letter with him), "pointing out my position . . . & stressing that had A.G. [attorney general] acted as I suggested all of this furor would have been avoided." The attorney general had brought up this matter at a cabinet meeting, Steelman advised

Roach, had fully presented Hoover's objections, but after consulting with army and navy intelligence officials had decided that "it was important that the Government win the Coplon case, and that we should win it at all costs." Truman's opinion had not been sought; the attorney general briefed the president only on "what was being done and that a decision had been reached to continue the case." The cabinet minutes in fact record that Clark had outlined his department's difficulties in prosecuting the case and his "determination to go forward with the prosecution."[10]

Hoover's concern over the "security of our files" reflected his public relations concerns rather than legitimate security interests. Production of the memoranda confirmed that FBI agents closely monitored liberal and radical political activities and that the FBI had wiretapped extensively, validating criticisms that FBI investigations focused on political activities. The reports also indirectly supported the motion of Coplon's attorney, Archibald Palmer, for a hearing to determine whether the FBI had wiretapped his client. U.S. Attorney John Kelly, Jr., urged the court to reject Palmer's motion as "primarily a fishing expedition which requires no answer." Siding with the government, Judge Reeves rejected Palmer's request.

During Coplon's second trial in New York, her attorneys again demanded a pretrial hearing to determine whether their client had been wiretapped. The presiding judge, Sylvester Ryan, ordered the hearing, which established that Coplon's phones at her office, her Washington apartment, and her parents' residence in New York had been tapped, and that these taps had been installed on January 6, 1949, and had continued for two months after her arrest. These revelations raised three questions. First, had the wiretaps provided the lead resulting in the FBI's uncovering her alleged criminal activities? Second, had these taps intercepted Coplon's privileged conversations with her attorneys, alerting government prosecutors to the defense's trial strategy? Third—and a question potentially most damaging to the FBI's image—why had FBI officials remained silent during Coplon's Washington trial when the U.S. attorney dismissed the defense motion as a "fishing expedition"? Had Justice Department officials even known of FBI wiretapping practices? The pretrial hearings at the second trial produced further embarrassment for the FBI: the agent who had originally denied under questioning any "previous knowledge" of whether the FBI had wiretapped Coplon, had in fact routinely received the records of these wiretaps and had destroyed "quite a number" of the tapes of these wiretaps "in view of the imminence of her trial."[11]

FBI officials also feared that Judge Ryan might honor Coplon's attorneys' subpoena for the records and testimony of AT&T officials regarding FBI wiretapping. If this request were honored, Hoover lamented, "all wiretapping is through."[12] Meeting with FBI assistant director Louis Nichols to discuss the prosecutive problems posed by these cumulative revelations of FBI wiretapping, Deputy Attorney General Peyton Ford suggested that the Justice Department disclose how the FBI learned of Coplon's recruitment. Ford proposed that they seek the agreement of Secretary of Defense Louis Johnson and "his intelligence people" to use the Venona information, as "this would be ample protection for the Bureau and the Department." Hoover counseled against this idea as "most unwise."[13] Ford's suggestion was either not pursued or was disapproved.*

Revelations of the FBI's questionable conduct led civil libertar-

*Nichols's memorandum on Ford's proposal records Ford's admission that only he and Attorneys General Clark and McGrath knew about the Venona source. Clark had been attorney general at the time of the discovery of Coplon's recruitment (through Venona) and then her arrest. Later promoted to the Supreme Court, he was succeeded by McGrath in August 1949. Ford's unqualified if suggestive statement leaves unclear whether President Truman had been briefed about Venona.

ians—from the liberal president of the Americans for Democratic Action, Joseph Rauh, to the radical National Lawyers Guild—to demand an independent investigation of the bureau. In June 1949 and again in January 1950, Lawyers Guild president Clifford Durr, a former chairman of the Federal Communications Commission, strongly urged President Truman to appoint a commission of "outstanding citizens, including representatives of the national bar associations and civil liberties organizations, to undertake a comprehensive investigation into the operations and methods of the Federal Bureau of Investigation." To buttress his recommendation, Durr submitted a detailed analysis of the Coplon trial record, focusing on FBI political surveillance, wiretapping, and agents' efforts to disguise this practice during the initial pretrial hearing.

Moving quickly to squelch any such presidential initiative, FBI officials launched a covert campaign. Forewarned of the Guild's plan through a wiretap of that organization's Washington office, Hoover forwarded to Attorney General McGrath (for submission to the president) a detailed report summarizing the National Lawyers Guild's "subversive" activities and membership. The Guild's purpose, Hoover warned, was to subvert the nation's security. Meanwhile Hoover's liaison to the media, Louis Nichols, worked closely with Lyle Wilson, the United Press's Washington bureau chief, to elicit from Truman's press secretary, Charles Ross, a firm denial that the president was even considering the proposal to investigate the FBI. Nichols and senior FBI officials were worried by Truman's jocular response to a question posed during a recent press conference about the possibility of such an investigation. In payment for his help in securing this denial, FBI officials gave Wilson an advance copy of the Guild's report, having obtained it through a break-in of the Guild's Washington office along with a copy of the minutes of an October 1949 Guild executive board meeting. In his wire service story, Wilson characterized the Guild's initiative as a campaign to "weaken" the FBI and to drive FBI director Hoover from office. This effort, Wilson continued, was "right down the [Communist] party line."

In another part of Hoover's campaign to discredit the Guild, FBI agents prepared a three-hundred-page report summarizing the Guild's "subversive" activities and its officers' and executive board members' past or current membership in the Communist party or their "Communist sympathies." In the spring of 1950 a copy of this report was leaked to the House Committee on Un-American Activities (HUAC), which in turn issued its own fifty-page *Report on the National Lawyer's Guild: Legal Bulwark of the Communist Party.* HUAC's report lifted passages verbatim or paraphrased sections from this FBI report, and demanded that the attorney general list the Guild as a "subversive" organization and require it to register "as an agent of a foreign principal."[14]

Having successfully contained the threat of an independent investigation of FBI practices, Hoover addressed the companion problem posed by the Coplon case: the vulnerability of FBI records. Through two carefully crafted initiatives, the FBI director sought to avoid potentially damaging disclosures.

On July 8, 1949, within weeks after the "furor" precipitated by the public release of the twenty-eight FBI memoranda during Coplon's first trial, FBI agents were ordered to eliminate from the text of their reports "gossip, rumors or any information that could *unjustifiably* embarrass any person or organization," any "verified or unverified information" that was not pertinent to or the basis for future investigations, any "unconfirmed or uncorroborated information" about associates of alleged subversives, and any "facts and information which are considered of a nature not expedient to disseminate, or which could cause embarrassment to the Bureau, if distributed." Such information should instead be conveyed "on the administrative pages attached to the regular report." Should the agent's report then be distributed outside the FBI, these pages could "be detached" without revealing that information was being withheld. The FBI director listed seven examples of the type of information that agents henceforth were to report on administrative pages. His first example: "An anonymous complainant alleges A . . . is a member of the Communist Party and further that A is a man of loose morals, a heavy drinker living with a known prostitute. . . . The allegation of Communist Party membership should be included in the investigative section while the allegation concerning loose morals should be included in the administrative section." Hoover's seventh example: "During the legal search of a white slave traffic [prostitution] act investigation there is found an address book containing data identifying prominent public officials. Unless the names appearing therein are material to the investigation, this information should be placed in the administrative section."[15]

Backstopping this action, on June 29, 1949, Hoover instituted a special June Mail procedure. All heads of FBI offices were to convey to FBI headquarters information "received from some highly confidential source" in a special letter "bearing the code word 'June' and then placed in the envelope addressed to the Director 'Personal and Confidential.'" On receipt at FBI headquarters, these letters would not be filed in the FBI's central records system but would be routed to a "separate confidential file" in the FBI's Special File Room "under lock and key." In turn, SACs at field offices would maintain copies of these letters in a locked "confidential file." The June Mail procedure, Hoover emphasized, was to be used "only for the most secretive sources, such as Governors, secretaries to high officials who may be discussing such officials and their attitude, or when referring to highly confidential or unusual investigative techniques." "Highly confidential" referred to FBI informers of particular sensitivity; "unusual investigative techniques" was a euphemism for illegal wiretaps, bugs, break-ins, and mail openings. A 1969 FBI memorandum explicitly described these techniques as "sources illegal in nature."[16]

After the embarrassing revelations about FBI wiretapping practices during Coplon's second trial, Hoover further refined the June Mail procedure. In December 1949 he ordered all FBI supervisors and SACs that when they assigned an agent to investigate a case "which might make him a competent witness in the event . . . it should be decided to proceed with prosecution," this agent must "have no specific testifiable knowledge of the existence of a technical surveillance [wiretap] in that particular case." Furthermore, all wiretap logs and "all administrative correspondence" relating to wiretaps—in other words, requests to wiretap, and FBI headquarters' approval of such requests—were to be captioned JUNE to ensure that they were "retained and filed separate and apart from the main file room."[17]

These records procedures had been instituted too late to ensure Coplon's conviction. Nonetheless, this sophisticated system to minimize discovery of the FBI's most sensitive and illegal actions did not enhance FBI efforts to indict any of the spies that its investigations had uncovered. The questions arise: Why had FBI officials never recommended that the Justice Department seek indictments of these individuals under the Foreign Agent Registration or the Espionage acts? And why were similar indictments not sought based on information developed under the COMRAP program?

A draft of proposed testimony that Hoover considered presenting to Congress in 1955 provides a partial answer to these questions. Seeking to convince members of Congress to amend the Communications Act of 1934 to authorize "national security" wiretapping, Hoover spelled out how the needs of counterintelligence undermined prosecution. He noted that the nation's security "has been weakened by the banning of evidence from leads secured from wire taps," and as an example he cited how FBI agents had learned the purpose of the April 1943 meeting between Zubilin and Nelson. The FBI's "first knowledge" of this meeting,

Hoover admitted, "came as a result of a wire tap." The FBI director continued: "The information arising from the meeting did not come from a wire tap as such [it was a bug of Nelson's residence, which would have posed similar prosecutorial problems] but the facts we learned there were valueless as evidence since the lead did come from a wire tap [of the headquarters of the American Communist party] and hence the two [Zubilin, Nelson] could not be prosecuted for espionage."[18]

The COMRAP investigation also produced no indictment of any Soviet official or American Communist, except indirectly in the case of Schevchenko. Owing to the massive redactions in the released COMRAP file, the reasons for this seeming inaction cannot be definitively established. Had FBI agents uncovered no evidence of espionage activities committed by Soviet officials and American Communists? Given their extensive use of illegal wiretaps, bugs, break-ins, and mail intercepts, had FBI officials decided that prosecution was foreclosed? It is impossible to say from the redacted COMRAP file. But one thing is clear: FBI director Hoover never recommended that the Justice Department seek indictments.

During the course of the two-year COMRAP investigation, Hoover's sole communications to Attorney General Biddle were to solicit his approval of proposed FBI wiretaps. Of the thousands of documents in the massive COMRAP file, only one memorandum even alludes to the possibility of prosecutive action. This partially unredacted memorandum records FBI assistant director Edward Tamm's discussion with Assistant Secretary of State Adolf Berle, the State Department official responsible for security matters. Berle informed Tamm that "this matter [spelled out in the preceding two redacted paragraphs] would then be discussed with the president and appropriate arrangements made to initiate a vigorous course of action." Tamm asked how Berle "contemplated handling this matter with the Attorney General, who would be the official responsible for any prosecution initiated." Berle responded by promising to "give this matter some study in order that the Attorney General would appropriately be considered in any program that was initiated."[19] Tamm's memorandum on this conversation suggests that the "matter" might have involved lodging a protest or demanding the recall of a Soviet official,* or perhaps seeking indictments of Communist party officials Earl Browder and Steve Nelson.

FBI officials' inaction in deciding not to seek the indictment of Nelson and Zubilin, or their wariness about Berle's proposed action, or their opposition to retrying Coplon, was not exceptional. It illustrates graphically the essence of the FBI's counterintelligence dilemma. The U.S. constitutional system was designed to prevent abuses of power by government officials, to safeguard privacy rights, and to preclude bureaucrats from advancing their personal views of the nation's security interests. Laws banning wiretaps, or constitutional amendments banning break-ins, made evidence gained through such techniques inadmissible in court. Yet FBI officials' eagerness to identify espionage agents, or to determine how Communists and radicals planned to influence public policy, invariably led them to authorize illegal investigative techniques. The scope of these practices remains unknown, for our only knowledge of them comes from the unprecedented release of traditionally secret grand jury records during the 1990s or embarrassing discoveries during adversary trial proceedings.

FBI practice, and the counterintelligence dilemma, is highlighted by FBI responses to Elizabeth Bentley's identification of the participants in a wartime Soviet espionage ring. To corroborate her testimony and, just as important, to prevent future espi-

*Zubilin and Kheifets would be logical suspects since both eventually departed the United States in August 1944. It is unclear, however, whether their departure resulted from the fallout of Kravchenko's defection in April 1944 or State Department pressure based on the COMRAP and CINRAD investigations. Robert Louis Benson and Michael Warner, eds., *Venona,* p. 112.

onage, FBI agents resorted to wiretaps, mail openings, and break-ins. They failed, however, to document that any of the named individuals continued to engage in espionage. (Having been alerted to Bentley's defection, KGB officials discontinued the activities of the Silvermaster and Perlo spy rings and recalled their supervising KGB agents in New York and Washington to Moscow rather than risk their defection and cooperation with the FBI.) FBI agents were able to determine only that those named by Bentley were "in frequent contact"—at dinner parties, other social gatherings, and political meetings.[20] Although they were aware of the lack of admissible evidence sufficient to sustain indictments, Justice Department officials nonetheless decided to present the case to a grand jury, hoping that one or more of the suspects might break under pressure and corroborate Bentley. Harry Dexter White, a high-level Treasury Department official, was considered a weak link, having been described by Bentley as an extremely cautious participant who feared being discovered.

Like other subpoenaed witnesses before the grand jury, White did not know what government prosecutors knew about his alleged activities and those of his colleagues in the Treasury Department. He could refuse to cooperate, denying any part in espionage. But a denial could render him vulnerable to a perjury indictment should another of the subpoenaed witnesses break and testify to his own and the other suspects' actions. To avoid this risk, White sought to concert his testimony with at least two other Treasury Department employees subpoenaed by the grand jury, Frank Coe and George Silverman. In so doing, White became vulnerable to indictment for obstruction of justice.

Subpoenaed to testify before the grand jury, White was first asked about his relationship with a number of the individuals whom Bentley had named as members of the Silvermaster-Perlo espionage rings. Then he was asked whether he had played a role in the hiring of specifically named individuals, and whether any of them were Communists or had solicited classified information. White acknowledged having a professional and in some cases personal association with some of these named individuals, but he explicitly denied any knowledge of their politics or their possible involvement in espionage, though he expressed his doubts about either matter. Until then a confident witness, White was blindsided when U.S. attorney Thomas Donegan asked whether, before his grand jury appearance he, Frank Coe, and George Silverman had discussed how each would respond to grand jury questions about their earlier relationship and activities. White admitted to an accidental meeting with Coe at which he had inquired in passing about Coe's subpoenaed appearance. Donegan followed up by asking whether White had telephoned Silverman and had arranged a second meeting among the three of them. Changing his testimony to admit to this second meeting, White described it as a social discussion over a beer, not a purposeful effort to frustrate the work of the grand jury.[21] Without explicitly admitting that his knowledge of White's actions came from an FBI wiretap, Donegan had subtly conveyed his awareness of this telephone conversation. An unprepared White did not realize that this information had been illegally obtained and thus could not be used to indict him. In any event, White denied that he had obstructed the work of the grand jury. Donegan could not press the matter, for to have done so would have required him to reveal that his question had been based on an illegal wiretap.

The FBI's counterintelligence dilemma surfaced anew in the course of an investigation that led to the arrest of six individuals in the so-called *Amerasia* case, one of the most celebrated "spy" episodes of the early cold war. A journal of Far Eastern affairs with a circulation of less than two thousand, the left-oriented *Amerasia* was at the time widely read and respected by officials, academics, and journalists.

The incident triggering the FBI investigation involved the

journal's publication of an article on Thailand in its January 26, 1945, issue. The article, as it turned out, had been based on a classified Office of Strategic Services (OSS) report outlining Anglo-American differences over the postwar status of Thailand. Upon reading this issue, the OSS analyst who had written the classified report recognized that the *Amerasia* article was an almost verbatim copy. He immediately brought this discovery to the attention of OSS security officials. Despite lacking any authority to conduct investigations within the United States, on March 11, 1945, they broke into *Amerasia*'s New York office. There the OSS agents discovered more than three hundred classified OSS, State Department, and Office of Naval Intelligence (ONI) documents, took with them twenty of these documents "as proof," and brought this discovery to the attention of senior State Department officials. These officials in turn solicited FBI assistance to identify the source of the leak.*

FBI agents began their investigation by focusing on *Amerasia*'s editor, Philip Jaffe, a known radical and Communist sympathizer. In the initial phase of the investigation, FBI agents broke into the *Amerasia* office six times during March, April, and May 1945, and filmed the stolen documents. They also wiretapped Jaffe's office and residence. Through these wiretaps, and by identifying those government employees who had access to the stolen documents, FBI agents were able to establish that Jaffe's sources

*By 1944–1945 the State Department's Far Eastern Division was riven by sharp differences over postwar U.S. policy toward China and the Far East in general. At the heart of this conflict was the question whether the United States should support the Chinese Nationalists in a possible recurrence of a civil war with the Chinese Communists, but also whether the United States should oppose the restoration of British colonial rule—the latter the very subject of the Thailand article. The principal antagonists were longtime China expert Stanley Hornbeck and John Carter Vincent. Hornbeck headed the Far Eastern Division until 1944 when he was unceremoniously displaced by his younger, more progressive colleague.

were State Department employee Emmanuel Larsen, a China specialist, and ONI officer Andrew Roth, a draftee and China specialist who had earlier been employed by *Amerasia*. Further investigation led to the identification of others affiliated with the journal who had access to the documents—*Amerasia* co-editor Kate Mitchell and freelance reporter Mark Gayn. In the course of this continuing investigation, FBI agents broke into the apartments of Jaffe and Mitchell, but uncovered no documents in either one; they did, however, find and photocopy documents when they broke into the apartments of Larsen and Gayn.* FBI agents also bugged the *Amerasia* offices and Jaffe's hotel room during his trip to Washington, D.C., on May 7, 1945.

Agents uncovered no evidence that the stolen documents were particularly sensitive, or that any of the suspects were engaged in espionage or were continuing to leak classified documents. One agent, for example, discovered that the government report that they observed Gayn reading while riding a bus, involved gossip about the marital relations between Chinese Nationalist president Chiang Kai-shek and his wife. At this point FBI assistant director D. Milton Ladd informed Assistant Secretary of State Julius Holmes, State Department security officer Fred Lyons, and Assistant Secretary of the Navy Mathias Correa on April 18, 1945, that the *Amerasia* investigation had reached "a dead end" with the identification of Roth. Holmes and Correa nonetheless urged Ladd to continue this investigation for another two months. Any future discovery, they argued, could provide valuable leverage for U.S. officials to use against the Soviet Union in already contentious diplomatic negotiations. Continuing the investigation, FBI agents discovered another suspected leaker, John Service, a Foreign Service officer who on April 12 had returned to Washington from a stint in China. FBI agents knew, through the bug of

*FBI agents also wiretapped Larsen's home phone.

the *Amerasia* office, that Jaffe had encouraged Service to write a book challenging the policy recommendations of his more conservative State Department colleagues on China.

The *Amerasia* investigation took an abrupt turn on May 28, 1945, when Hoover learned that Roth was about to be transferred to Hawaii. He now recommended seeking indictments of the six identified suspects and for the first time briefed Justice Department attorneys in the Criminal Division about the FBI's resort to illegal investigative techniques. Based on this briefing, junior Justice Department attorneys concluded that the FBI had not uncovered "the necessary legal evidence" to convict the alleged suspects. "Most of the foregoing [FBI] information regarding the contacts made by the various principals and the documents which were exchanged," a Justice Department attorney pointed out, "were obtained through highly confidential means and sources of information [wiretaps, bugs, break-ins] which cannot be used in evidence." Assistant to the Attorney General James McInerney, however, devised a strategy to finesse this evidentiary problem: FBI agents were to arrest Jaffe and Mitchell at the *Amerasia* office and Larsen and Gayn at their homes "in order that agents could conduct a [lawful] search of these premises." From the earlier FBI break-ins of the office and residences, FBI agents knew that such an arrest strategy—by "making possible searches of the premises of the subjects incidental to arrest"—could produce the desired admissible evidence. McInerney also pointed out that in 80 percent of all criminal cases, arrested suspects could be pressured into making "damaging admissions" when confronted, as expected in this situation, by "incriminatory documents."[22]

The proposed arrest of the six suspects was temporarily aborted on June 2, 1945. Secretary of the Navy James Forrestal objected, fearing that these arrests would adversely affect U.S.-Soviet relations, given the delicate negotiations over the United Nations Charter then occurring at the San Francisco Conference. But President Truman overruled Forrestal, insisting that he "wanted to use this case as an example to other persons in Government Service who may be divulging confidential information." Truman personally instructed Myron Gurnea, Hoover's liaison to the White House, to proceed with the case, adding that Gurnea should notify him directly if FBI officials encountered any difficulties from other federal agencies.[23] The president's concern stemmed not from his belief that the *Amerasia* case involved a possibly damaging espionage ring* but a different loyalty issue—Roosevelt holdovers in the executive branch leaking information to the media and to prominent liberals in Washington as part of a concerted effort to counteract Truman's more conservative domestic and foreign policies. In sum, the president's primary concern was insubordination, not espionage.

Truman's concern about leaks had earlier led him to request a special investigation of suspected White House employees, which FBI officials code-named the White House Security Survey program. In conveying the president's wishes, White House aides Edwin McKim and James Vardaman demanded that the FBI "investigate suspected White House aides, wiretap Edward Prichard [an aide to the director of the Office of War Mobilization and Reconversion, Fred Vinson] and study the operations of the White House with the objective of offering recommendations to improve

*The sole report by Hoover to the Truman White House based on the *Amerasia* investigation involved an intercepted conversation in which Jaffe claimed that "President Truman has on his desk a Japanese peace offer which was furnished through the Argentine Government." Truman had White House aide Harry Vaughan thank the FBI director for this information, observing that "Apparently the gentleman knows more than the President does." Personal and Confidential Letter, Hoover to Vaughan, May 21, 1945, and Memo, Vaughan to Hoover, May 26, 1945, PSF, FBI, Truman Presidential Library. In addition, the FBI wiretap intercepted conversations in which the *Amerasia* editor encouraged Larsen and Service to write books about Far Eastern developments.

its efficiency." The Prichard wiretap disclosed this liberal New Dealer's regular contacts with Supreme Court Justice Felix Frankfurter, syndicated national columnist Drew Pearson, and former Roosevelt aide Thomas Corcoran, and confirmed Prichard's suspicions about the new president's commitment to Roosevelt's domestic and foreign policies.* After reading the FBI's summary of these intercepted conversations, Truman ordered White House aide Edwin McKim to request FBI wiretaps of Pearson and Corcoran. The president hoped that the Corcoran wiretap would identify "any other sources" that the former Roosevelt aide and prominent Washington attorney might have in the administration. Fully aware of the sensitivity of this request, given the prominence of both Pearson and Corcoran, McKim emphasized that these "highly confidential" taps "should never become known." Hoover agreed to the Corcoran tap† but deemed wiretapping Pearson too risky. The FBI director did so on the understanding that should the Corcoran tap "ever become known it would be our [FBI] baby" and the White House "would deny any knowledge."[24]

The White House Security Survey investigation resulted in no arrests, but it did alert the White House to Corcoran's political plans and those of other New Deal liberals with whom he was in contact, some intended to advance more liberal domestic and foreign policy objectives than those of Truman.[25]

*The transcripts of these wiretapped conversations and Truman's responses are reprinted in Theoharis, *From the Secret Files of J. Edgar Hoover,* pp. 204–209.

†The Corcoran wiretap also uncovered information that proved of crucial importance to FBI officials later, as leverage against the Truman Administration. Recruited by State Department counselor Benjamin Cohen to serve as John Service's attorney, Corcoran capitalized on his high-level contacts in Washington and directly interceded with Attorney General Tom Clark and Assistant Attorney General James McGranery on Service's behalf. These intercepted conversations are included in the massive (6,250-page file) Technical Summaries Sent to White House folder, Folder #2, Hoover O&C.

Proceeding with the *Amerasia* case, FBI agents on June 6, 1945, arrested Jaffe, Mitchell, Gayn, Larsen, Roth, and Service, charging them with conspiring to violate Title 50, Section 31 of the Espionage Act, unauthorized removal or possession of classified documents. On August 10, 1945, indictments were returned against only Jaffe, Larsen, and Roth, the grand jury voting 20 to 0 not to indict Service, 15 to 5 not to indict Gayn, and 18 to 2 not to indict Mitchell. Many of the jurors who voted not to indict Service, Gayn, and Mitchell criticized executive department controls over classified documents, concluding that this laxity invited leaks. The jurors also noted that many other reporters, beyond the defendants, had regularly obtained classified material. In his own grand jury testimony, Service admitted to meeting Jaffe but denied acting any differently than in other meetings with reporters; Gayn admitted to having used the documents in writing articles on the Far East.

Jaffe, Larsen, and Roth, though indicted, were never tried—the result of the risky strategy of finessing the evidentiary problems by seizing the leaked documents when the arrests were made. An unanticipated crisis occurred when Larsen confronted the manager of his apartment, E. R. Sager, who admitted to having given FBI agents a key to his apartment weeks before his arrest and without having been served a warrant. (Larsen had been struck by how easily the arresting agents located the State Department documents he had brought home. He correctly suspected that the agents had earlier obtained entry to his apartment.) Larsen thereupon filed a motion, on September 28, 1945, to suppress his indictment on grounds of an illegal FBI entry. At the time, Justice Department attorneys were negotiating with Jaffe. Realizing that Jaffe's attorney would soon learn of Larsen's motion and file his own discovery motion, Justice Department officials offered Jaffe a plea bargain, later extended to Larsen. Jaffe would plead guilty and in return would receive no jail sentence but be fined $2,500; Larsen would plead no contest, with Jaffe paying his fine of $500. Justice Department officials also decided to drop the case against Roth. For one, their only evidence of Roth's involvement was that he had apparently typed or handwritten several pages of the leaked documents. Justice Department attorneys were also aware that Larsen would testify that Roth did not know that Larsen had forwarded these documents to Jaffe.[26]

Justice Department attorneys decided not to prosecute Jaffe and Larsen because of the FBI's illegal investigative activities. FBI director Hoover did not concur in this decision. His rationale reflected a tortuous reading of the law and evidentiary standards—that because the FBI had broken into an apartment from which Larsen had later moved,* the documents found in Larsen's second apartment were legally admissible; that when installing the bug, FBI agents had not actually broken into Larsen's apartment because the janitor had given them a key to the apartment; and that this janitor had not known of the FBI's earlier break-in to Larsen's first apartment. These circumstances, Hoover contended, would place the burden on Larsen's attorneys of proving that evidence used to indict him had been illegally obtained.† Hoover's confidence, however, was not shared by the FBI's legal counsel. When the counsel later evaluated the problems posed by the case, he concluded that because the sources of the FBI's discovery of the contacts were bugs and wiretaps, this evidence "was tainted and

*Larsen had moved to a new apartment weeks before his arrest on June 6. Thus, of the two FBI break-ins, the first (at his old apartment) located his possession of classified documents, and the second (at his new apartment) led to the installation of a bug.

†An emboldened Hoover later claimed that "at no time did any Agents of the Bureau obtain by improper or illegal means any documents whatsoever in connection with the Larsen aspect of the case or any other aspect of it. . . . All of the documents were obtained as an incident to a lawful arrest upon a duly issued warrant." Theoharis and Cox, *The Boss,* p. 242.

that there is [sic] no definite cases available to substantiate that the evidence secured is admissible."[27]

Justice Department officials' decision to offer fairly liberal terms to Jaffe and Larsen provoked limited criticism in 1945, and later in a relatively unpublicized 1946 congressional investigation. The *Amerasia* case, by contrast, became a major political scandal in 1950 following Senator McCarthy's charges that there were eighty-one "known Communists in the State Department"—one of whom was John Service. The ensuing congressional and media investigations into McCarthy's eighty-one cases soon focused on the question of why Justice Department officials had failed to indict Service in 1945. Hearst columnist George Sokolsky and reporter Frederick Woltman in fact wrote exposés in which they attributed Service's exoneration to a Truman administration conspiracy to downplay the seriousness of the Communist internal security threat. (The Scripps-Howard chain published in pamphlet form Woltman's investigative series on this alleged administration conspiracy.) Seeking to defend their own conduct in negotiating the plea bargain, Justice Department officials drafted a lengthy report on the history of the case. Their principal defense was that FBI agents' illegal break-ins of the *Amerasia* office and the residences of some of the defendants left them with no alternative but to drop the charges.

Upon learning of this planned response by Justice, FBI assistant director Louis Nichols warned Deputy Attorney General Peyton Ford that should department officials not defend the FBI's conduct during testimony before the so-called Tydings Committee, FBI officials would be forced to release information about Corcoran's behind-the-scenes contacts in 1945 with Attorney General Clark and Assistant Attorney General McGranery, documented through the FBI's wiretap of Corcoran. The deputy attorney general replied that "of course, we would never [publicly] admit this." Nichols threatened that "we wouldn't want to admit [that the FBI had wiretapped this prominent Washington attorney], but if we were ever forced into a position the only thing we could do would be to tell the truth and point out we were ordered [by President Truman] to do this." Nichols's threat worked. Justice Department officials softened their public defense and instead emphasized the difficulties of securing a conviction owing to evidentiary problems. While the Corcoran wiretap was presumably a closely held secret from the time of its installation, it surfaced in 1950 in public comments about Corcoran's dealings by Robert Morris, minority counsel for the Tydings Committee; radio commentator Fulton Lewis, Jr.; and reporters Willard Williams and Frederick Woltman—though they did not disclose that their source was FBI officials and that Corcoran's actions were confirmed by wiretaps.[28]

Explaining their decisions in the *Amerasia* case, Justice Department officials received limited exoneration from a federal grand jury. Convened in 1949 to hear testimony about alleged espionage activities, this body initiated an investigation of the *Amerasia* case that included questioning Justice Department and FBI officials—specifically, James McInerney, assistant to the attorney general, who had had supervisory responsibility over the *Amerasia* case in 1945, and Deputy Attorney General Peyton Ford. No indictments were issued; instead the grand jury on June 15, 1950, released a presentment of its observations. All the officials involved in the handling of the case, the grand jury concluded, had "acted in a responsible manner," the FBI had "properly performed its duty . . . not only conditioned on bringing criminals to justice, but on the equally important considerations of thwarting further crime, and protecting national security," and "no evidence [was "found"] to indicate that the Department of Justice was remiss in its prosecution of the case" under prevailing law.[29]

In 1950, FBI officials had threatened to play the Corcoran wiretap card in a defensive strategy to ward off criticism of their own illegal conduct. By 1953 an emboldened FBI director considered playing the same Corcoran wiretap card, but this time for offensive reasons: to discredit President Truman. Hoover intended to exploit the opportunity of a friendly congressional inquiry convened for the purpose of enabling Attorney General Herbert Brownell to rebut sharp criticisms of the former president.

In a November 6, 1953, speech to a businessmen's group in Chicago, the Republican attorney general, who had been Dwight Eisenhower's campaign manager during the 1952 presidential election, delivered a subtly partisan attack on Truman. Praising the Eisenhower administration's more vigorous approach to internal security, Brownell contrasted its handling of FBI reports with the Truman administration's laxity or indifference. He specifically cited the former president's failure to act on FBI reports documenting Harry Dexter White's disloyalty when White's name was submitted for confirmation as director of the International Monetary Fund. Truman responded immediately, claiming that he had arranged with Hoover to let White's nomination go forward in order to keep secret an ongoing FBI investigation into White and others—the investigation triggered by Elizabeth Bentley's allegations. After justifying his actions, Truman concluded by accusing Brownell of McCarthyism. To defend himself and the accuracy of his criticisms, Brownell arranged to testify (accompanied by Hoover) before the Senate Internal Security Subcommittee.

In preparing for his testimony, Hoover ordered his aides to review the record of his reports to the president and senior Truman administration officials about White's loyalty. He also purposefully weighed this opportunity to revisit the *Amerasia* case and raise questions not about Clark's or McGranery's roles but whether Truman knew of their actions and had done nothing. Accordingly, on November 8, 1953, the FBI director demanded a search of FBI files for any record documenting that FBI officials had briefed Truman about these intercepted Corcoran conversations.

Beginning in 1945 and extending through 1948, the duration of the FBI's wiretapping of Corcoran, Hoover had regularly sent transcripts of the Corcoran wiretap intercepts to the White House. Because of the massiveness of these transmissions (more than 6,250 pages) and the fact that the cover letters accompanying the transcripts were addressed to White House aides George Allen and Harry Vaughan, the FBI director needed to know whether any FBI reports called Truman's attention to the Corcoran conversations with Clark and McGranery. FBI assistant director Nichols responded to Hoover's order, advising his chief that "there are no such letters that I can recall or find." Such explicit documentation was needed given the uniqueness of the Corcoran wiretap—installed solely on the authorization of the FBI director in violation of established departmental rules requiring the attorney general's prior notification and approval, and on the FBI director's clear understanding that this wiretap "should never become known" and "should [the tap] ever become known, it would be our [FBI] baby" as the White House "would deny any knowledge."[30]

In 1953, Hoover could have disclosed that Corcoran's phone had been tapped, and that the intercepted conversations recorded Corcoran's intercession on Service's behalf while his case was being presented to a grand jury. But Hoover's willingness to accompany Brownell and testify in the partisan setting of the Senate Internal Security Subcommittee proceeding was sharply criticized by Southern Democrats and other commentators as politicizing the FBI. Thus, had Hoover recounted the history of this wiretap operation, he would have raised further questions about the FBI's independence. For the released records would have confirmed that Hoover had willingly furthered the political interests of one president (Truman) in 1945 and now willingly broke this confidence to further the political interests of another president (Eisenhower) in 1953. Hoover thereupon dropped the idea.

Not only had Hoover's indifference to the rule of law undermined the prosecution of the *Amerasia* defendants. Just as important, the FBI director's expansive view of the FBI's counterintelligence responsibilities led to the wiretapping of individuals as respectable as a White House aide and a prominent Washington attorney whose sole "crimes" were to oppose the political interests of the president. Hoover's handling of information about the Corcoran wiretap confirms how FBI practices were no longer determined solely by law enforcement considerations but by an equal desire to preclude discovery of illegal investigative techniques. This was pointedly underscored by the special records procedures instituted in the wake of the Coplon revelations. Hoover's success in immunizing specially sensitive FBI records from public discovery also averted future embarrassment of his agency's abuses of power and politics of counterintelligence.

CHAPTER FIVE

• • •

Politicizing Justice: The Hiss and Remington Indictments

THE COUNTERINTELLIGENCE DILEMMA produced by the FBI's use of illegal investigative techniques does not alone explain why the FBI failed to apprehend and prosecute Soviet agents and their American recruits. The fact is that FBI counterintelligence investigations never focused solely, or even primarily, on suspected spies. Dating from World War I and the Bolshevik Revolution, FBI officials authorized wide-ranging investigations to identify members of the American Communist party and those individuals and organizations suspected of being Communist sympathizers. Their principal objective was to determine how Communists might influence government policy, labor organizations and strike activities, movements for racial equality or social change, higher education, and the media (newspapers, movies, and books).* FBI

*This is indirectly confirmed by the COMRAP file. Although heavily redacted and authorized for the purpose of monitoring suspected Soviet re-

investigations of Communist and radical movements intensified after 1936, encouraged by President Roosevelt's verbal request of August 1936 that Hoover determine whether American fascist and Communist movements were directed by Nazi Germany and Soviet Russia.

FBI initiatives of 1940 and 1945 highlight this broader political surveillance purpose. In December 1940, "in connection with the [FBI's] investigation of united front organizations," FBI assistant director Edward Tamm proposed investigations of organizations "of the labor union type" as well as "Communist-front organizations." Tamm identified specific organizations that fell in these two categories: the American Civil Liberties Union, the American Newspaper Guild, the Consumers Union, the Consumer National Federation, the Needle Workers Council for Peace and Civil Rights, the Southern Tenant Farmers Union, the National Lawyers Guild, the Farmers Union, the League of American Writers, the Transport Workers Union, and the Sharecroppers Union. Hoover endorsed Tamm's proposal, requesting Justice Department approval for FBI investigations of suspected "Communist-dominated or controlled" organizations. His request named all those cited by Tamm except the American Civil Liberties Union.[1] Five years later, in 1945, Hoover rejected Tamm's recommendation to discontinue FBI wiretaps on three unidentified "CIO units." Despite having uncovered information about "Communist activities in these units, in strikes and in various other every-day occurrences," Tamm lamented, when intercepted information was conveyed to the White House, the attorney general, or the secretary of the navy, "nothing whatsoever is done by the policy-making agencies

cruitment of American Communists to conduct military and industrial espionage, this code-named program ended up monitoring Communist political activities and efforts to influence public policy. See also Regin Schmidt, *Red Scare: FBI and the Origins of Anticommunism in the United States, 1919–1943* (Copenhagen, Denmark, 2000), pp. 9–23, 61–68, 83–360.

of the Government about this Communist activity." Conceding that some FBI wiretaps were "unproductive," Hoover nonetheless concluded that these "3 cases are highly informative on an aspect of Communist activities of considerable importance."[2]

From 1942 through 1950 the FBI extensively wiretapped and bugged the American labor movement. While the scope of this surveillance cannot be definitively established owing to continued restrictions on relevant FBI records, a released index-card file on the FBI's most sensitive wiretaps and bugs confirms that the targets included at least the CIO Council; the CIO Maritime Committee; the Food, Tobacco, Agricultural & Allied Workers of America (CIO); the International Longshoremen's and Warehousemen's Union; the National Union of Maritime Cooks & Stewards; the United Public Workers of America; the United Automobile Workers; the United Electrical Radio & Machine Workers of America; and the United Mine Workers.[3]

Because of procedures instituted to destroy all records of FBI break-ins, the scope of these practices also cannot be definitively established. Owing to an inadvertent failure to destroy the office file of FBI assistant director Louis Nichols, however, we know that targets of two 1941 FBI break-ins were the American Peace Mobilization and the Washington Committee for Democratic Action, and that FBI agents photocopied their membership files. FBI director Hoover thereupon discovered that some Justice Department employees or their wives were members of one or both of these organizations and immediately urged Assistant Attorney General Matthew McGuire to dismiss these employees. Among those he identified were Assistant Solicitor General (and later federal judge) Charles Fahy; and department attorneys Edward Prichard, a later White House aide and prominent New Deal activist;* Thomas Emerson, a distinguished First Amendment scholar

*In March 1941, FBI officials prepared a memorandum summarizing

and later Yale Law School professor; and Herbert Wechsler, another distinguished scholar and later Columbia University Law School professor. At the same time the FBI initiated a Hatch Act investigation (under which federal employees found to be members of fascist or Communist organizations were to be dismissed) of State Department employee Alger Hiss, "based on the allegation that he was a member" of the Washington Committee for Democratic Action.[4]

FBI officials also discreetly investigated "subversive activities at educational institutions," inquiries that required the recruitment of informers on college campuses. In 1948–1949, for example, the FBI looked into allegations "concerning Communist infiltration and instruction being given at the Sarah Lawrence College." Officials hesitated to launch a direct investigation, fearing an adverse reaction should it become known, and instead ordered FBI agents to obtain "discreetly" a copy of the college's catalogue to check the names of faculty members against FBI files. This tactic would blunt any allegation that the FBI was investigating the college rather than the "individual instructor."[5]

FBI officials also intensively investigated the Federation of American Scientists (FAS). Formed after World War II, the FAS wanted to be sure that scientists had a voice in setting governmental policy on the international control of atomic energy and the military use of the atomic bomb. FBI agents carefully monitored the public activities of FAS leaders and their various efforts to influence public policy, having been ordered to determine their "political orientation," possible links to Communists or suspected Communists, and "agitation and pressure activities aimed at influ-

Prichard's Communist sympathies: his opposition to alien, sedition, and poll tax laws and his support for anti-lynching and mental health legislation. Tracy Campbell, *Short of Glory: The Fall and Redemption of Edward F. Prichard Jr.* (Lexington, Ky., 1998), p. 73; see also pp. 137–152, 157, 159, 164–165, 173.

encing the dissemination of technical and other information concerning it [policy toward the atomic bomb]."[6]

This obsession with Communist influence also led FBI officials to target the Hollywood community and other authors, reporters, and influencers of public opinion. FBI resources and personnel were thus diverted from legitimate and necessary counterintelligence investigations.

Despite the intensity of the FBI's COMRAP investigation, until Elizabeth Bentley's defection in 1945 and Whittaker Chambers's altered testimony of November–December 1948, the FBI had failed to develop admissible evidence to prosecute or even to identify Soviet espionage agents in wartime Washington. Not dissuaded by this failure, FBI officials continued their efforts to contain the "Red Menace." With the Justice Department they succeeded in indicting and convicting only 2 of the more than 150 individuals accused by Chambers and Bentley—Alger Hiss and William Remington—and then only on charges of perjurious testimony before a federal grand jury. Yet to secure these indictments and convictions, FBI and Justice Department officials either abused or purposefully politicized the grand jury system. Their eventual success stemmed from the secrecy of grand jury proceedings, not from the evidence developed by the FBI.

Despite Whittaker Chambers's production in November–December 1948 of notes in Hiss's handwriting, and typed and microfilm copies of State Department documents that he claimed Hiss had given him in 1938, Justice Department and FBI officials confronted real prosecutorial problems. These stemmed from Chambers's credibility as a witness. In his August 1948 testimony before the House Committee on Un-American Activities and in earlier FBI interviews, Chambers had dated his own defection from the Communist party as 1937. And he had consistently described his relationship with Hiss, and Hiss's activities, as those of members of a Communist underground group whose purpose was to influence government policy. At no time, including his October 14–15, 1948, testimony before a federal grand jury, had Chambers accused Hiss of having engaged in espionage.

Chambers's grand jury testimony of October 1948 proved to be the most troublesome for the Justice Department, especially since this grand jury had been convened to hear testimony about Soviet espionage activities. At this hearing a grand juror directly asked Chambers if he "could give one name of anybody who in [Chambers's] opinion, was positively guilty of espionage against the United States? Yes or no." Seemingly searching his memory, Chambers equivocated, "Let me think a moment and I will try to answer that. I don't think so but I would like to have an opportunity to answer you more definitely. Let me think it over overnight." The same juror renewed this query the next day. When asked by Chambers if he meant by espionage "the turning over of secret or confidential documents," the juror replied, "Or information—oral information." Chambers then replied, "Or oral information. I do not believe I do know such a name."[7]

A month later, however, Chambers produced the typed copies and handwritten notes of State Department documents which he then claimed to have received from Hiss in 1938. On December 2–3, 1948, moreover, Chambers gave HUAC investigators microfilm copies of State Department documents which he also claimed to have received from Hiss. Assistant Attorney General Alexander Campbell's initial response, conveyed to FBI officials on December 3, was that he did not intend to recall Chambers before the grand jury as "an indictment against him [for perjury and obstruction of the grand jury] was contemplated."[8] Campbell soon had second thoughts and subpoenaed Chambers to testify before the grand jury on December 6.

Chambers encountered deep skepticism, even hostility when questioned by U.S. attorneys Thomas Donegan and Raymond Whearty and members of the grand jury about the disparity between his October responses and his recent production of documents, which he claimed to have received from Hiss. Their questions reflected doubts of his credibility and an underlying conviction that he had willfully committed perjury and obstructed the work of the grand jury.

Chambers was intensively questioned by Whearty on December 6 about his new account of his awareness of Communist espionage activities. Shifting the thrust of his questions on December 9, Whearty expressed bewilderment as to the "real reason why you held out these documents and failed to disclose their existence prior to" November 17 and December 2–3, 1948. Responding, Chambers claimed that when he met with Assistant Secretary of State Adolf Berle in November 1939 to tell him of the Communist "underground," he had expected that an investigation "would begin at once" and that he would be "called to Washington quickly and that the whole story would then be developed." Pressed by Whearty, Chambers conceded that he had "made no reference to having possession of any documents." When no investigation resulted, Chambers added, "the documents had dimmed in my mind, for one thing, and my old feeling that I did not want to involve human beings in such a tragic difficulty any more than necessary became paramount again." Chambers repeated this explanation when asked why he had not produced the documents for FBI agents when interviewed in 1942, 1945, and 1946: he had forgotten their existence until retrieving them in November 1948 from a nephew to whom he had given them for safekeeping in 1938. A grand juror then sarcastically asked if Chambers had "additional documents, film, et cetera that you have completely forgotten," to which Whearty equally sarcastically added "that are so important that you have forgotten them." Chambers responded, "No, I don't believe so."

The grand jurors found equally incredible Chambers's explanations that he had been purposefully vague because he had not wished to damage Hiss or other individuals. Reflecting skepticism over this explanation, one juror observed that neither the typewritten nor handwritten documents contained the names of Chambers's sources. Why then had Chambers not given them to government agents? Chambers repeated that it was "a question of the degree of damage I would have done to a man like Alger Hiss, for example." A juror then asked Chambers to reconcile his denial "under oath before this Grand Jury" on October 14–15 of any knowledge of "an espionage group" with "your answer this time that it was an espionage group." "It was my desire," Chambers repeated, "not to inflict greater damage on these people than was necessary in the course of revealing Communist activities." Pressed whether he considered this "more important than the fact that you were perjuring yourself before the Grand Jury," Chambers conceded that "I ran that risk" and reiterated that "I wished to shield certain people." Had he then decided on October 14 to "perjure yourself rather than reveal information and injure those people?" Chambers responded that his intent was not to "perjure myself, but if the result is technically perjury, I can only say that my mind is at peace." Donegan asked Chambers why, having "withheld" information about espionage during his October testimony before the grand jury, he had changed his mind since then. Donegan particularly inquired whether Chambers was in effect a "co-conspirator" since he had failed to give these documents either to Berle or to the FBI. Chambers disputed this characterization, adding that he thought the "F.B.I. was doing as good a job as it could do." Concluding this line of questioning, Whearty asked whether Chambers would have produced the documents had it not been for Hiss's libel suit. Chambers replied that he had forgotten their existence.[9]

During his questioning of HUAC counsel Robert Stripling on December 9, 1948, Whearty again returned to Chambers's withholding information from the grand jury. Stripling agreed "there is no question" that Chambers had deliberately withheld information and had thereby "misled the investigators with reference to this information." "The Grand Jury is particularly interested" in action, Whearty emphasized, signaling an intention to pursue a perjury and obstruction of justice indictment of Chambers.[10]

In his own first appearance before the grand jury in March 1948, Hiss had been asked almost exclusively whether he had been a member of the Communist party, the International Juridical Association, and the Washington Committee for Democratic Action, and about the nature of his relationship with a series of named individuals. This limited questioning was consistent with the information the FBI had developed, based primarily on earlier interviews in which Chambers contended only that Hiss had been a member of a Communist cell composed of identified federal employees. Hiss denied membership in the Communist party and the Washington Committee, but admitted to membership in the Juridical Association. His relationship with the named individuals, Hiss asserted, was professional and/or social, and he did not know whether any were Communists or Communist sympathizers. Asked if he knew an individual "by the name of Whittaker Chambers," Hiss admitted having been "asked that question before, but I do not know Mr. Chambers." Hiss categorically denied having "furnished any information to any person known to you or suspected by you to be a member of the Communist Party or a representative or connected with the Soviet Government."[11]

Armed with the documents that Chambers had provided in November 1948, the grand jury's line of questioning of Hiss changed abruptly in December. Both the U.S. attorneys and the grand jurors showed deep skepticism about Hiss's responses to questions of how Chambers could have produced typed and handwritten copies of State Department documents, the latter in Hiss's handwriting and the former typed on a typewriter owned by the Hisses. Hiss had "no idea how Mr. Chambers got hold" of the handwritten notes, adding, "he did not get them from me," though he said he regularly discarded his notes, some in the wastebasket. Questioned about the typed documents, following the testimony of FBI experts that the Chambers-produced documents had been typed on the same machine used by Mrs. Hiss to type personal correspondence during the 1930s, Hiss claimed that Chambers "has framed me." He was convinced that Chambers "is not a man of sound mind and I believe that he has some abnormal and, to me, not clearly understood reason for wishing to destroy me." Questioned how Chambers could have had access to his typewriter, Hiss replied that Chambers "must have obtained access to the typewriter without my knowing it." Had Chambers broken into his residence then, Hiss was asked pointedly, to which he replied, "I would certainly not put that beyond him." Hiss might have gotten "rid of the typewriter before these dates [January 5–April 1, 1938, of the typed State Department documents] and he [Chambers] somehow obtained it," or Chambers could have first stolen and then returned the Hisses' typewriter after typing the documents. Hiss's explanations struck one grand juror as "more and more fantastic" and as going beyond "the realm of anything that anybody can believe." Hiss blandly responded that Chambers "is a fantastic personality."[12]

The grand jury records confirm that its members had initially found both Chambers's explanations for his changed testimony and Hiss's explanations about the typed documents incredible. The records further confirm that the grand jury would have indicted Chambers for perjury but, owing to the statute of limitations, could not indict Hiss for espionage. Both of these possibilities deeply troubled Congressman Richard Nixon.

From August 1948, Nixon had assumed a leading role in HUAC's highly publicized hearings into the Hiss-Chambers relationship. At first HUAC wanted to know whether Hiss and Chambers had known each other as fellow Communists during the

1930s, and whether their relationship confirmed that Communists had successfully infiltrated New Deal agencies to influence public policy. Unknown at the time, Nixon worked closely with FBI officials to raise doubts about Hiss's credibility and thereby to substantiate HUAC's partisan charge that the Truman administration was indifferent to the Communist threat. Through "informal contacts with a lower level [FBI] agent" (whom Nixon never identified) and with the Catholic priest John Cronin as an intermediary, Nixon obtained "the results of the Bureau's investigation into Hiss—the car, the typewriter, etc." Under this arrangement, FBI agent Ed Hummer informed Cronin what the FBI "had turned up," and Cronin then telephoned Nixon's private line "frequently between August and December 1948" to supply "the F.B.I. tidbits." As a result, Nixon "then knew just where to look for things and what he could find."[13]

Senator Karl Mundt's recently released grand jury testimony further confirms this covert FBI-HUAC relationship. In 1948, Mundt had also been a member of the House Committee on Un-American Activities. He testified that HUAC, not just Nixon, had a "fairly good liaison with the F.B.I." FBI officials, Mundt clarified, "would never come to us originally with tips," but "sometimes" helped by keeping "us from getting off on a wrong track." "Most of our work with the F.B.I.," Mundt continued, "had to be on a personal basis, rather than an official basis."[14]

Nixon's and HUAC's "informal" relationship was meant to ensure that senior Justice Department officers could not discover that FBI officials were assisting the Truman administration's partisan adversaries. The relationship moreover was not confined to low-level FBI agents. By late 1948 Nixon had established a close working relationship with FBI assistant director Louis Nichols, the third-ranking FBI official and Hoover's liaison to Congress and to the media. The closeness of their collaboration proved to be of crucial importance in December 1948.

An FBI memorandum of that month confirms the scope and nature of this relationship. It records the responses of senior FBI officials to what became the defining event in the Hiss-Chambers matter—Chambers's production on December 2 and 3 of microfilm copies of State Department documents for HUAC investigators.

This dramatic development had its origins on December 1, when Nicholas Vazzana, an investigator hired by Chambers's attorneys to help in defending against Hiss's libel suit, told Nixon and HUAC Counsel Robert Stripling that Chambers had turned over documents to Hiss's attorneys that could "break the case."[15] Intrigued by this tip, Nixon and Stripling traveled to Chambers's farm in Westminster, Maryland, that night. When they returned from this meeting in the middle of the night, Nixon immediately telephoned Nichols to report "on a strictly personal and highly confidential basis" about a dramatic new development and HUAC's plans to deal with it.

Nixon began by reporting that Chambers had earlier delivered to Hiss's attorneys, who then turned them over to the Justice Department, "highly incriminatory documentary evidence"—the handwritten and typed documents. Chambers "still has other documents and materials," Nixon added, which had not yet been "publicly known." HUAC intended to subpoena these "other documents and materials" and would hold hearings on December 18. (Nixon was leaving on vacation the next day and would not return until December 15.) The "purpose of his call," Nixon emphasized, was "merely to apprise the Bureau so that the FBI would not be caught off base." Assuring Nichols that the committee "intended to handl[e] the matter so that there will be no criticism of the FBI," Nixon "particularly urged that we [FBI] do nothing about the information which he had just furnished as he feels the statute of limitations [for an espionage conviction of Hiss] has run." Nichols thereupon briefed Hoover about Nixon's call and the congressman's specific request that "we [FBI] not tell the Attorney General [Tom Clark] that we were told of this information as the Attorney General undoubtedly would try to make it impossible for the Committee to get at the documents. He also asked that the Bureau not look for the documents themselves." Despite the audacity of this freshman congressman's proposal, the FBI director agreed to defer to the committee, and merely ordered his aides to inquire of Assistant Attorney General Campbell about the "documentary evidence" that Chambers had turned over on November 17.[16]

Before leaving on vacation, Nixon ordered Stripling to subpoena Chambers to produce the "documents and materials." Chambers thereupon took two HUAC investigators to a pumpkin patch on his farm and removed from a carved-out pumpkin three rolls of undeveloped microfilm. Stripling had the Veterans Administration laboratory develop the film; he realized that contacting the FBI Laboratory would have required FBI officials to alert their superiors in the Justice Department. Upon receipt of the developed microfilm, and having learned that the film contained "reproductions of confidential documents from the State Department," Stripling briefed FBI assistant director Nichols on this matter "for our [FBI] confidential information and he [Stripling] specifically asked that the information not go out of the Bureau." Stripling promised to keep "in close touch" with Nichols upon learning of HUAC's plans for dealing with this dramatic development and hoped to obtain committee authorization "to furnish us [FBI] with a copy." The microfilm confirmed Hiss's guilt, Stripling emphasized, but would also raise questions about "Chambers withholding information." Nichols again briefed FBI associate director Clyde Tolson and Hoover about this development, pledging to "keep in touch with him [Stripling] from time to time." The FBI, Nichols recommended, should not "make any formal request for the material because obviously it would be difficult to take prosecutive action for espionage on actions that occurred in 1938."[17]

Having already learned from his FBI allies that Assistant Attorney General Campbell might indict Chambers for perjury, Nixon convened public hearings on December 8 to foreclose this possibility. During these hearings, the congressman minimized Chambers's perjurious testimony of October 14–15 as merely "technical perjury"—despite the fact that the grand jury had been convened explicitly to consider indicting anyone who had committed espionage for the Soviet Union, and that Chambers's response in October had thwarted this inquiry. A Justice Department indictment of Chambers, Nixon insisted, would undermine any case against other more guilty espionage participants, since the principal witness would be a convicted perjuror. Should Hiss or others not be indicted on a technicality—the expiration of the statute of limitations—Nixon warned, HUAC would pursue the matter.[18]

But Nixon now reassessed his plan to have HUAC simply publicize this matter. He decided instead to pressure Justice Department officials to indict Hiss, realizing that while an espionage indictment was foreclosed by the statute of limitations, Hiss could be indicted for perjurious testimony before the grand jury. To achieve this objective, Nixon sought to exploit the leverage deriving from HUAC's physical possession of the microfilm. Chambers's production of the microfilm would not have been sufficient to prove that Hiss had committed espionage, since it would not confirm that Chambers's State Department source was Hiss. Government prosecutors nonetheless needed to test the authenticity of the microfilm if they were to present it as supportive evidence to the grand jury or during any resultant trial. The typed documents, on the other hand, were crucial for a perjury conviction: they provided a direct link between Chambers and Hiss.

Nixon's recognition of the perjury indictment option led to his December 8 meeting with two former FBI agents, Patrick Coyne and Bob King. Nixon could not risk contacting Nichols or any other FBI official directly (as he had done as recently as his December 2 telephone call to Nichols), given the hostility between HUAC and the Justice Department created by HUAC's December hearings and Nixon's charges of a Justice Department cover-up. Having somehow obtained "copies" of the typed documents, Nixon showed them to Coyne and King and expressed his desire to "obtain, if possible, specimens of the typewriting, from the typewriter which was formerly used by Mrs. Alger Hiss for comparison with the typing of the [State Department] documents." (The FBI had already obtained such specimens, and provided expert testimony to the grand jury linking them to the Hisses' typewriter.) Nixon further conveyed to Coyne and King his bitterness toward Attorney General Clark and Assistant Attorney General Campbell for "not having more vigorously prosecuted this whole matter," and his high praise for the FBI and Hoover. He then volunteered to the former agents that he "had worked very close with the Bureau and with Mr. Nichols during the past year" on the Hiss-Chambers "matter." Coyne and King immediately relayed Nixon's request to FBI assistant director D. Milton Ladd, who in turn briefed Hoover.[19]

Not surprisingly, no extant FBI record describes whether senior FBI officials honored Nixon's indirect request for copies of the Hiss "typewriter specimens." In any event, Nixon moved quickly to exploit the opportunity of his subpoenaed appearance before the grand jury on December 13. The sole purpose of the U.S. attorney's invitation was to pressure Nixon to turn over to the grand jury the original microfilm documents in HUAC's possession. Nixon, however, immediately sought to pressure the grand jurors to indict Hiss, but also not to indict Chambers.

During this session, Nixon refused the prosecutors' direct request to turn over the original microfilm, claiming that he lacked the authority to relinquish control without a formal vote by the

House of Representatives, which was then not in session. He would willingly allow the FBI to examine and establish the authenticity of the microfilm, Nixon stated. Further, should the grand jury indict, "and if the Department of Justice then was faced with the necessity of a criminal prosecution of individuals involved and if then the original document itself would have to be submitted in evidence, certainly it could be made available at that time for this purpose." Nixon questioned the Justice Department's commitment to pursue the matter. He claimed—dishonestly—that HUAC's decision to have the Veterans Administration develop the microfilm was due to the fact that "the Department of Justice has issued instructions to the FBI not to cooperate with the Committee on Un-American Activities," thus HUAC was "unable to avail itself of the very fine work the FBI has done and does." Nixon regretted that the Justice Department "feels as it does concerning the Committee and thereby has seen fit to inform the FBI that that should be its attitude toward the Committee."

Stressing that HUAC's sole purpose was to determine the "truth," while characterizing the Justice Department as partisan and obstructionist, Nixon proceeded to lecture the jurors on their duty—in the process countermanding the authority of the prosecutors. Implying that Hiss had unquestionably committed espionage, he outlined lines of inquiry that the jurors should pursue and emphasized that HUAC had discovered that the "only way that Mr. Hiss can be cross-examined is by obtaining basic information and then confronting him with that information and then cross-examining him relentlessly and I mean relentlessly, until the truth comes out." Shrewdly distinguishing between the jurors and the Justice Department, Nixon expressed personal confidence in the jurors "provided the Department of Justice does a proper job in presenting all the facts to the jury, providing it does a proper job in relentlessly and ruthlessly in cross-examining all that are involved before the jury—I am confident that the jury will reach the decision that will be in the best interests of the country." He concluded his peroration with an explicit threat: if the statute of limitations and "legal technicalities" allowed that the "individual who furnished this information to Chambers might go Scot-free," HUAC fully intended to "go ahead with our investigation" of the case.[20]

Nixon's intrusion into the grand jury's deliberations violated constitutional procedures intended to ensure that such bodies would not be subject to political pressure. The very reason for secrecy in grand jury proceedings was to ensure both that a decision to indict would be based solely on the jurors' independent evaluation of the evidence, and that their deliberations would be free from political pressure. Nixon's success in politicizing the process had the desired consequence of gaining Hiss's indictment and not Chamber's: first, by casting doubt on the Justice Department's presentation of the case, and, second, by ensuring that the jurors recognized his and HUAC's continuing intent to establish Hiss's guilt. The covert FBI-HUAC relationship, unknown to the attorney general and government prosecutors, also helped ensure this result.* On December 15, the last day of its tenure, the grand jury indicted Hiss on two counts of perjury: denying having met Chambers after 1937 and having given classified State Department documents to him. At the same time the grand jury returned no indictment against Chambers for perjury or obstruction of justice.

Almost immediately after the grand jury indictment, the Justice Department convened a new grand jury. Its purpose was not simply to secure additional indictments based on Chambers's revised December 1948 grand jury testimony (none were returned); government prosecutors also sought to use the grand jury process to pressure the named individuals to corroborate Chambers's testi-

*Nixon lied to the grand jury about his own and HUAC's relationship with the FBI. Mundt's admission was made to a later grand jury in May 1949.

mony. Such corroboration was of crucial importance given Chambers's questionable credibility as the prosecutors' key witness. Hiss's attorneys predictably adopted the same skeptical questioning of Chambers about his changed testimony that U.S. attorneys Donegan and Whearty and the grand jurors had employed earlier. If the government could get those named by Chambers to admit to their espionage relationship with Chambers, Chambers's credibility would be strengthened.

Ironically, the government's strategy was complicated by its successful indictment of Hiss. The stark lesson for subpoenaed witnesses was that they risked indictment not for what they might have done but for denying Chambers's charges under oath. Their safest course was to take the Fifth Amendment and, when confronted by potentially troublesome questions, to avail themselves of the right to consult with their attorneys before answering. Confronted by this uncooperative stance, government prosecutors resorted to tactics that raised serious questions about their abuse of the secrecy of grand jury proceedings. This was particularly true in the case of two witnesses subpoenaed to corroborate Chambers's identification of "Felix," the individual whom Chambers claimed had in 1936–1938 photographed the State Department documents he had received from Hiss.

In December, government prosecutors had subpoenaed Samuel Pelovitz to testify before the grand jury that had indicted Hiss. A former Communist, Pelovitz had for a time lived on Callow Avenue in Baltimore, the street address and city cited by Chambers as the location of the filming operation. Pelovitz, however, denied knowing Chambers and, more important, claimed to have lived in New York City in 1936–1937, to be a printer by trade, and to have no photographic skills. Testifying immediately afterward, Chambers positively identified Pelovitz as "Felix." Following a short recess, however, Chambers abruptly changed his testimony. He had been mistaken, he now testified, and attributed his revised account to Pelovitz's different build and facial structure and that Pelovitz "is Jewish and Felix was not Jewish."

Identifying "Felix" had been at best a peripheral concern of government prosecutors in early December. But by January, identifying "Felix" acquired greater significance. Chambers's credibility would be enhanced should "Felix" admit and testify to having photographed State Department documents for Chambers. An intensive effort was thus made to locate the real "Felix." Relying on earlier intensive FBI investigations of Communist activists in Baltimore during the 1930s, FBI officials in January 1949 identified Felix Inslerman as Chambers's "Felix." Chambers was then brought before the grand jury to testify that Felix Inslerman was "Felix" and to describe in detail their photographing operation.[21] Inslerman was thereupon subpoenaed.

A reluctant witness who nonetheless recognized his own vulnerability, Felix Inslerman responded to questions from the U.S. attorneys and grand jurors by pleading an inability to recall, or by requesting the right to consult with his attorney before answering, or by taking the Fifth Amendment. Seeking to pressure Inslerman to corroborate Chambers, U.S. attorneys threatened him with an indictment for obstructing the grand jury. When Inslerman took the Fifth Amendment rather than deny the charges, U.S. attorneys pointedly questioned his loyalty and willingness to cooperate. Indeed, jury foreman John Brunini characterized Inslerman's actions as a "refusal" to help the grand jury. "We are going to drag it out of you, so open up and give it to us," Brunini threatened, challenging Inslerman's reliance on counsel before answering questions. Inslerman should "help out with the investigation," Brunini counseled, for by doing so "It's going to be very much more to your advantage and the advantage of your wife and child and those who are close to you if you do." Repeating this admonition, Donegan urged Inslerman to cooperate, adding ominously, "You are in a bad position, and I think you should consider trying to improve your position." Standing his ground, Inslerman refused to abandon his Fifth Amendment rights. For this he was threatened by one grand juror, who told him that should he leave "without divulging the information that is in your possession," it could leak out eventually and affect his chances for future employment. Inslerman's persistence in not answering, U.S. attorney Whearty added, "gives the Grand Jury and the Government no other course than to leave no stone unturned to get to the bottom of the story you gave." By cooperating, Inslerman would benefit his own position, Donegan advised, for if he were tried the government would inform the court of his full cooperation. When Inslerman persisted, another juror threatened to indict him "for everything we can." Inslerman "either tells the truth or suffers the consequences."[22]

In a companion tactic to pressure Inslerman to cooperate, government prosecutors unsuccessfully attempted to launder illegal FBI wiretap information. Inslerman's intercepted conversations underpinned a series of questions as to whether he had sought to obstruct justice. U.S. attorney Donegan pointedly questioned Inslerman about his "telephone conversation" with his wife. (Inslerman had telephoned her at their home from New York City, where he had gone to prepare for his grand jury testimony.) Donegan asked Inslerman why he had asked his wife to bring his Leica camera to New York but leave their other two cameras at their farm. The implication of this line of questioning was that Inslerman's intent was to deny FBI access to the Leica.* Donegan also questioned Inslerman about his telephone conversation with his friends Mr. and Mrs. Richard Lotus. Had Inslerman sought to influence their possible statements to the FBI, Donegan asked, and did they

*In fact Inslerman had used the Leica to photograph documents for Chambers—as FBI agents later established during Hiss's trial.

know whether Inslerman had known Chambers and had photographed government documents?[23]

The U.S. attorneys employed the same tactics in questioning Elizabeth Inslerman, Felix's wife, badgering her to cooperate and asking her questions based on FBI wiretap information. At the outset of her testimony, Elizabeth Inslerman had asserted her privilege not to testify against her husband. Regardless, prosecutors and the grand jurors did not confine their questions to what she had done but to what she might have seen her husband do or might have done—inquiring specifically about Felix's employment status in the 1930s. As in the questioning of her husband, Elizabeth was chastised whenever she exercised her right to consult counsel before answering specific questions. At one time she was even pressured to answer questions about her attorney's advice to her. Donegan implied that Elizabeth's answers were perjurious and obstructed the investigation, and threatened to take her "before a Judge, because a Grand Jury cannot be treated lightly or in a contemptuous manner by a witness." Whearty and Donegan also asked about her husband's telephone conversation with the Lotuses, asking her why he had sought their advice and whether he had coached the Lotuses on how to respond to questions from the FBI. Concluding his brutal questioning, Donegan warned Elizabeth of the perils of her refusal to answer questions: "The Grand Jury is all-powerful, as far as what they do," and she and her husband could minimize their future risk if they cooperated. Brunini interjected to emphasize the importance of Felix Inslerman's testimony, adding that if her husband "persists in being a non-cooperative witness, I think you are going to find, even if there is no legal action against you, that you can have an extremely difficult time in getting along."[24]

Brunini's threats to both Felix and Elizabeth Inslerman proved prophetic. The Inslermans paid a heavy price for refusing to corroborate Chambers's account of the Baltimore photographing operation. After losing his job with General Electric, a chastened Felix Inslerman recanted in 1954 and admitted to FBI agents that he was indeed Chambers's photographer. He further admitted to having traveled to the Soviet Union in 1935, where he had been trained in the use of the Leica camera. The FBI already knew of Inslerman's 1935 trip and training. This knowledge underlay U.S. attorneys' persistent questioning of the Inslermans during the January grand jury proceedings. Inslerman might have expected questions about his employment status in 1936–1937, the time of the microfilm operation, but not about his 1935 employment. He took the Fifth Amendment, suspecting correctly that government attorneys already knew of his 1935 trip to the Soviet Union.[25]

The politicization of the grand jury process to ensure Hiss's indictment (owing once again to the FBI's inability to develop admissible evidence of espionage activities) was replicated in the case of William Remington. The foreman of the grand jury that returned Remington's indictment, John Brunini; U.S. attorney Thomas Donegan; and senior Justice Department officials combined to politicize the grand jury process and thereby secure Remington's perjury conviction.

Remington's travails had their origins in Elizabeth Bentley's defection in November 1945, when she informed FBI agents of her role as a courier for a wartime Soviet espionage ring, then identified the Communist federal employees who comprised it. Bentley eventually named 150 individuals during her FBI interviews. Nathan Silvermaster and Victor Perlo, she claimed, had headed two separate espionage operations. Remington did not figure prominently in Bentley's original account of Soviet espionage.

An intensive FBI investigation was launched to corroborate Bentley's account, during which FBI agents broke into Remington's residence, intercepted his mail, and tapped his phone despite his peripheral status in Bentley's account. As in the cases of the others named by Bentley, FBI agents could not develop any admissible evidence to indict Remington for espionage. Nonetheless the Justice Department convened a federal grand jury in 1947, hoping to pressure one or more of the subpoenaed witnesses into admitting their role and implicating others. Remington was among those subpoenaed. In his grand jury testimony he was questioned about his relationship with Bentley and specifically whether he had been a member of the Communist party or had paid party dues. He was not indicted by this grand jury—nor, for that matter, were any of the others named by Bentley.

When no indictments were returned, two congressional committees initiated public hearings in the summer of 1948, one focusing on Bentley's testimony and the other on that of Whittaker Chambers. These hearings proved damaging to both Remington's and Hiss's reputations. Remington's problems stemmed from two factors. First, he did not take the Fifth Amendment when responding to the committee's questions—in striking contrast, for example, to Silvermaster and Perlo. Second, by then most of the individuals named by Bentley were no longer federal employees while Remington continued to hold a sensitive appointment in the Commerce Department. He was one of only three named by Bentley who was currently employed in the federal government.

In her July 27, 1948, testimony before the Senate Subcommittee on Expenditures in Government, Bentley accused Remington only of having paid his Communist party dues to her and of having given her secret information on aircraft production in the belief that this information was to be given to Earl Browder, executive secretary of the American Communist party. Remington did not know, Bentley explained, that this information was delivered to the Soviet Union. Subpoenaed to testify before the Senate subcommittee, Remington admitted having met Bentley in Washington during the war years, to having thought she was a freelance journalist for leftist publications, and to having given her only public information about war production in order to rebut Communist and radical suspicions that the U.S. government was "an appeasement government but [instead] was going to fight the war and win."[26]

Despite Remington's benign account of his wartime relationship with Bentley, her charges led a Commerce Department loyalty board in 1948 to deny him a loyalty clearance. Remington successfully appealed this adverse ruling to the Civil Service Loyalty Review Board and at the same time filed a libel suit against Bentley and the producers and sponsor of the *Meet the Press* radio program for her claim on this interview show that he had been a member of the Communist party. The Review Board reversed the Commerce Department's denial of clearance. Because of this reversal, and specifically because of Bentley's refusal to appear and testify under oath before the Review Board, NBC and General Foods, the sponsor of *Meet the Press*, agreed to a settlement in February 1950, paying Remington $9,000 to drop the suit. (Bentley was not party to this agreement.)[27]

Remington's exoneration proved to be short-lived. The New York grand jury that had been convened to corroborate Chambers's December 1948 testimony voted unanimously on June 8, 1950, to indict Remington on one count of perjury: denying that he had been a member of the Communist party. Remington was convicted of this charge on February 7, 1951. A unanimous Court of Appeals, which included Justice Learned Hand, reversed Remington's conviction on August 21. The court ruled that presiding judge Gregory Noonan's charge to the jury was "too vague and indefinite" about what constituted Communist party membership, and that Noonan had also erred when denying Remington's attorneys' motion for access to the grand jury testimony of Remington's estranged wife. The Court of Appeals allowed the indictment to stand but ordered that the case be retried. Rather than retry the case, however, government prosecutors convened another grand jury, which indicted Remington for perjurious testimony during his trial. Its five-count indictment involved his denials of (1) knowingly attending Communist party meetings, (2) asking others to join the Communist party, (3) knowing of the Young Communist League while a student at Dartmouth College during the 1930s, (4) paying Communist party dues, and (5) giving classified or secret information to Bentley. Remington was convicted on January 28, 1952, but on only two of the five counts—denying giving information to Bentley and knowing of the Young Communist League. He appealed this conviction, but this time the Court of Appeals denied his appeal in a 2 to 1 vote.

Justice Department officials had good reason to seek a new indictment rather than retry Remington, given the prosecutorial problems posed by jury foreman Brunini's and U.S. attorney Donegan's politicization of the grand jury. In their appeal of his conviction in his second trial, Remington's attorneys had raised the issue of grand jury improprieties. They won over Justice Hand, but the majority of the appeals court ruled that Remington had been properly indicted and convicted for his perjurious testimony during the first trial.

This decision ensured that questions about the politicization of the grand jury system were not addressed. In Remington's case, the catalyst was not a partisan congressman but a partisan grand jury foreman, John Brunini.

In May 1950, Brunini learned of a renewed HUAC and FBI investigation into whether Remington had joined the Communist party while employed with the Tennessee Valley Authority during the 1930s. Brunini also learned that Ann Remington, Remington's estranged wife, had not been called as a witness. Fearing that Justice Department officials would bypass the New York grand jury (which he headed) and instead present this matter to a grand jury in Washington, D.C., Brunini subpoenaed Bentley's attorney and then Ann Remington to testify before the New York grand jury.

At first Ann Remington expressed ignorance about her husband's membership in the Communist party and his first meeting with Bentley. She was unwilling to testify against her husband, emphasizing her dependence on his support payments. Questioned for hours by Brunini and Donegan about her husband's suspected Communist affiliations and relations with Bentley, and not having eaten since an early breakfast, at one point she protested, "I'm hungry. I would like to get something to eat. I haven't eaten since a long time ago, and I don't think I am going to be coherent from now on. I would like to postpone the hearing. . . . I want to consult my lawyers and see how deep I am getting in." When Donegan renewed his question whether her husband had paid Communist party dues, Brunini interjected by affirming how "kind and considerate" the grand jury had been until then. "A witness before a Grand Jury hasn't the privilege of refusing to answer a question," he pointedly warned. "When we get a witness who is contemptuous, who refuses to answer questions, we can take them before a Judge" who could order them to answer. Repeating Donegan's question, Brunini asserted, "You have no privilege to refuse to answer the question." Ann Remington then admitted that her husband had paid Communist party dues. After a thirty-minute recess, she returned to recount in detail her husband's membership in the Communist party and his relationship with Elizabeth Bentley.

Brunini's and Donegan's badgering raise troubling questions about grand jury proceedings. The most troubling aspect involved Brunini's unqualified threat that Ann Remington had no privilege and must respond to any question. A silent Donegan did not intercede to advise Ann Remington of her right not to respond either by taking the Fifth Amendment or the marital privilege. From the outset, moreover, she had expressed a reluctance to testify against her husband, and then she had expressed her sense of fatigue and her desire to consult her attorney. In 1953, when he evaluated the record of these grand jury proceedings, Justice Hand likened this treatment to a medieval Star Chamber proceeding. Hand conceded that Brunini might have been ignorant of a witness's privilege not to testify, since he was not a lawyer (though Elizabeth Inslerman had exercised her Fifth Amendment and marital privilege rights before the same grand jury). But he sharply rebuked Donegan for not intervening "to correct the mistake." As the historian Gary May writes, "In Hand's view the foreman and the prosecutor were guilty of misconduct, coercion, and deceit."[28]

Brunini was not simply an anti-Communist zealot. He also had a personal pecuniary interest in discrediting Remington. In January 1950, when the grand jury was in recess, Brunini met with Elizabeth Bentley, at which time he learned of her financial difficulties. He urged her to write a book recounting her experiences as a Communist agent, arranged a meeting with the publisher Devin-Adair, and helped secure a contract for her, including a $2,000 advance. Under the terms of the original contract, Brunini was to receive a share of the royalties for his collaboration as a ghostwriter.

Brunini later tried to cover up this questionable relationship, claiming to have severed any formal contact with Bentley after she received the contract from Devin-Adair. The testimony of two secretaries employed by Devin-Adair, Eileen Collins and Leyla Sefa, and FBI records contradict this account.

During the first Remington trial, the two secretaries approached Remington's attorney to advise him that Devin-Adair had rewritten its contract with Bentley. Sefa later testified during the trial that Bentley's original contract with Devin-Adair contained a clause entitling Brunini to a share of the royalties, but that this clause had later been deleted. Collins, who was the administrative assistant to Devin Garrity, the publisher, testified that in May 1950 Garrity had introduced her (in her capacity as Devin-Adair's publicity director) to Bentley and Brunini, telling her that Bentley "is going to do a book for us, and this is John Brunini who is helping her do it." She further testified that a contract had been written stipulating that Bentley and Brunini were to share in the royalties, that both had signed the contract, but that later this contract had been destroyed and replaced by another dated June 2, 1950.[29]

Prosecutors challenged Sefa's and Collins's testimony, implying that they were disgruntled employees and had coordinated their stories. Yet the prosecutors already knew about this problematic relationship. Their knowledge is documented by recently released FBI records. On October 16, 1950, before the start of Remington's trial, Brunini, who feared that detectives hired by Remington might have learned of his relationship with Bentley, informed Donegan that he had helped Bentley find a publisher and had then collaborated on her book but had received no compensation. Brunini asked whether he should accept a collaborator's fee offered by Bentley and her publisher. An appalled Donegan insisted that Brunini not accept any payment. Briefed by Donegan about this development, Justice Department officials at first considered obtaining a new indictment against Remington. Should Remington's attorneys learn of these improprieties, Justice Department officials reasoned, they could challenge the indictment. On further reflection, they decided—and Attorney General J. Howard McGrath agreed—to proceed with the trial on the hope that the Brunini-Bentley relationship could be kept secret.[30]

Remington's attorney, William Chanler, had not known that Brunini had initiated the grand jury investigation of Remington and had pressured Justice Department officials to recommend Remington's indictment. Nor did he know that Justice Department officials had decided that the contradictory testimony of Bentley and Remington was insufficient but that Brunini had pressured the grand jury to indict. Nonetheless Chanler had moved to dismiss the indictment on grounds of grand jury impropriety, based on Sefa's and Collins's account of the Bentley book contract. Judge Noonan summarily rejected his motion.[31] Noonan's indifference foreclosed any possibility that Brunini's questionable relationship with Bentley, and his improper questioning of Ann Remington, would be uncovered during Remington's first trial—abuses that had caused even Justice Department officials to weigh the possibility of a mistrial.*

Motivated by a desire to convict Remington, Justice Department officials decided to seek a new indictment rather than retry him or dismiss the case. Their actions do not simply raise questions about fairness and the violation of procedural rights. The release of the secret Remington (and Hiss) grand jury records document how even perjury indictments depended on political aims, not lawful investigations.

The Hiss and Remington indictments were not the only actions by which FBI officials looked to offset their failure to develop admissible evidence to sustain espionage indictments and convictions. Their covert collaboration with Nixon and HUAC was replicated and soon expanded to underpin a politics of counterintelligence. It relied on secrecy to shroud the bureau's efforts to influence public opinion and help promote a McCarthyite politics.

*John Haynes and Harvey Klehr's account of the Remington case replicates their distorted discussion of the Coplon case. First, they do not acknowledge that Remington's name was not cited in any of the 2,900 deciphered Venona messages. Second, after recounting Bentley's allegations against Remington, they blandly assert that in his testimony before a grand jury he had "made statements that the government was able to prove to have been false. Among other points, Remington denied having taken part in Communist activities, a fact easily refuted with, among other evidence, the testimony of his former wife." Haynes and Klehr, *Venona,* pp. 161–162.

CHAPTER SIX

• • •

The Politics of Counterintelligence

> I do think that it is long overdue for the Communist infiltration in Hollywood to be exposed, and as there is no medium at the present time through which this Bureau can bring that about on its own motion I think it entirely proper and desirable that we assist the Committee of Congress [the House Committee on Un-American Activities] that is intent upon bringing to light the true facts of the situation.
>
> —FBI Director J. Edgar Hoover, June 24, 1947

IN THEIR massive monitoring of the American Communist party and other left-wing political and labor union organizations from the 1920s on, FBI investigations focused not on espionage but on Communist influence in American society. FBI agents were directed to uncover the role of Communists in organizing labor unions, in promoting labor strikes, in challenging racial segregation, in lobbying for reform of a corporate-dominated capitalist economy, and in forming alliances with or seeking to influence liberal and left-liberal groups. Employing both legal and illegal investigative techniques, FBI agents amassed information about the personal and political activities of American activists. In the process, they and their supervisors at FBI headquarters in Washington often failed to uncover information about Soviet espionage activities and successful recruitment of American spies.

From a law enforcement or legitimate counterintelligence standpoint, the information accumulated through these investigations of Communist and left-wing political activities had little value. This was because the information either was illegally obtained—thus negating prosecution, unless Justice Department officials were willing to risk discovery during the adversarial proceedings of a trial—or did not document the violation of a federal statute. Nor was it inadvertent that many such investigations sought only to uncover information about the plans and objectives of radical activists. Hoover himself conceded that not all FBI investigations were intended to uncover federal crimes—pointedly distinguishing between "intelligence" and "investigative" activities. Spelling out this difference, the FBI director affirmed that "investigative" activity was predicated on "a specific violation of a Criminal Statute" and was intended to develop "facts and information that will enable prosecution under such legislation." On the other hand, "intelligence" activity sought information about "Communists and subversive elements" which "does not, in its original stage, involve an overt act or a violation of a specific statute." "These subversive groups," Hoover warned, "direct their attention to the dissemination of propaganda and to the boring from within processes, much of which is not a violation of a Federal Statute at the time it is indulged in, but which may become a definite violation of law in the event of a declaration of war or of the declaration of a national emergency."[1]

For example, Hoover responded to the upsurge of civil rights activism during the 1960s by ordering all FBI field offices to evaluate "Communist influence in racial matters." It would be "reasonable to assume," he emphasized, that the American Communist party would "inject itself into and to exploit the struggle for equal rights for Negroes." Accordingly, all heads of FBI field offices were ordered to be "extremely alert to data indicating interest, plans or actual involvement of the Party in the current Negro movement." The culmination of this was a formal code-named "Racial Matters" program, which coordinated the accumulated information.[2]

This decision to monitor civil rights activities was not exceptional. It replicated Hoover's earlier authorization of investigations into suspected Communist influence. These included the code-named COMPIC program to investigate "Communist influence in the motion picture industry," and the COMINFIL program to determine Communist infiltration of liberal social and political movements. Both programs lacked any law enforcement purpose.

"Intelligence" information, moreover, was to be disseminated—at first only to the White House and other executive agencies, alerting the president to the plans and objectives of radical activists. This information was also useful in federal employee clearance programs, instituted temporarily during World War II and then made permanent after 1947, to dismiss potentially "disloyal" federal employees or preclude their employment. Then, during the cold war era, FBI dissemination practices exploded. The need, first, to promote a politics of militant anti-communism, and then to exploit public concerns about the "Red Menace," led Hoover and senior FBI officials to launch a purposefully secret politics of counterintelligence.

The catalyst to this shift stemmed from Hoover's frustration over the limited consequences of his intelligence work. Since the mid-1930s he had regularly forwarded reports to the Roosevelt White House detailing the efforts of Communists and other "subversives" to influence public policy. Similar reports were sent to military and naval intelligence officials. Fearful of an adverse reaction should these investigative activities become known, FBI officials episodically disseminated information about "subversive" activities to ideologically sympathetic reporters and members of Congress—on the strict understanding that the recipient not disclose the FBI's role.

The onset of the cold war profoundly reshaped FBI dissemination activities. The FBI director continued to forward reports on Communist influence to the Truman administration and succeeding administrations, and to military and naval intelligence. But increasingly after 1945, the FBI director expanded his informal practice of selective leaks. He authorized a series of formal and informal dissemination programs that successfully exploited the shared anti-Communist politics of reliable reporters and politicians. The explicit purpose of Hoover and his senior officials was to legitimate and sustain an anti-Communist politics. Publicly projecting the image of a disinterested, professional law enforcement agency which disdained the role of a national police force and respected the First Amendment and privacy rights of American citizens, FBI officials privately took great care to ensure that their purposeful leaking of derogatory political and personal information could not be discovered. They succeeded partly because of Hoover's ingenious special records procedures—blind memoranda, JUNE Mail, administrative pages, Do Not File documents. These procedures ensured that records of illegal conduct or of the dissemination of information were not incorporated in the FBI's Central Records System. Such records were routed to senior FBI officials and maintained in their secret office files. These dissemination activities could not have succeeded, in any event, without the witting cooperation of reporters, members of Congress, and prominent anti-Communist activists who accepted Hoover's strict condition not to disclose the FBI as their source.

With the intensification of the cold war, and the McCarthyite consensus that more effective measures were needed to protect the nation's internal security, FBI officials were emboldened to abandon an earlier sense of caution. They instituted a series of formal programs that relied on more aggressive tactics, including the COMINFIL program targeting Communist "sympathizers" and the COINTEL program to "harass, disrupt, and discredit" radical organizations such as the American Communist party, the Trotskyite Socialist Workers Party, black nationalist groups, the Ku Klux Klan, and the New Left.

Under COMINFIL, FBI agents compiled information on the efforts of Communists to infiltrate "the entire spectrum of the social and labor movement," encompassing youth, civil rights, labor union, and political groups active in organizational and legislative lobbying. This information was correlated and then forwarded to the White House and federal agencies to "fortify" the government against "subversive pressures." One COMINFIL target, authorized by the FBI director in October 1962, was the recently established Southern Christian Leadership Conference and its president, Martin Luther King, Jr.[3]

The COINTEL program differed from COMINFIL and similar FBI containment programs in that it resulted in the creation of discreet files. The result was a comprehensive record documenting FBI agents' proposed "disruptive" and "harassment" tactics and their review, approval, and commendation by senior FBI officials. The COINTEL program, however, was not the only FBI effort directed at radical and left-liberal activists. Similar tactics were employed to harass and discredit organizations such as the Southern Christian Leadership Conference and individuals such as Martin Luther King, whose activities FBI officials had concluded threatened the nation's internal security. The records of these harassment and disruption tactics were not incorporated in the COINTEL program files but were scattered through FBI individual case files. Both kinds of actions disseminated derogatory information and shared the common premise of required secrecy—recipients were cautioned that FBI assistance must never become known.

This wall of secrecy immunizing FBI records from independent scrutiny was first breached in the mid-1970s—by the unprecedented congressional investigations of the so-called Church and Pike committees in 1975–1976, and then by the mandated release of FBI files with the enactment in 1974 of key amendments to the Freedom of Information Act. Numerous books and articles have since been based on the released if often heavily redacted FBI files. These publications confirm that FBI investigations were not confined to criminals or spies but extended to political activists and prominent citizens. Some of the subjects were liberal political activists (First Lady Eleanor Roosevelt, Democratic presidential nominee Adlai Stevenson), popular culture celebrities (Frank Sinatra, John Lennon), and prominent authors (Ernest Hemingway, Norman Mailer) and reporters (Harrison Salisbury, Peter Arnett). The released records further confirm that FBI officials also recruited the covert assistance of prominent informers (Joseph Kennedy, Walt Disney, Ronald Reagan).[4] This rich and expanding literature, however, does not fully chronicle how FBI officials launched and then succeeded in promoting a McCarthyite politics.

The origins, methods, and operational assumptions that governed the FBI's politics of counterintelligence are best illustrated by two case studies. One involves an initially close but ultimately abortive relationship between FBI officials and the liberal Catholic priest John Cronin. The second involves the COMPIC program, initiated in 1942, the fruits of which were shared in 1947 with the chairman and chief counsel of the House Committee on Un-American Activities.

Influenced by the social justice teachings of the Catholic church, Father John Cronin became active in the burgeoning organized labor movement in Baltimore during the late 1930s and early 1940s. His support for the CIO's strategy of organizing workers along industrial lines and its success in transforming labor-management relations drew sharp criticism from other, more conservative Catholics. At the same time his questioning of the motives of Communists active in the Baltimore CIO led to the liberal priest's bitter confrontation with these Communists and to a close working relationship with FBI agents in the FBI's Baltimore field office.[5] A seemingly audacious request by this liberal priest underscores the closeness of that relationship.

In October 1943 two local Communist leaders, Roy Hudson and Al Cannon, sought to meet with Cronin. Their stated purpose was to seek an end to their confrontational relationship, given their shared goals in the changed circumstances brought about by U.S.-Soviet cooperation during the war. Cronin was leary of Hudson's and Cannon's purpose and feared they might exploit this meeting to "frame" him. So he asked the FBI's Baltimore field office to bug this meeting and create a record that would protect him from future misrepresentation. FBI assistant director Edward Tamm approved this request.[6]

Cronin's conflict with Baltimore's Communists had also commanded the attention of the hierarchy of the Catholic church. At a November 1944 meeting of the Catholic bishops conference, the bishops decided to commission a report on "the specter of Communism in the United States." To write this report, they turned to Cronin. After lengthy research, he completed the report in November 1945.[7]

To obtain evidence that could be publicized in this report, Cronin solicited FBI assistance. His request was readily honored. FBI officials astutely recognized the potential influence of the Catholic bishops and the strong anti-Communist proclivities of the intended audience. In response, FBI agents prepared nine blind memoranda for Cronin's use, totaling 164 pages and dated June 13, August 3, 6, 7, 25, and 30, 1945. The subjects of these memoranda were Communist "Organizational System and Tactics," the Communist party's "Financial Resources," Communist "Activities in the Labor Movement," Communist "Infiltration of Government Agencies" and of the "Armed Forces," Communist "Exploitation of the Negro People and Their Organizations," the Overseas News Agency, the leadership and sponsors of Communist-front organizations, and Communist "Attacks upon the Vatican." Cronin relied heavily on these FBI memoranda in writing his report, in some cases lifting paragraphs verbatim and in other cases citing specific information, data, or allegations.[8]

Cronin's cooperative relationship with the FBI continued into 1946. On the one hand, the Catholic priest provided FBI assistant director Edward Tamm with copies of his draft and then his final report to the Catholic bishops. Appreciative of FBI assistance, Cronin solicited Tamm's input about this draft regarding "the elimination of any data or information which might embarrass Bureau informants or operations." On the other hand, Cronin and his FBI contacts shared information that each had independently uncovered. In March 1946, for example, in return for Cronin's providing copies of the letters of Catholic bishops rallying behind Hoover's continuance as FBI director (triggered by a report that Hoover was to be replaced), FBI assistant director Louis Nichols "confidentially and off the record" briefed the Catholic priest about Communist labor strategy and foreign policy objectives, which the FBI had obtained by bugging a Chicago meeting of Communist officials. Nichols specifically "pointed out" that "if this information ever became public that it would be known that it could come only from one place and it might make it more difficult to secure information as in the past." Cronin assured the FBI assistant director that "such information should be kept confidential and should never be used publicly." Although he concurred in Nichols's action, FBI director Hoover nonetheless emphasized the need to "be *most* circumspect in giving information" to Cronin.[9]

Cronin had nonetheless become a valued intermediary for FBI officials, who willingly provided him with information, for example, to promote the shared interests of and "for the use of" prominent Catholic officials, notably Francis Cardinal Spellman of New York.[10] FBI officials also sought to ensure the success of another Cronin assignment. In early 1946 officials of the U.S. Chamber of Commerce decided to launch their own campaign to influence public opinion about "the menace of Socialism in Europe and its effect upon this country." Having learned about Cronin's report to the Catholic bishops, Chamber officials asked him to write their report as well. Although the author was publicly identified as the head of the Chamber's Committee on Socialism and Communism, Francis Matthews, Cronin actually wrote the report. He demanded anonymity to avoid criticism should it be discovered that "there was any Vatican influence." Released in October 1946 and entitled "Communist Influence in the United States," the Chamber report was based on the FBI information provided to Cronin in 1945. More than 200,000 copies were distributed in pamphlet form, with copies sent to every Catholic bishop and to 80,000 Protestant ministers. Not surprisingly, the pamphlet emphasized Communist influence in the labor movement—a persistent theme of Chamber of Commerce publications and press releases—and in government agencies, notably the State Department.

Although the Chamber's plans, and Cronin's role, were not known publicly at the time, FBI officials had been fully briefed about it in advance. Matthews met with Hoover in January 1946 to discuss the Chamber's publication plans and its decision to have Cronin write the report. After completing his final draft, Cronin again solicited FBI assistant director Tamm's evaluation. Because this report was to be publicly released, Tamm responded (after clearing the matter with Hoover) that he could not "officially or personally" comment. This refusal, Tamm emphasized, "should not be construed either as approval or disapproval of the accuracy or desirability of the contents of this material."[11]

FBI officials in fact had no disagreement with the report's emphasis on the seriousness of the Communist threat and its recommended actions to combat communism. To the contrary, an FBI analyst privately commended the report's analysis, "easy reading style," recommended bibliography, and avoidance of citing individuals by name, thereby averting "possible law suits."[12]

This burgeoning collaborative relationship between Cronin and the FBI was soon severed—but not because of disagreement over Cronin's continuing efforts to promote a militant anti-communism. By June 1946, Hoover and senior FBI officials had come to reassess their covert relationship with Cronin. Their concerns were triggered by the Catholic priest's penchant for publicity, indiscretion, and a seeming inability to keep FBI assistance secret.

The first breach in a heretofore harmonious relationship stemmed from a private talk by Cronin at a communion breakfast in Arlington, Virginia. The Catholic priest charged that more than 2,000 "active" Communists were employed in the federal government, of whom 130 held "key positions" and could thereby influence government policy. American Communists, Cronin added, "regularly transmit reports to the Soviet [Union]." A *Washington Post* reporter, present at this breakfast, filed a story on Cronin's dramatic charges; it was picked up by the wire services and received nationwide coverage. Briefing Hoover about this publicity, FBI assistant director D. Milton Ladd observed that Cronin's statistics about "active" Communists probably combined both Communists and those who had been identified as members of Communist front organizations. By so doing, Cronin had enabled

Civil Service Commissioner Arthur Fleming to rebut his "Communists in Government" charge. A discomfitted Hoover responded that Cronin "is making the mistake so many others have made—popping off *prematurely* & thereby giving his enemies basis for branding him a 'red-baiter.' "[13]

Cronin's talk previewed his decision to launch a campaign that year to publicize the Communist threat. Given his status as an FBI favorite, Cronin in early February briefed Hoover on his plan to establish an organization "patriotic in nature, subsidized by general contributions but of unquestioned integrity, unconnected with the [Catholic] Church, capital, labor, or any political group" to uncover and publicize the facts concerning the Communist threat. Hoover commended these efforts as "most interesting" and asked to be "kept informed as they progress."[14] Later that year, working with Alfred Kohlberg* and former FBI agents, Cronin helped launch the anti-Communist periodical *Plain Talk* and the anti-Communist screening organization American Business Consultants and its publication *Counterattack.*

FBI officials had no problem with Cronin's purpose. They became deeply concerned, however, that the Catholic priest might publicly compromise their covert relationship. These concerns intensified when FBI officials first learned—from a former agent whom Cronin had recruited—of Cronin's claim to the other organizers of this anti-Communist network that he "has been promised cooperation by the Bureau only upon assurance that it would be carefully guarded and also the [proposed] corporation will furnish to the Bureau confidential information in return." According to this former agent, Cronin had assured those funding his organization that he would have to secure "official approval [of FBI offi-

*A wealthy businessman active in anti-Communist politics, Kohlberg was the reputed head of the so-called China Lobby, which later charged that the Truman administration had lost China to the Communists.

cials]" in order to "assure his [Catholic] superiors that you [Hoover] have been consulted and approved this program."

FBI officials became particularly worried by Cronin's bragging about his covert relationship with the FBI. But these were private matters. Their concerns soon intensified upon learning that Cronin might have to disclose that the source for his charges was in fact the FBI.

Cronin's visibility, his apparent expertise with statistics about Communists in government, and his claim that American Communists had regularly transmitted reports to the Soviet Union had come to the attention of the House Committee on Un-American Activities. Learning that he might be subpoenaed to testify before HUAC, Cronin met with FBI assistant director Ladd to discuss how he should respond. Ladd emphasized that "any information which had been furnished to him [Cronin] by the Bureau had been done on a confidential basis for his assistance in preparing a report for the College of Bishops." In the future, Ladd urged, Cronin should be general, focusing his attack on communism without citing specific names or statistics on the number of Communists in government, thereby averting congressional scrutiny. Ladd concluded by urging Cronin to make no *public* charges unless he could document them through his own sources.[15]

Already disturbed by Cronin's lack of discretion, FBI officials soon decided to end their covert relationship. The final straw came in June 1946 when FBI assistant director Tamm learned that Cardinal Spellman had discussed the proposed formation of the "patriotic" anti-Communist organization with the pope, based on "statements that Father Cronin has been assured Bureau cooperation." Hoover immediately ordered, "There must be no further cooperation with Father Cronin as it is obvious that he twists contacts with different meanings." The head of the FBI's Washington, D.C., field office was instructed that henceforth no agent could "contact" Cronin without first obtaining the approval of senior

FBI officials. Briefed in September 1946 about Cronin's request for a meeting with Tamm to discuss "a very important matter," the FBI director ordered Tamm to "be most discreet as he obviously talks too much & unwisely." By August 1947, FBI officials had decided that, owing to Cronin's "lack of prudence," the FBI had no alternative but to sever all future contacts as "we can't deal with him on a confidential basis." In June 1949, when a chastened Cronin sought to renew this earlier relationship, assuring the Washington special agent in charge of his "continuing cooperation with the Bureau and that he will do anything possible in an effort to assist the Bureau in their work," Hoover dismissed this assurance as "just a lot of double talk."[16]

Cronin's experience highlights the importance that FBI officials placed on ensuring the secrecy of their practice of leaking information to influence public opinion. It also helps explain how information developed through the COMPIC program was handled.

The catalyst to this ongoing program stemmed from FBI director Hoover's apparently onetime request of August 1942 that Richard Hood, the special agent in charge of the FBI's Los Angeles field office, prepare a "comprehensive report indicating Communist infiltration and control of the motion picture industry." A massive fourteen-year investigation was launched that terminated only in January 1956 when FBI officials concluded that Communist influence in Hollywood was "practically nonexistent at the present time."[17]

Hoover's request did not mean, however, that FBI interest in Hollywood dated only from 1942. FBI agents had begun investigating Communist influence in Hollywood during the 1930s. Their interest at that time was part of a broader effort to monitor labor organizing and strike activities. In the case of the film industry, this involved technicians, writers, and even actors. The FBI's interest took a new tack in the late 1930s and early 1940s when, as the result of intensive monitoring of Popular Front activities, agents uncovered the active participation of Hollywood artists. Hoover's August 1942 request to Hood thus merely marked a shift in FBI priorities. FBI agents were now to ascertain suspected Communist influence in the making of films. Ironically, this interest coincided with the wartime U.S.-Soviet alliance, when American Communists—including those in the film industry—enthusiastically endorsed and actively promoted the U.S. war effort.

The FBI's Los Angeles office did not complete the requested comprehensive report until February 1943. At 211 pages, it reaffirmed what had been a long-term concern of FBI officials over Communist influence in Hollywood's 39 labor unions and in the establishment of "many Communist controlled front organizations." The report also addressed Hoover's new focus on "subversive" influence on the popular culture. For the FBI director had ordered the Los Angeles office to determine whether the "cultural group" of actors, producers, directors, and writers "appear to be under the control and direction of the Communist Party and follow the Communist Party line in all details and revise their position without difficulty when the Communist Party changes its policy." The evidence for the Los Angeles office's report came from accounts in Los Angeles newspapers or trade publications, through culling names from the letterhead stationery of Popular Front organizations, and from the uncorroborated allegations of FBI informers (volunteered and paid) who had either infiltrated the Los Angeles Communist party and Popular Front organizations or were themselves employed in the film industry.

The Los Angeles office attributed its failure to identify Hollywood Communists to the actions of the Los Angeles Communist party leadership. The party had purposefully created "closed" units for actors, writers, or directors, to ensure that other Communist party members could not identify these artists' "official connection" with the party. The party also regularly destroyed all membership records, dues payment receipts, and "other documentary" evidence. The Los Angeles office concluded its report by assuring Hoover of its commitment to "compile information showing the Communist Party connections of many of the most influential personages in the motion picture industry" and to identify the "large number of books, pamphlets, scenarios, plays, newsreels, speeches, letters, and other material . . . which indicate the enormous effort that has been made and is now being made by the Communist Party to get complete control of the motion picture business and use it for propaganda purposes."[18]

The report's examples of Communist influence in fact involved no actions that diverged fundamentally from the Roosevelt administration's domestic and foreign policies. Regardless, Hoover remained convinced that a serious internal security threat existed. Dissatisfied with the February 1943 report, four months later he demanded an "up to date" report on "significant developments." His follow-up request was triggered by "recent events"—the release of the film *Mission to Moscow* and the imminent release of other anti-fascist films which Hoover concluded "demonstrated the extent to which the influence of the Communist Party has been felt in Hollywood."[19]

In July 1943 the Los Angeles office submitted a preliminary report citing seven films that contained "Communist propaganda"* and nine other films that "have been made or are now in the process of being made but have not been released" that contained "information of a propaganda nature."† As evidence, the report identified screenwriters "who write propaganda material who are known to be Communists or followers of the Communist Party

*The seven were *Mission to Moscow, Action in the North Atlantic, Hangmen Also Die, Keeper of the Flame, Edge of Darkness, Our Russian Front,* and *This Land Is Mine.*

†The nine were *North Star, For Whom the Bell Tolls, Through Embassy Eyes, Russian People, Song of Russia, Boy from Stalingrad, Girl from Leningrad, Seventh Cross,* and *Secret Service in Darkest Africa.*

line." But, just as in its February report, the evidence cited here was primarily ideological, and the sources upon which these contentions were based were anti-Communists employed in the film industry who either had made these charges publicly or had privately volunteered the information to FBI agents.[20]

Nevertheless, Hoover's renewed pressure did produce a major breakthrough. Later that month, FBI agents broke into the office and photocopied the membership files of the Hollywood section of the Los Angeles Communist party. These records listed only the member's first name and initial of the last name. Also photocopied during this break-in were the addresses of the private residences where cell meetings were held, and the dates of these meetings. From this essential information, FBI agents were able to identify Hollywood Communists. Agents then linked them with specific films by searching the public credits. The Los Angeles office sent the resultant lists of names and films to Hoover in August 1943 and again in February 1944 as a "complete memo of influence of Communists in motion pictures."[21]

In these reports the Los Angeles office confidently reported how Hollywood Communists exploited "the present apparent patriotic position of the party to recruit new members, and control fellow travelers and sympathizers." Hollywood Communists, the reports charged, "bore within" the film industry's labor unions; "spread propaganda within and without unions to create sympathy for the Soviet Union and their system of government"; and "browbeat and terrorize public officials by such tactics as demonstrations, letter writing campaigns, slander campaigns, and personal attacks." More ominously, the Los Angeles office reported, Hollywood Communists were able to "force the making of motion pictures which glorify the Soviet Union and create sympathy for the Communist cause," pressure producers to make "motion pictures delineating the Negro race in most favorable terms as part of the general line of the Communist Party," and propagandize un-American themes.[22] Assuring Hoover of its intention to continue monitoring "the production of motion pictures having a propaganda effect favorable to Communist ideology," the Los Angeles office pledged to "obtain evidence of activities of directors, producers, writers, actors, and distributors engaged in producing and distributing pictures of a propaganda nature."[23]

Hoover's continued pressure for follow-up reports on "all developments indicating Communist infiltration of motion picture field"[24] led to repeated FBI break-ins of the local Communist party office to photocopy membership records—in November 1943; August 1944; January, February, and November 1945; and February and May 1947. These photocopied records confirmed whether Communists already identified had continued their membership, and the names of new recruits. These lists enabled FBI agents to identify, by October 1947, 47 actors, 45 actresses, 127 writers, 8 producers, and 15 directors as former or current Communist party members.[25]

FBI agents' intensive monitoring of Communist activities in Hollywood never uncovered evidence that Hollywood Communists engaged in espionage or violated any other federal law. Moreover, the Los Angeles office never reassessed its contentions about the Communist threat despite having concluded in August 1944 that Hollywood Communists "injected small portions of propaganda into pictures" and "almost completely abandoned the idea of putting over any pictures filled with propaganda and are just as active to see to it that propaganda pictures favorable to America are kept to a minimum."[26] FBI reports soon stopped examining the "propaganda" nature of specific films and instead merely compiled and regularly updated a "ready reference" of all Hollywood employees "who are members of the Communist Party or of Communist front organizations," broken down into categories of "producers, directors, writers, actors, labor union figures and miscellaneous."[27]

An emboldened FBI director first briefed Attorney General Francis Biddle in October 1944 about the FBI's discovery of "Communist influence" in Hollywood. No "direct investigation" of the motion picture industry had been conducted, Hoover claimed—technically truthful since the FBI's approach was indirect. The FBI director nonetheless pinpointed the seriousness of this threat—"the growing Communist influence in that industry, which industry is recognized not only as a great medium for propaganda but also as one of the most influential agencies of education."[28] Given the ideological tenor of Hoover's report and its failure to cite any instance of illegal conduct, an unimpressed attorney general did not even respond.

Hoover was not dissuaded by Biddle's indifference. A new opportunity to use the Hollywood intelligence arose shortly thereafter in the highly charged political climate of the cold war era. Yet despite the deterioration in U.S.-Soviet relations between 1945 and early 1947, FBI officials were stymied. Documenting Communist employment in the film industry could not lead to prosecution, for no evidence had been uncovered that Hollywood Communists either committed espionage or conspired to overthrow the government "by force or violence." Nor was Communist employment in Hollywood covered under the Federal Employee Loyalty Program instituted in 1947 by President Truman. Frustrated by his inability to use the FBI's accumulated information for legitimate law enforcement or counterintelligence purposes, Hoover soon decided to disseminate this information covertly to the chairman of the House Committee on Un-American Activities, J. Parnell Thomas, and the committee's chief counsel, Robert Stripling. Hoover's decision marked a reversal in FBI policy toward this committee.

As recently as 1945, FBI officials had purposefully avoided any association with HUAC's plan that year to investigate Communist influence in the film industry. Hoover took steps to ensure that the FBI could not be linked with this proposed but soon aborted investigation.[29] Hoover reaffirmed this policy of careful avoidance in March 1947 when he explained to Attorney General Tom Clark why he would not honor HUAC's request that month for "certain summaries of [FBI] files on subversive activities." Were the FBI to comply with HUAC's request, Hoover emphasized, the committee would disclose this cooperation and then "our sources of information will dry up and we will not be able to obtain the coverage [of Communist activities] that we now have." The importance of confidentiality, Hoover conceded, had to be balanced against the value of maintaining "harmonious relations with members of Congress and Committees thereof." The FBI director observed that congressional committees have "powers broader than those of this Bureau . . . [to] compel witnesses to appear and testify and also compel the production of records and documents which this Bureau cannot do unless there is a case pending in a court of law." These advantages were counterbalanced, however, by the public's antipathy toward Congress's "irresponsible" investigations. "This has been particularly true of the Committee on Un-American Activities," Hoover stressed, "and if now that committee can put in a 'pipe-line' to the files of this Bureau, even though it be in the form of synopsis of our files, I think there is going to be a very bad public reaction ultimately."[30]

Two months later, unaware of Hoover's reservations, Thomas and Stripling traveled to Los Angeles to conduct a preliminary investigation of Communist influence in Hollywood. Quickly recognizing the limitations of their own resources, they solicited Los Angeles SAC Richard Hood's appearance before their subcommittee. Briefed about this request, Hoover worried that the FBI would become publicly involved in HUAC's announced investigation. Hood was therefore instructed to inform Thomas that he "could not appear before the Committee in open session because to do so would spotlight the things we are trying to do with respect to keeping in touch with the Communist situation." Thomas should be assured of the FBI's desire to "cooperate but that a public hearing would necessarily disclose confidential information and would make it difficult for us to do our work." However, while the FBI could not provide "any confidential information in our files," "if any individuals in the motion picture industry had been the subject of publicity which is available to anyone, there would be no objection to pointing out [to Thomas] such instances."[31]

Meeting Hood the next day, Thomas quickly allayed Hoover's concern that HUAC planned to involve the FBI publicly in its investigation. The HUAC chairman understood FBI officials' concerns and assured Hood that he intended to avoid "any misunderstanding." HUAC would not do "anything that might in any way interfere with any Bureau activity." Nonetheless Thomas emphasized that "information in the Bureau's files ought to be made available to [himself and Stripling] in order that they better put the spotlight of public opinion on the Communist movement." Thomas then spelled out the difficulties that he and Stripling had encountered during their preliminary inquiry, citing the example of their recent questioning of Hanns Eisler, a suspected Communist film writer, about his known attendance at a Communist party meeting. Eisler had admitted this onetime action, but without further evidence of Eisler's Communist activities, Thomas and Stripling could not "question him further along this line." The lack of such evidence "severely handicapped" HUAC's efforts and could undermine the purpose of his and Stripling's trip to Los Angeles: to determine whether a full-scale HUAC investigation of Hollywood could succeed. Only if they developed sufficient evidence of Communist influence in Hollywood could the full committee be persuaded, during a meeting scheduled for June 16, to "send investigators" to Los Angeles in preparation for public hearings. Thomas then asked Hood to check FBI files for "any data that might be of assistance to them concerning" nine named persons. The HUAC chairman did not want anything that "might embarrass our Sources of Information or interfere with our investigations." He simply was looking for "background and other definite data" that could be of "assistance."

FBI assistant director Nichols briefed Hoover about Thomas's request and suggested how the FBI could safely assist Thomas and Stripling. The bureau could furnish "the names of known Communists who have some basis for knowledge of Communist activities, the known Communist front groups and officers whom the Committee might investigate," and could prepare "summary" memoranda on the nine "individuals about whom [Thomas] has requested specific information." Approving Nichols's recommendations, Hoover ordered: "Expedite. I want to extend *every* assistance to this Committee."[32]

The very next day Hood personally delivered the requested summary memoranda to Thomas. They covered eleven individuals—the additional two being spouses of the nine named by Thomas. These eleven included two of the so-called Hollywood Ten,* Edward Dmytryk and Adrian Scott. The memoranda on each of the eleven specifically identified their Communist party and Communist Political Association "membership book number." Hoover authorized the release of this sensitive information to HUAC on the understanding that "the disclosure of this data will not in any way embarrass the Bureau." Hood also gave Thomas an FBI-prepared memorandum "Re: Communist Activities in Hollywood." Nine "non-Communists"—including Ronald Reagan, Robert Montgomery, Robert Taylor, Richard Arlen, Leila Rogers, and Jack Warner—were identified as "cooperative and

*Ten individuals—producers, directors, and writers—who were later indicted for contempt of Congress for refusing to answer questions about their Communist activities during HUAC's October 1947 hearings. The Ten were Dmytryk, Scott, Alvah Bessie, Herbert Biberman, Lester Cole, Ring Lardner, Jr., John Lawson, Albert Maltz, Sam Ornitz, and Dalton Trumbo.

friendly witnesses" while twenty-four "hostile witnesses and uncooperative" were "identified with the communist movement, together with positions or activities" about which they could be questioned. Hood was specifically ordered to ensure that Thomas and Stripling understood that this information "is furnished strictly for their confidential information and . . . under no circumstances will the FBI source of this material be disclosed." After delivering the materials, Hood reported back that Thomas and Stripling were "very friendly and appreciative of this cooperation."[33]

Thomas and Stripling remained in Los Angeles until mid-June. As a result of their preliminary inquiry, the full committee approved a full-scale investigation. Skeptical that their investigation could succeed based solely on HUAC's efforts, a concerned Thomas met personally with Hoover on June 24. HUAC might not have "worked harmoniously" with the FBI in the past, Thomas conceded, but it intended to "work even closer." The HUAC chairman lamented that his and Stripling's preliminary inquiry had failed to develop the "necessary information" owing to pressures on many potential witnesses not to cooperate. He then outlined a series of problems that could only be redressed through FBI assistance were the committee to hold successful hearings scheduled for September 1947. First, he solicited the FBI director's counsel as to whether the committee should hire former FBI agent H. Allen Smith as an investigator. (Hoover assured Thomas of Smith's excellent record.) Second, and more important, Thomas raised the matter of direct FBI assistance. FBI files, he acknowledged, must be kept confidential, yet those files contained "vast knowledge of subversive activities." "Entirely off the record and with absolute assurance that it would not pass beyond him as Chairman of the Committee," he asked Hoover to provide "leads and information of value to the Committee."

The FBI director was willing to be "as helpful to the Committee as we could," and promised to order a search of FBI files "to see what help we might be able to be to the Committee insofar as submitting leads and material that might be used as a basis of interrogation." But he would do so only if Thomas agreed that "the Bureau could not be publicly drawn into the investigation nor be called to appear in any capacity." When Thomas accepted these conditions, Hoover spelled out how this covert relationship would work: committee requests could be forwarded only by the HUAC chairman, through FBI assistant director Nichols.

Hoover immediately informed senior FBI officials about his decision to be as "helpful to this Committee as I can." He described his political purpose in assisting the committee and his insistence that this not become known:

> We will not be able to disclose the confidential sources of our information and no doubt in some instances by reason of the extreme confidential character of information . . . may not be able to divulge some of the information we have, but I do think that it is long overdue for the Communist infiltration in Hollywood to be exposed, and as there is no medium at present through which this Bureau can bring that about on its own motion I think it entirely proper and desirable that we assist the Committee in Congress that is intent upon bringing to light the true facts in the situation.[34]

Assisting the committee became an FBI priority. FBI files in Washington, Los Angeles, and New York were culled, and summary memoranda on the "leading Communists and pro-Communists" in Hollywood and "all the motion pictures in which Communists and Communist sympathizers have participated" were prepared for HUAC's "utilization." Great care was taken not to include information that could compromise the FBI's confidential sources—wiretaps, break-ins, and informers.[35]

The next month FBI supervisor John Mohr met HUAC's recently hired investigator H. Allen Smith to discuss the parameters of FBI assistance and to ensure "close harmony . . . in connection with the work of the Committee." Mohr reaffirmed that no information would be furnished by the FBI's Los Angeles office to Smith. Should Smith desire any FBI assistance, such requests must be directed through HUAC chairman Thomas. Smith honored this condition in the succeeding months, at the same time "fully" briefing the FBI's Los Angeles office "of his activities," the names of proposed committee witnesses, and then, following the final scheduling of HUAC's hearings for October, the names of the friendly and unfriendly witnesses whom the committee had subpoenaed and the order of their appearance.[36]

By mid-August, HUAC investigators had identified forty unfriendly witnesses whom they were considering subpoenaing for the scheduled hearings on September 24. The forty included the remaining eight of the eventual Hollywood Ten. Submitting this list to Nichols on August 21, Stripling asked "unofficially" for "blind memoranda giving [their] background, associations, Communist Party membership, etc."* FBI assistant directors Edward Tamm and D. Milton Ladd were immediately ordered by Hoover to "get to work on the list."[37]

Before doing so, Ladd described how the requested memoranda would be prepared to ensure that the FBI's covert assistance could not be discovered. Each memorandum would: "1. Include all pertinent public source data; 2. Exclude all data received from technical [wiretap] and microphone surveillances, as well as from other highly delicate media [break-ins, informers]; and 3. If the public data alone does not suffice, the memoranda will have included therein on a selected basis information received from live

*Blind memoranda were prepared on non-letterhead stationery and identified neither the sender nor the recipient of the report, thereby disguising that the FBI was the source.

confidential informants which will be prepared in such a fashion to obviate the possibility of jeopardizing our informants." Hoover nonetheless required his own and FBI associate director Clyde Tolson's advance "approval" before any memorandum could be given to Thomas. The process of culling the FBI's massive records and ensuring that the FBI's assistance not become known or FBI sources compromised proved to be time consuming. The first ten of the requested forty memoranda were completed only on September 12; an additional twenty were completed the next day, and the remaining ten by September 16.[38]

Because of the delay in securing this information from the FBI, HUAC's public hearings were rescheduled for October. Each blind FBI memorandum cited but did not identify "highly confidential sources," and reported background information on the individual's membership in, affiliation with, or attendance at meetings sponsored by various Communist or left-wing organizations. The memoranda further proposed questions that the committee might ask the various witnesses during the hearings.[39]

Because of the FBI's restrictions on reporting information obtained through wiretaps, microphones, and break-ins, the value of the information offered to HUAC was somewhat limited and thus might impair the committee's hearings. Recognizing this, Hoover partially relented on this restriction. On September 13 and 17, Los Angeles SAC Hood was ordered to forward photostats of the "Communist Party membership cards" of twenty-five named individuals to FBI officials in Washington. The twenty-five included the remaining eight of the Hollywood Ten; Thomas had earlier, in May, provided Dmytryk's and Scott's Communist "membership book number."[40]

The blind memoranda and the photostats proved to be devastating to the First Amendment strategy adopted by the subpoenaed Hollywood Ten in responding to HUAC's questions during the October hearings. After each of the Ten refused to answer on

First Amendment grounds whether they were or had been Communist party members, HUAC counsel Louis Russell took the stand to introduce photostats of their Communist membership cards; Stripling followed by reciting into the record their organizational affiliations and the meetings they had attended.[41]

Unknown to the Hollywood Ten and to the reporters covering the hearings, HUAC was able to document that the recalcitrant witnesses were Communists only because of FBI assistance. Indeed, after the conclusion of the October hearings, an elated Thomas telephoned FBI assistant director Nichols to convey his "heartfelt appreciation" to Hoover "because the Director more than any other person is responsible for his Committee not being put out of business." Thomas specifically cited how this assistance enabled Russell, for example, to produce John Lawson's Communist party membership card and then cite his Communist affiliations. When briefing Hoover on this call, Nichols bragged that this information had been "provided" by the FBI.[42]

Owing to their refusal to answer HUAC's questions, the so-called Hollywood Ten were indicted for contempt of Congress. Yet the completion of the HUAC hearings did not mark the end of FBI officials' covert campaign to promote public awareness of the Communist threat. Instead they continued to seek to neutralize the efforts of the Hollywood Ten to raise First Amendment concerns. FBI agents continued monitoring the Ten's post-hearings public relations activities as well as those of their allies in the film, liberal, and radical communities. Agents also intensively monitored the accused's strategies to defend themselves from being convicted for contempt of Congress. Through illegal wiretaps of three of their attorneys—Bartley Crum, David Wahl, and Martin Popper—FBI officials obtained advance intelligence about how these attorneys planned to avoid trial and conviction. The Popper wiretap proved to be the most valuable, as his Washington, D.C., office became the clearinghouse for communications among the various attorneys handling aspects of the Ten's defense.[43]

Hoover immediately relayed this intercepted intelligence to Attorney General Tom Clark and Assistant Attorney General T. Vincent Quinn, who headed the Justice Department's Criminal Division and supervised the government's prosecution of the Hollywood Ten. Between November 26, 1947, and May 7, 1948, the FBI director regularly briefed Clark or Quinn about the crucial intelligence learned from the Crum, Wahl, and Popper wiretaps—disguised as having been obtained from a "highly confidential source."[44]

Thus Clark was alerted to Crum's and Popper's plan to seek to convince the Justice Department not to present to a grand jury the House's approval of the contempt of Congress citation. Clark further obtained advance warning about Popper's and another attorney's plans to convince him to delay arraigning the Ten, and of their intent to request a continuance of the trial until the Supreme Court had ruled in a pending contempt of Congress case. Clark was also briefed about the defense attorneys' plans to have liberal Democratic Senator Claude Pepper intercede with the attorney general personally while Crum concurrently contacted the Truman White House to secure support for a continuance. The two senior Justice Department officials were also alerted to Popper's claim that the attorney general, during his meeting with Senator Pepper, allegedly expressed an interest in making a "deal," and that the Ten hoped to exploit Pepper's White House connections.

Clark and Quinn were also fully briefed about the Ten's trial strategies. These included the defense attorneys' intention to have Methodist Bishop G. Bromley Oxnam file an *amicus* brief; to subpoena all of John Lawson's films (Lawson was the first of the Hollywood Ten to be tried), seven of Dalton Trumbo's films (the second to be tried), and specified HUAC records; to invite Henry

Wallace to testify as a defense witness; to subpoena actors Burgess Meredith and John Huston; to recruit three experts on the film industry (Irving Pichel, Lewis Milestone, and Howard Koch) and five actors and actresses (Lena Horne, Marsha Hunt, Frederic March, Florence Eldridge, and John Garfield) to demonstrate that HUAC's investigation was unjustified; and finally to hire the prominent black attorney Charles Houston as co-counsel, on the premise that black jurors might be influenced by his presence, thereby increasing chances of a hung jury.

In addition, Justice Department officials were apprised of the divisions among the Ten's defense attorneys over whether to accept Clark's proposal to delay the trials of the remaining eight until the Supreme Court had ruled on the Lawson and Trumbo verdicts. Some of the attorneys had wanted to accept Clark's offer only if he would agree to urge film industry executives to abolish the blacklist. Finally, Clark and Quinn were fully briefed on the various public relations strategies of the Ten: their plans to hire a public relations expert (John Stone, Irving Lichtenstein, or Jack McManus), to bring "big name" people to Washington to focus attention on the trial's civil liberties issues, and to solicit labor union support, on the premise that compelling congressional testimony could compromise union organizing efforts.

The wiretaps of Crum, Wahl, and Popper were illegal. They violated the 1934 Communications Act and Supreme Court rulings, first, that the ban on wiretaps applied to federal agents, and, then, that any indictment based on an illegal wiretap tainted and required the dismissal of the case. Wiretapping Crum, Wahl, and Popper had also compromised the attorney-client privilege, since the intercepted information was immediately relayed to senior Justice Department officials who not only supervised prosecution of, but were under great political pressure to win, the case.

Clark and Quinn never inquired as to the identity of the FBI's "highly confidential source." Their indifference is troubling. The obviously confidential nature of the reported information confirmed that the FBI either had an informer on the defense team or had obtained this information from an illegal wiretap or bug. Clark's and Quinn's indifference allowed them to avoid notifying the court of this intelligence-gathering operation while they benefited from the information. Their only communication to Hoover involved Quinn's request (on behalf of U.S. attorney George Fay) that the FBI investigate "the April and May panels of petit jurors to be called . . . in connection with the trial of the several Hollywood writers" and specifically check "indices, credit reports, and other available sources" "for the purpose of ascertaining the background of members of the panels." This investigation was to be completed at "your earliest convenience after the names are made available" in view of the "importance of these contempt cases."[45]

In mounting a First Amendment defense, the Hollywood Ten erroneously assumed that their Communist party membership and their trial and public relations strategies would remain confidential. They had not anticipated that FBI agents could illegally obtain, and then covertly disseminate, their Communist membership cards and their attorneys' privileged conversations.

Motivated to discredit and convict the Hollywood Ten, FBI officials relied on the bureau's vast resources to initiate a politics of counterintelligence aimed at alerting the public to the Communist menace. Their reason for targeting Hollywood Communists had never been to anticipate and deter suspected Soviet espionage activities. FBI officials instead were concerned about these individuals' role as producers, directors, writers, or performers of popular entertainment—and how their "subversive" ideas might influence the popular culture. FBI officials' further decision to assist HUAC was intended to pressure reluctant motion picture executives to dismiss employees holding radical political beliefs and associations. Until the adverse publicity of the October 1947 HUAC hearings, Hollywood executives had been unwilling to cooperate with

HUAC, primarily because they valued the professional talent of these writers, producers, directors, and actors. That talent promoted their own interest in creating a commercially successful product. First in 1945 and then again in early 1947, they resisted HUAC's announced plans to investigate Communist influence in the film industry. But they abandoned this stance after the adverse publicity engendered by HUAC's October 1947 public hearings and the Hollywood Ten's citation for contempt of Congress. Already wary about the potential economic threat posed by the fledgling television industry, film executives shifted their stance in November 1947. Their employment decisions would no longer be based on talent and creativity alone. That month the Hollywood Ten were suspended without pay, and it was announced that none would be rehired until "he had purged himself of contempt or been acquitted or declared under oath that he was not a Communist." The film executives further affirmed their future intent not "knowingly" to employ Communists.[46]

FBI officials did not confine their concerns over Communist influence on the popular culture to the film industry. Twenty months before HUAC's October 1947 Hollywood hearings, Hoover had instituted a covert program to educate the public to the threat posed by the Communist party and to the "support which the Party receives from 'liberal' sources and its connections in the labor unions." To achieve this propaganda objective, FBI agents prepared "educational material" to "be released through available channels so that in the event of an emergency we will have an informed public." These channels eventually included governors, prominent conservatives, sympathetic reporters, columnists, members of Congress, and congressional committees—HUAC and the Senate Internal Security Subcommittee. In a 1960 directive, Hoover identified six categories of individuals who should be closely scrutinized owing to their being "in a position to influence others against the national interest or are likely to furnish financial or other material aid to subversive elements due to their subversive associations and ideology." These six categories were: "(1) Professors, teachers and educators; (2) Labor Union organizers and leaders; (3) Writers, lecturers, newsmen and others in the mass media field; (4) Lawyers, doctors and scientists; (5) Other potentially influential persons on a local or national level; (6) Individuals who could potentially furnish financial or material aid."[47]

FBI assistant director D. Milton Ladd, who headed the FBI's Internal Security Division, succinctly articulated the concern underlying FBI officials' politics of counterintelligence—to contain ideas that were particularly dangerous because an unsuspecting public was ignorant about their Communist provenance. In a memorandum to Hoover, Ladd characterized Gordon Kahn's critical book on HUAC's Hollywood hearings, *Hollywood on Trial,* as "not truth but falsehood; not fact but fiction" and further as "polemical," "dull, devious, deceptive in style, and defamatory in content." Despite having chronicled these blatant deficiencies, Ladd worried that the book's publication "will serve to further confuse and divide unsuspecting American citizens on the question of Communists in Hollywood. It is another example of a foreign-born writer abusing American liberties. It is another example of what a Herculean task confronts all persons who seek to maintain truth in the face of falsehood."[48]

Their command of vast resources to acquire confidential information—primarily by illegal means—enabled FBI officials to meet this challenge and successfully educate public opinion about the Red Menace. At the same time this covertly organized and executed politics of counterintelligence succeeded in diverting attention from the FBI's failure to apprehend and convict Soviet spies.

CHAPTER SEVEN

• • •

The Politics of Morality

IN FEBRUARY 1950, Senator Joseph McCarthy catapulted to national prominence by claiming in a speech before a Republican women's club in Wheeling, West Virginia, that there were 205 "known Communists in the State Department." McCarthy revised this figure in other speeches later that month, first citing 57 and then 81 cases. The specific nature of McCarthy's charges—his citation of a precise number—and his focus on federal employees holding sensitive policy positions commanded far more attention than had similar "Communists in government" charges leveled by conservatives since the 1930s. For McCarthy had reframed the issue from an oblique partisan attack on the New Deal to an apparent national security threat that resonated in the cold war era. Were Communists in fact employed in the State Department and thus in a position to undermine the nation's foreign policy? At the same time, McCarthy's charges capitalized on recent events—notably the perjury conviction the previous month of Alger Hiss—that seemed to confirm that the Truman administration had knowingly permitted Communists and Communist sympathizers to gain influential positions. Owing to his relative obscurity, McCarthy appeared to be a disinterested advocate—a freshman Senator not readily identified with the Republican congressional leadership.

Despite his initial impact and his confident assertions, McCarthy met an ambivalent response from his Republican colleagues. His Republican colleagues willingly lent him moral and research support. Indeed, Republican Senate minority leader Robert Taft urged McCarthy that "if one case doesn't work out, bring up another." McCarthy's Republican colleagues really had no alternative but to rally to his defense, since the publicity he had provoked was quickly exploited by the Democratic Senate leadership to authorize a special Senate investigation. The creation of the so-called Tydings Committee, named after its chairman, Maryland Democratic senator Millard Tydings, to investigate the eighty-one cases McCarthy had cited in a February 20, 1950, Senate speech had personalized the issue—thus the coining of the phrase McCarthyism. On the other hand, Senator Taft's private response to McCarthy's February 20 speech—a "perfectly reckless performance"—reflected a wariness among many Republicans who feared that McCarthy's sweeping allegations could not be proven and could thus discredit this line of attack. After all, President Truman in March 1947 had instituted a Federal Employee Loyalty Program to purge "subversives" from the federal government. Unwilling to link their political fortunes to the senator's anti-Communist crusade, leading Republicans immediately latched onto another national security theme, which McCarthy had also indirectly catalyzed: the seeming threat posed by homosexual federal employees.[1]

This parallel security theme had first arisen during the Senate's preliminary inquiry into McCarthy's claims. Responding to Republican senator Styles Bridges's queries about State Department security procedures, Assistant Secretary of State John Peurifoy defended the department's dismissal procedures. Challenging McCarthy to identify by name his eighty-one cases, Peurifoy further emphasized how ninety-one State Department employees had been allowed to resign while under investigation for possible dismissal under the Federal Employee Loyalty Program, and that "most of them were homosexuals." McCarthy counterattacked by promising to name all eighty-one cases except those involving "morals charges." State Department officials had allowed a "flagrantly homosexual" employee to resign, McCarthy added, and this individual had found employment with the CIA. This was a serious security breach, McCarthy charged, since homosexuals were vulnerable to blackmail.[2]

Republican National Committee Chairman Guy Gabrielson seized on this issue. "Sexual perverts who have infiltrated our Government in recent years," Gabrielson maintained, posed "perhaps as dangerous [a threat] as the actual Communists." In a newsletter to Republican activists, Gabrielson jumped on Peurifoy's admission to having dismissed homosexuals, and added, "The country would be more aroused . . . if it were not for the difficulties of the newspapers and radio commentators in adequately presenting the facts while respecting the decency of their American audiences." Republican members of the Tydings Committee repeated this oblique charge of an administration cover-up and demanded that the special committee established to investigate McCarthy's eighty-one cases be expanded to encompass homosexual employees. As justification, Senator Karl Mundt cited Peurifoy's admission that ninety-one homosexuals had been dismissed. Continuing this line of attack in a speech on the Senate floor, Republican Senate minority whip Kenneth Wherry claimed that one of McCarthy's eighty-one cases had resigned because of his homosexuality. Senator Tydings responded to Wherry's charge by affirming that the committee was already investigating this specific case. He implored his Republican colleagues to "stop this continual heckling about homosexuals and let us get on with the main work of finding Communists." His plea fell on deaf ears. Instead, in a speech at a New York Republican fund-raiser, the former Republican presidential nominee and current New York governor, Thomas E. Dewey, accused the Truman administration of "tolerating spies, traitors and sex offenders in the Government service."[3]

The issue of a serious homosexual security threat would not die. A subcommittee of the Senate Appropriations Committee in fact initiated a preliminary hearing, conducted by Democratic senator Lister Hill and Republican senator Wherry, into the potential security risk that homosexual federal employees posed. The principal witness at these hearings, Roy Blick, head of the metropolitan Washington, D.C., police vice squad, suggested, as a "quick guess," that 3,500 federal employees were homosexuals, of whom 300 to 400 were State Department employees. Based on this assertion, Senator Wherry demanded a special Senate inquiry into this security threat. As a basis for comparison, Wherry noted that there were only an estimated 55,000 Communist party members throughout the United States.[4]

In the ensuing weeks, Senators Wherry and Clyde Hoey, a Democrat from North Carolina, proposed that the Senate Committee on Expenditures in Government initiate this special inquiry, to be conducted in the "strictest secrecy" in order to preclude any injury to innocent persons. Their proposal was endorsed by the full committee on May 24 and by the Senate on June 9. Their joint resolution authorized a special investigation by a subcommittee of the Senate Committee on Expenditures into whether the employment of homosexuals and "moral perverts" posed a serious security risk. As chairman of this subcommittee, Senator Hoey pledged a "complete and thorough" investigation, one that would protect both the government and the public interest, obtain "all of the pertinent facts," and "not transgress individual rights" or "subject any individual to ridicule." Hoey further promised that the investigation would not "become a public spectacle."[5]

As it turned out, Blick's statistics on homosexuals in government, and in the State Department, were as phony as McCarthy's statistics on Communists in the State Department. Blick admitted that his "estimate" of 300 to 400 State Department employees was "not based on factual knowledge." He had derived this figure from an estimate of the U.S. Public Health Bureau that only one in ten persons who had a venereal disease actually reported it. Relying on the revised State Department figure of 86 dismissed homosexual employees, Blick admitted to having multiplied this figure by ten and then halved it to reach the number of 300 to 400. Blick's figure of 3,500 homosexual federal employees was similarly conjectural, based on his estimate that there were "at least" 4,000 homosexuals in Washington, and that 75 percent of Washington residents were "connected with the Government." Blick discounted Washington police arrest files as a source of the actual number of homosexual employees. Conceding that these were a matter of public record, the vice squad detective claimed to have "his own personal files on perverts," but he refused to turn these over to the State Department officials. The D.C. arrest records, which FBI director Hoover obtained "confidentially" in April 1950, identified by name only 393 individuals whom the Washington police had arrested on homosexual charges since early 1947. Of the 393 arrestees, only 47 were federal employees, and only two were employed by the State Department. The arrestees also included one White House employee (a porter) and two congressional assistants, one of whom was an aide to Senator McCarthy.[6]

Statistical evidence, however, proved irrelevant in the ensuing inquiry, or in formulating public policy on an alleged homosexual crisis. The inquiry was instead driven by political considerations. Forced on the defensive, Truman administration officials met frequently with Hoey Committee investigators to work out arrangements for committee access to relevant government records and to reach agreement on the conduct of the investigation. The administration refused to grant the committee access to personnel files but did agree to provide raw statistics on the numbers of employees identified and dismissed, and relevant policy documents. A consensus was also reached that the committee would conduct only executive session hearings, both to protect privacy rights and to avoid sensationalizing the investigation.

From its inception, the committee's investigation was based on the premise that "homosexuals should not be employed in government under any circumstances and that doubt should always be resolved in favor of the government." This conclusion was based neither on medical evidence nor confirmed cases of security breaches. In the words of State Department security official Carlisle Humelsine, "most homosexuals are weak, unstable, and fickle people who fear detection and who are therefore susceptible to the wanton designs of others," making them unsuitable for employment. Humelsine admitted that "no evidence" existed that "these designs of others have caused a breach of security." In fact, security personnel from the State Department, military and naval intelligence, and the CIA told committee investigator Francis Flanagan that they could not "produce much dope or documented instances in which homosexuals had endangered security," except for one instance of an Austrian army officer during World War I. Despite the absence of confirmed cases, Flanagan nonetheless concluded that "homosexualism represents a serious security threat."[7]

Throughout its discussions with the Hoey Committee, the Truman White House accepted the committee's assumption that homosexuals in fact threatened the nation's security. Already battle-scarred by the Tydings Committee's inquiry into McCarthy's charges of Communists in the State Department, White House officials worried that Senator Hoey might become "a dupe of the Republicans" and that Republican members of the committee might be "working up a very sordid smear campaign to the effect that the President is protecting the homos." "The charges of homosexuality," they were convinced, "have struck home with far greater effect in certain quarters, than the Communist allegations." Emphasizing that this "has nothing to do with the alleged security risks" but rather was the product of homophobic attitudes, White House aides evaluated the Hoey Committee investigation as one that "represents a political problem of considerable magnitude."[8]

But White House concerns about Republican partisanship and widespread public anxiety proved to be unfounded. The delicacy of exploring the sexuality of government employees led the committee to decide against holding public hearings or even interrogating suspected or accused homosexuals, and this decision ensured limited media coverage. Furthermore the committee's delay in releasing its published report defused the homosexual charge as a campaign issue during the 1950 congressional elections—in striking contrast to the Communist issue.

The Hoey Committee's final report was never debated, thereby precluding a critical evaluation of its assumptions. Homosexual employees, the committee had concluded, posed a serious security threat owing to their "lack of emotional stability which is found in most sex perverts, and the weakness of their moral fiber [which] makes them susceptible to the blandishments of foreign espionage agents" and "easy prey to the blackmailers." Communist and Nazi espionage agents, the report added, had sought to obtain U.S. secrets "by threatening to expose their abnormal sex activities"—but the report was silent as to whether these efforts had met with any success. Federal officials were criticized for failing to "take adequate steps to get these people out of Government." The report specifically condemned the State Department's "mishandling" of the ninety-one cases, first by allowing these employees to resign "for personal reasons" and then by not taking adequate measures to ensure that they would be barred from employment in other federal agencies. Federal officials, the committee insisted, must "investigate each complaint of sex perversion" to ensure that "these perverts can be put out of Government and kept out." This objective specifically required tighter Washington, D.C., laws on sexual perversion, closer liaison between federal agencies and the local police, and thorough investigation by all branches of the federal government of all reasonable charges of homosexuality.[9]

The Hoey Committee's report might not have commanded public attention, but it provided an opening for FBI officials to utilize information that agents had been collecting about homosexuals since 1937. FBI director Hoover moved quickly to exploit Congress's insistence on purging homosexuals as justification for an increase in FBI appropriations. During April 1951 testimony before a House appropriations subcommittee, Hoover emphasized that 3,225,000 current or prospective federal employees had been investigated by the FBI since the inception of the Federal Employee Loyalty Program in 1947, with the FBI uncovering derogatory information on 14,484. Of these, Hoover observed, the FBI since April 1, 1950, had identified 406 "sex deviates in government service."[10]

Two months later, on June 20, 1951, Hoover instituted a code-named Sex Deviate program "for furnishing" to specified executive, legislative, and judicial officials "information concerning allegations" of homosexuality on the part of "present and past employees." The FBI director soon expanded this reporting program "in appropriate instances where the best interests of the Bureau is served" to other "proper" officials and "institutions of higher learning or law enforcement agencies." Two known recipients of this expanded program were officials at George Washington University and New York University.[11]

Did Hoover unilaterally institute this program, without consulting the attorney general or the Truman White House? Had the FBI director's April 1951 testimony signaled an intention to establish such a formal program? Did the FBI reports contain confirmed information or mere allegations and suspicions? Did the operation of the Sex Deviate program include a public relations component to heighten security concerns and thereby poison national politics? What factors led Hoover to expand this reporting program outside the federal government to universities and police agencies? When did this expansion occur, and was it made known to the attorney general or the White House? None of these questions can be answered definitively, owing to the destruction of relevant FBI records. In 1977–1978 senior FBI officials obtained National Archives approval to destroy two headquarters files—Sex Offenders Foreign Intelligence and Sex Perverts in Government Service—and one policy file—Sex Degenerates and Sex Offenders.

While this record destruction precludes a definitive understanding of the scope, nature, and results of the FBI's Sex Deviate program, its general character can be partially reconstructed from a smattering of FBI documents that escaped destruction.

Hoover's decision to institute the Sex Deviate program, for example, is recorded in the minutes of the FBI Executives Conference, the regular meetings at which senior FBI officials reviewed current FBI policy and recommended changes to Hoover. The minutes of two such meetings, held in 1953 and 1954, record the deliberations of senior FBI officials concerning current programs in which information was disseminated outside the executive branch. At the time the Executives Conference participants were evaluating whether or not to continue such programs, and the Sex Deviate program was among those reviewed. A section in the minutes briefly describes the date of inception, purpose, and operation of the Sex Deviate program. Other memoranda in this file record that within two years the program was expanded to certain "institutions of higher learning and law enforcement agencies," citing George Washington University and New York University.[12]

A second source about this program that escaped record destruction was the National Archives records responding to the FBI proposal to destroy the Sex Deviate program files. Following enactment in 1974 of key amendments to the 1966 Freedom of Information Act, FBI officials became worried over their loss of control over FBI records after receiving a flurry of FOIA requests for FBI files. Accordingly, they drafted a series of plans to destroy specified FBI records, and these were then submitted for National Archives approval under provisions of the 1950 Federal Records Act. One of these plans recommended the destruction of the three Sex Deviate files noted above. National Archives officials approved the plan, but in the process created a permanent record which described in general terms the contents of these files: 99 cubic feet (approximately 330,000 pages), including index cards, abstracts, photographs, and related documents covering the years 1937 through 1977. An Archives official characterized the contents of these three files as having "some evidential value for documenting the FBI's interest and activities in gathering information on sexual offenders and homosexuals" and as containing "massive amounts of material that relates to matters of individual sexual conduct." This material, he continued, "infringed on personal privacy," and most of the reported information "involved unsubstantiated accusations and allegations." Because of this, the archivist argued, the records could not "be made available for research purposes without threatening damage to the reputations of numerous private citizens," and the volume of this material diminished its "value" "in terms of systematic use for research purpose."[13]

Other surviving FBI records offer insights into how FBI officials used this Sex Deviate information to influence government hiring practices and promote a politics of counterintelligence. For example, a copy of one of the captioned Sex Deviate index cards remains extant—having escaped destruction because it was included in Hoover's Official and Confidential File. This card was maintained in Hoover's secret office file owing to its sensitivity—its subject was Adlai Stevenson, Democratic governor of Illinois and the 1952 and 1956 Democratic presidential nominee.

On April 17, 1952, Edward Scheidt, head of the FBI's New York office, informed Hoover that a detective in the New York district attorney's office, "on a strictly confidential basis," had identified Illinois governor Adlai Stevenson and Bradley University president David Owen as homosexuals. According to Scheidt's information, Stevenson was well known as "Adeline" and "would not run for President because of this." The sources for this information, Scheidt reported, were Bradley University basketball players recently arrested for fixing basketball games. On the basis of this uncorroborated allegation, a Sex Deviate index card was prepared on Stevenson (another was prepared on Owen), which listed Stevenson's name, occupation, and the FBI serial number assigned to the document supporting this allegation (Scheidt's memo to Hoover). Then, on June 24, 1952, at Hoover's specific request, FBI assistant director D. Milton Ladd prepared a "blind memorandum"—a special FBI records procedure that disguised the FBI as the source of the information—summarizing this discovery: namely that Stevenson was "one of the best-known homosexuals" in Illinois, was "allegedly well-known as Adeline," and that because of his homosexuality Stevenson "would not run for President in 1952."[14] Hoover's office file, however, contains no other records describing why Hoover ordered this "blind memorandum" prepared just a month before the Democratic National Convention (at which Stevenson won the Democratic presidential nomination) and to whom it was given.

Over the next few years Stevenson's alleged homosexuality became the subject of a flurry of FBI reports. Owing to their political sensitivity, all of them were also filed in Hoover's secret office file. Some of these memoranda record FBI officials' unsuccessful efforts to confirm these uncorroborated rumors and allegations.

For example, after Stevenson's defeat in the 1952 presidential election, C. Robert Love, a former FBI agent then employed as a security officer for a San Bruno, California, corporation, advised the FBI director that Hearst columnist and radio commentator Fulton Lewis, Jr., had "information" that Stevenson "was homosexual" and that Lewis was "attempting to gather evidence to support this allegation." Conceding that the FBI had "no investigative jurisdiction in a matter of this kind," Love nonetheless thought that the FBI director should be alerted to this allegation owing to its "gravity" and Stevenson's "national stature." A grateful Hoover thanked Love for "bringing this matter to my attention."[15]

FBI officials thereupon sought to run down the Lewis lead, contacting him directly. FBI assistant director Alan Belmont reported back that one of the columnist's investigators had questioned Stevenson's estranged wife as to her reasons for divorcing Stevenson, and that she had mentioned her husband's "queer friends." According to Lewis's investigator, Stevenson's former wife had told him that he "could interpret the words in any manner that he wished, but out of consideration for her son she would not attempt any explanation."[16]

FBI officials learned of another similar rumor about Stevenson in December 1952, triggered by a report from Illinois Republican senator Everett Dirksen. Bradley University trustees, Dirksen informed Alan Belmont, had placed Bradley president David Owen on extended leave, having learned about his alleged homosexuality. Assigned to run down this allegation, the head of the FBI's Springfield, Illinois, office learned through a "discreet inquiry" that former Bradley basketball player Gene Melchiore was the source of this allegation about Owen, and that Melchiore had tried to pressure Bradley officials to stop investigating his role in fixing basketball games.[17]

Dirksen reported that Bradley trustees had hired the Pinkerton Detective Agency to investigate this allegation. The detective agency's report, among other matters, concluded that Owen was "a sex deviate and was probably a member of a group of homosexuals meeting secretly in Chicago and New York," but it conceded that "it could not prove the statement in court." According to a Bradley trustee, the Pinkerton agency had also discovered that Stevenson "was homosexual and possibly met with Owen in Chicago and New York and may have been meeting with the same group of sexually abnormal individuals." Responding to this briefing, the Springfield SAC contacted this trustee and was told that this information was "unconfirmed" and had been conveyed "orally." Nonetheless the trustee assured the SAC that the Pinkerton agency's "source would be available to the [FBI's] Chicago Division." The report of the Pinkerton agency, the trustee affirmed, had described Owen and Stevenson as members of "an elite club in New York of homosexuals where Stevenson had the feminine name of 'Adelaide.'" The Springfield SAC thereupon "made discreet inquiries" of the Pinkerton agency to learn the identity of this source but discovered that "all known copies of the Pinkerton report reportedly had been destroyed."[18]

The reports of these various unsupported allegations about Stevenson did not simply repose in Hoover's secret office file. They were incorporated in summary memoranda that FBI officials automatically prepared about Stevenson in both 1952 and 1956 upon learning of his candidacy for the Democratic presidential nomination.[19] Hoover's office file contains no record of how and when FBI officials used these detailed summaries. Other contents of that office file, however, suggest that this information was disseminated, but in ways that could not be traced to the FBI.

On August 29, 1952, following Stevenson's selection as the

Democratic presidential nominee, Milt Hill, a former national correspondent of Federated Publications, advised FBI assistant director Louis Nichols of his assignment "to do the official Republican biography of Governor Stevenson." His purpose in contacting Nichols, Hill explained, was to corroborate information he had learned from a former FBI agent, Orville Yarger. Yarger had told him, Hill said, about alleged corruption in an Illinois governmental agency and "scuttlebutt" that Stevenson had been arrested in New York City "on a morals charge, put up bond, and elected to forfeit." Briefing Hoover about this meeting, Nichols claimed that Hill had "furnish[ed] me this information on a strictly personal and confidential basis."[20] Nichols's delicately worded memorandum, however, does not record whether the FBI assistant director—acting independently or after obtaining Hoover's approval—honored Hill's request for FBI corroboration. Given the sensitivity of his meeting with a Republican operative seeking information helpful to a partisan adversary during a presidential campaign, it is not surprising that Nichols did not record in writing his actions or Hoover's response.

The same political risk was posed by a second, far less discreet initiative. Earlier that same month, the assistant SAC of the FBI's Washington, D.C., field office learned from a contact in the metropolitan Washington police department that Frank Barry, a former Secret Service agent and then the advance man for the Stevenson campaign, claimed that Washington SAC Guy Hottel had been "spreading word that STEVENSON was a 'queer,' that the FBI had a file on him." FBI officials moved quickly to quash this story, having learned that Barry had conveyed this information to Attorney General James McGranery and to White House press secretary Matthew Connolly. They first pressured Hottel to sign a statement that he could not have been overheard making this statement at the Mayflower Hotel and that he did not know whether the FBI did or did not have "such a file." At the same time FBI officials interviewed the individuals identified as the sources for this report, including Barry, to rebut this allegation about the FBI—again carefully wording their denials of such an FBI "file." These denials finessed the fact that such information was not maintained in official FBI files but in Hoover's office; in addition, Barry and his sources had never claimed to have overheard Hottel conveying this information at the Mayflower Hotel.[21]

FBI denials did not convince President Truman, in part because such misinformation about Stevenson had been quietly circulating, even during the Democratic National Convention. In one of his last actions before leaving office, on January 19, 1953, Truman ordered his administrative assistant, Donald Dawson, to contact the FBI's liaison to the White House, Ralph Roach, to convey his understanding that "the Bureau had investigated Adlai E. Stevenson and desired to obtain copies of the reports" that afternoon. Roach first briefed senior FBI officials about Dawson's request, then advised the White House aide that "it was not recalled that the Bureau had ever investigated Stevenson and that if he, Dawson, had reference to some old investigation that we had made, it would be necessary for the Bureau's files in the Archives to be checked." When Dawson expressed an interest only in any investigation conducted in the last four to five years, Roach responded that "the Bureau had not conducted an investigation in recent years and that if it was desired, a further check would be made into the old records." Dawson thought that unnecessary, and the discussion ended.[22]

Had Dawson pursued the matter, FBI officials would have admitted to having conducted an applicant investigation of Stevenson in 1937 at the time of his appointment as an attorney in the Justice Department. Such a response, like that of the Hottel denial, amounted to word games. It would have been technically truthful, since the FBI had not directly investigated or created a file on Stevenson which had then been incorporated in the FBI's central records system. But in fact FBI officials had in 1952 compiled summaries and other "informal"—that is, nonrecord—memoranda reporting derogatory personal and political information about Stevenson, some of which was then safely retained in Hoover's office. Had the intent of Truman's request been honored, FBI officials would have had to disclose their interest in this uncorroborated information, the memoranda on Nichols's contact with Hill, and the Hottel matter. The memoranda would have confirmed Truman's suspicions and could have triggered a congressional investigation into the purposes and scope of FBI activities.

The information about Stevenson was directly used by FBI officials at least twice. The first known use was in response to President-elect John Kennedy's request for an FBI security clearance investigation of Stevenson, before submitting his nomination for confirmation as U.S. ambassador to the United Nations. Personally delivered to Lawrence O'Brien, the President-elect's liaison, the FBI's summary report cited, among other matters, two allegations of Stevenson's homosexuality. The first involved the Pinkerton Detective Agency source that Stevenson belonged to an "elite" homosexual group in New York, and the second that a "Queens Morals Squad" (or "State's Attorney") had in either 1950 or 1951 "raided a gathering of homosexuals at an unknown place in New York City and Stevenson and Owen were found to be present." FBI officials, however, could offer no corroboration for these allegations, having failed to obtain a copy of the Pinkerton report and then, after contacting the deputy commissioner of the New York Police Department, learning that there was "no 'Queens Moral Squad' or 'State Attorney's office.'" Not surprisingly, President-elect Kennedy did not find the FBI's reported allegations convincing, and submitted Stevenson's name for confirmation.[23]

The specific report delivered to O'Brien is not extant. It is cited and its contents summarized in an October 1964 memorandum included in Hoover's office file. It remains unclear why this memorandum was written in 1964, though the timing suggests a possible interest in briefing President Lyndon Johnson about the Stevenson homosexuality allegation. Whether or not Johnson was so informed in 1964, he was in July 1965—but in a way that implied that FBI officials had inadvertently learned about Stevenson's rumored homosexuality. (Hoover did not disclose that the FBI had been interested in such reports dating back to 1952.) In a letter to President Johnson's special assistant, Marvin Watson, the FBI director called attention to a chapter in right-wing activist Frank Capell's book that cited "case studies on several so-called security risks." Among these was Stevenson's "acquaintance with a known homosexual," Robert Woetzel, who had been arrested by the metropolitan Washington police in November 1955. Hoover did advise Watson that Capell had made similar false allegations of homosexuality about California Democratic senator Thomas Kuchel, but that in this case Woetzel had in fact been arrested in November 1955. Hoover remarked in passing that Woetzel's arrest record "contained no information concerning Ambassador Stevenson."[24] Hoover's crude attempt to smear Stevenson's reputation with the Johnson White House is striking, since the FBI had uncovered no evidence that Woetzel was "acquainted" with Stevenson. Furthermore, Woetzel had been arrested in Washington while serving in the military, at a time when Governor Stevenson resided in Springfield, Illinois.

Hoover might have failed to dissuade Kennedy and Johnson from retaining Stevenson as U.S. ambassador to the United Nations, but the FBI director had been far more successful in influencing Republican President-elect Dwight Eisenhower's decision not to appoint Arthur Vandenberg, Jr., as White House secretary.

The son of a powerful Republican senator from Michigan,

Vandenberg had played a key role in Eisenhower's successful 1952 campaign for the presidency. To reward Vandenberg for his loyalty and demonstrated administrative abilities, Eisenhower offered him the position of secretary on his White House staff. As in the case of other White House and cabinet appointments, as a condition for this appointment Vandenberg had to undergo an FBI security clearance investigation. Eisenhower's decision to extend security investigations beyond career civil service bureaucrats was intended to convey his administration's commitment to an effective internal security program. During the campaign he had sharply criticized President Truman for loose loyalty procedures.

At the very time the FBI launched its security clearance investigation of Vandenberg, FBI assistant director Nichols was contacted by Milt Hill who, in addition to writing the Republican biography on Stevenson, had played an important role in the campaign and in the transition period. Hill relayed a request from Ed Green, personal assistant to President-elect Eisenhower, for an FBI file check on an individual (whose name the FBI has withheld) recently arrested by the Washington, D.C., police on "a morals charge" and as a result "has been bounced out of the Navy." This individual, Hill advised Nichols, "has been advanced for some kind of job" and "is being sponsored by Arthur Vandenberg, Jr." Nichols promised to look into this matter, and immediately briefed Hoover about this request, adding that this individual was "presently" being checked in connection with Vandenberg's security clearance investigation.[25]

Unaware of Green's request, Vandenberg the next week met Nichols to arrange a meeting between President-elect Eisenhower and Hoover. In the course of this meeting, Vandenberg inquired in passing about the status of his own security clearance investigation, "as he was waiting for our [FBI] report to come through in order to get away" for a planned post-election vacation. Such investigations, Nichols counseled Vandenberg, "would take a little time," particularly in light of Vandenberg's lengthy and distinguished career. Nichols and FBI assistant director Nicholas Callahan formally interviewed Vandenberg four days later.[26]

At the outset of this interview, Vandenberg raised the matter of how the FBI reported "rumors," identifying this as the purpose behind President-elect Eisenhower's requested meeting with Hoover. The President-elect, Vandenberg claimed, was "somewhat concerned about [FBI] reporting unfounded rumors," a concern based on the FBI's report on postmaster general–designate Arthur Summerfield. "As a general rule," Nichols responded, whenever the FBI "picked up gossip and rumors," these allegations were checked out "and if definitely disproven, they were not included in reports." If the allegations were "the subject of widespread dissemination," Nichols added, "they had a logical place being in the reports," for otherwise the recipients of the reports "would have no way of knowing whether this had been covered in the investigation if there was some future question." Vandenberg expressed satisfaction over the handling of this matter. Three days later, Vandenberg informed Nichols that "he was entering the hospital in New York" and reiterated that Eisenhower still wanted to meet Hoover.[27]

Hoover and the President-elect met on December 30, 1952, at which time they discussed Eisenhower's concern about "the contents" of some FBI reports and specifically the reporting of rumors. The FBI did not normally disseminate "uncorroborated information" to federal officials, Hoover assured Eisenhower, but "included complete information in the reports being made to [the White House] upon applicants in view of the importance" of their positions. To allay the President-elect's concerns, Hoover promised to institute new procedures whereby all future FBI reports would be "carefully screened to eliminate any uncorroborated rumor or gossip." Hoover's and Eisenhower's conversation then turned to the FBI's investigation of Vandenberg. Outlining "briefly" "some of the angles" and "other phases" of this investigation, the FBI director informed Eisenhower of Vandenberg's request that the FBI "not interview the young man at present living with Vandenberg until he, Vandenberg, came out of the hospital, to which he had gone for a physical check over the last week end." Hoover's carefully phrased wording masked the delicacy of the matter—the FBI's discovery of Vandenberg's homosexuality. Eisenhower and Hoover then reached an agreement under which "should Mr. Vandenberg decide that he did not desire to continue in the position to which he had been appointed as Secretary to the President, that I could inform Vandenberg that no report would be submitted as it would then be a moot question." Vandenberg at first preferred to have the FBI investigation continue, but eventually he changed his mind. Availing himself of his publicized hospitalization, he withdrew his candidacy for health reasons, thereby obviating the need for an FBI report that could have revealed his homosexuality to White House staff and cabinet officials.[28]

Appointing Vandenberg would have posed no national security threat. Indeed, his impeccable record and his close relationship with Eisenhower during the 1952 campaign confirmed his discretion and loyalty. The Hoover-Eisenhower arrangement instead reflected the prevailing assumptions—summarized in the Hoey Committee report—about the political risks posed by such appointments. In April 1953, President Eisenhower institutionalized this as policy. The president issued an executive order barring the employment of any homosexual on "security" grounds. Eisenhower's stringent security program, however, proved to be error-prone, precipitating a later purge of the White House staff and actions intended to compromise the career of a prominent journalist.

In early April 1957 an employee in the correspondence section of the Executive Office of the President was arrested for making a homosexual advance to an undercover agent of the metropolitan Washington vice squad. A police interrogation and polygraph testing identified two other employees of the correspondence section as homosexuals. The resignations of all three employees were then requested and accepted. Secret Service officials now launched an investigation to "ascertain whether any other" White House employee was homosexual "and also whether the broad field of security had been breached." This broader inquiry was triggered by the response of one of the three arrestees to a Secret Service query. The White House employee admitted to having seen a "confidential" report in the Executive Office which had referred to British prime minister Anthony Eden "being in the same category," and to having told one of the other arrestees "about this." Because all three employees had received a security clearance before their appointment to the correspondence section, the White House ordered the Secret Service to "turn over" the matter to the FBI. White House officials conceded that the "possible breach of security" might indicate that other homosexuals had also secured employment "in other branches of the Government."

Hoover was quick to defend the thoroughness of FBI security clearance investigations and the FBI's "original" reports on the three homosexual White House employees. In his report on why the three had received clearance, the FBI director began by citing a letter he had sent to the White House in 1953 involving Vandenberg and two other suspect individuals.* The FBI had uncovered no evidence of their homosexuality, Hoover conceded, but the submitted FBI reports should have raised questions about the personal character of these three individuals, adding that one of them "could never be classified as a conservative." Implying that admin-

*The report on this investigation has not been released. Apparently the FBI uncovered no security breach or sinister homosexual ring.

istration officials were responsible for their clearance, Hoover urged Andrew Goodpaster, deputy assistant to the president, to look "into the backgrounds of these three cases since they had gotten appointed, and this might be something to keep in mind in future cases."[29]

The dismissal of the three White House employees had another dimension, triggered by the report that had led to the broader inquiry. After submitting the FBI's report on whether other homosexuals had obtained employment in other branches of the government, Hoover sought a conference with Assistant to the President Sherman Adams. There the FBI director briefed Adams on "the Joseph Alsop matter." One of the arrestees, Hoover told Adams, had admitted to having seen the "confidential" report referring to Eden as a homosexual, adding that "in the Alsop matter, both Alsop brothers [Joseph and Stewart] were intimately acquainted with Eden, though there was no indication of impropriety." Andrew Goodpaster had earlier directed Hoover to delete this reference to Alsop from his report on whether other federal employees were homosexual.[30]

The "Alsop matter" began in February 1957 when the syndicated columnist visited Moscow to interview Soviet prime minister Nikita Khrushchev. Lured into a trap by KGB agents, Alsop was arrested in his hotel room on February 18 during a homosexual tryst with a young man whom he had met the previous night at a Moscow restaurant. (The arresting officers identified themselves as Moscow police officers and the "vice director" of the hotel.) After warning Alsop that he had violated Soviet law, the KGB officers expressed their desire not to make a formal arrest but rather to ensure "absolute security." They urged Alsop to "help them a little if they were going to help" him. Alsop's conversation with these three KGB agents lasted three hours, ending only when Alsop explained that he had a scheduled dinner meeting at the U.S. embassy and "would be missed if" he did not appear. Assuring Alsop that he was free to go, the KGB agents arranged to meet him the next day at a Moscow restaurant "to try to find a way out" of Alsop's problem.

At this meeting the KGB agents made it clear that they were aware of Alsop's status as a syndicated columnist and tried to pressure him to "assist the cause of peace." A further meeting was arranged in Leningrad. Alsop by this time recognized the delicacy of his position, and fearing that he might be arrested gave a friend employed at the U.S. embassy a "sealed" envelope in which he briefly recounted what had happened. Alsop instructed his friend to deliver this envelope to U.S. Ambassador Charles Bohlen with the explicit instruction that the envelope not be opened for two weeks, and then only if Alsop had not departed Moscow for Paris. Bohlen, however, opened the letter immediately. The ambassador acted quickly to stymie the KGB, telephoning Alsop at his hotel to come at once to the embassy—claiming to have received an urgent message about the health of Alsop's mother. Bohlen's action enabled Alsop to leave Moscow.[31]

On reaching Paris, Alsop arranged a meeting with a CIA officer, at which time he wrote and signed a detailed account of the Moscow episode. He did so on the understanding that this statement would be brought to the "attention" of CIA director Allen Dulles and FBI director Hoover, and "would be kept out of the general file and placed in a special file."

Dulles immediately briefed Hoover about this episode and communicated "the substance of the memorandum" to Secretary of State John Foster Dulles. Hoover in turn informed Attorney General Herbert Brownell about the Moscow incident and further promised to have his aides prepare a memorandum summarizing all information contained in the FBI's and the Defense Department's files about both Joseph and Stewart Alsop—in the case of the Defense Department, owing to Joseph Alsop's military service during World War II. Upon receipt of this summary, Brownell contacted Hoover to advise him that he intended to arrange a meeting between himself, CIA director Dulles, and Hoover "to discuss what further action could be taken."[32]

The FBI had already compiled a massive file on Joseph Alsop. Its contents were then summarized, the highlights citing the columnist's "recent contacts" with Soviet officials, FBI investigations of unauthorized classified information that Alsop had published in his columns, and two instances of his alleged homosexuality. One of these involved a homosexual relationship with a State Department employee in Germany in 1954 (to which the employee had admitted); the other repeated the allegations of a "confidential source" who claimed to have observed Arthur Vandenberg, Jr., in bed with Alsop, and who said that Vandenberg, Joseph Alsop and his brother Stewart, and another individual "were members of a group of homosexuals." Hoover's summary memorandum reached Brownell on April 2, along with the original letter and enclosures about the Moscow incident that CIA director Dulles had sent to the FBI director.[33]

Whether Brownell, Hoover, and Dulles met is unclear. In any event, Hoover and Dulles exchanged a series of memoranda. In his communications with Dulles, Hoover specifically demanded "any information coming to your attention concerning any future contacts [Alsop] may have with the Soviets either abroad or within the United States." Dulles had already pledged to keep Hoover informed on "any important developments" but on the condition that the FBI director coordinate with him "any dissemination of this information outside the Bureau, or other action which might bear upon the counter intelligence aspects of this case while subject [Alsop] remains abroad."[34]

Dulles did send Hoover a detailed report on the CIA's April 3 interview with Alsop. At the outset of this interview, Alsop had admitted to being an "incurable homosexual since boyhood," to having unsuccessfully sought medical advice, to having concealed his homosexuality "from my family and friends," and to having initially considered suicide rather than succumb to KGB pressure to cooperate. Troubled by inconsistencies in Alsop's account of the Moscow incident and his refusal to act on the CIA's demand that he make an "open" confession, Dulles was particularly concerned about the columnist's "announced intention to travel" again to the Soviet Union and Eastern Europe. Sharing this concern, Hoover requested that the CIA alert the FBI to "any data relating to Alsop's plans to travel." The FBI director further complained about Alsop's unwillingness "to furnish the identities of his homosexual contacts in the United States, particularly in Washington, D.C., and New York City." Hoover concluded by reiterating his demand for "any additional information which [Dulles] may develop concerning contacts between Alsop and representatives or agents of Russia and satellite countries, as well as any information which may be developed concerning his homosexual contacts in this country, particularly any which may be in Government circles."[35]

The FBI director thereupon briefed Assistant to the President Sherman Adams, Attorney General Brownell, and Deputy Attorney General William Rogers about the Alsop matter "in view of the implications," citing specifically his alleged "intimate" relationship with British prime minister Eden. No FBI investigation into this matter had been initiated, Hoover assured Brownell, since it did not fall within the FBI's jurisdiction, but the CIA had agreed to report any information "indicating that [Alsop] had had any additional contacts with the Soviets."[36]

For Hoover and Eisenhower administration officials, the central issue was never whether Alsop could be blackmailed by the Soviets. Both before and after the Moscow incident, Alsop continued to endorse a militantly anti-Soviet position on military and foreign policy matters. But he had naively assumed that his chief problem was Soviet blackmail, and he believed he had neutralized this threat by immediately briefing the CIA and the FBI about this delicate personal matter.

Ironically, Alsop's anti-Soviet columns provoked a wholly unexpected response, because they contained sharp criticisms of the Eisenhower administration's fiscal conservatism as having undermined U.S. defense and security interests. In a series of columns published in 1958 and 1959, Alsop condemned the Eisenhower administration's fiscal conservatism for creating a "missile gap" that favored the Soviet Union. In a particularly harsh attack on March 4, 1959, Alsop accused the administration of "playing Russian roulette with the whole course of human history at stake." He was referring to the Soviets' 1957 launch of Sputnik and the subsequent inquiry of the Gaither Commission, which recommended substantial increases in defense spending, including a crash program to enhance U.S. missile capabilities. "The USSR will probably achieve a significant ICBM delivery capability with megaton warheads by 1959," the commission concluded, adding that without a substantially increased effort the "U.S. will probably not have achieved such a capability. . . . This appears to be a very critical period for the U.S."[37]

Infuriated by these criticisms and the columnist's influence on public opinion, Attorney General William Rogers in April 1959 decided to brief Secretary of Defense Neil McElroy about "the Joseph Alsop incident in Russia when Alsop admitted to certain acts of homosexuality." Before doing so, Rogers asked Hoover to "get together what we [FBI] have on Alsop as he [Rogers] believed very few people knew of this and he was not aware that the President was aware of it." (Adams had already briefed Eisenhower in 1957.) Rogers specifically asked for a copy of Alsop's statement. On receipt of the requested report and statement, Rogers told the FBI director, he intended to see that "certain individuals were aware of Alsop's propensities," specifically naming the president, the secretary of defense, Under Secretary of State Christian Herter, White

House aide Wilton Persons, and Secretary to the Cabinet Robert Gray. Rogers refused, however, to "take the responsibility for such information going any further."[38]

After advising Hoover of his briefing of McElroy, Rogers added that the chairman of the Joint Chiefs of Staff, air force General Nathan Twining, "has just heard of it and wondered how Alsop could be trusted." Alsop could be confident, Twining complained, that "there would be no disclosure by this government but knew he was vulnerable to blackmail by the Russians." The chairman of the Joint Chiefs argued that "there might be an obligation to let some of the [newspaper] publishers know of this incident."[39]

Released FBI records do not document whether Twining or Eisenhower administration officials alerted the publishers of Alsop's column to the columnist's homosexuality and the incident in Moscow. In any event, by 1961 Alsop had come to regret his decision to provide the CIA a signed account of his sexual history. In April that year, and by exploiting his friendship with the new Democratic president, John F. Kennedy, Alsop informed CIA director Dulles that he intended to "ask the President to take possession of the Central Intelligence Agency (CIA) file concerning the matter." Characterizing this proposal as "highly irregular," Dulles stated that "naturally [he] would be obligated to comply" should the president make "such a request."

The Bay of Pigs fiasco of that same month temporarily delayed any such initiative while also serving to poison President Kennedy's relations with CIA director Dulles. Eventually, the following October, Attorney General Robert Kennedy asked Dulles to turn the CIA's file on Alsop over to him. Consulting with Hoover, Dulles pointed out to his FBI ally that the attorney general was "very likely" acting for the president. Nonetheless Dulles decided to brief the president and the attorney general on all the ramifications of this case and specifically that "Alsop's involvement with the Soviets is a matter which cannot be buried." Furthermore, Dulles emphasized, if the CIA or the FBI were to receive any future name check request about Alsop, they "will be obliged to produce the facts." The British government, Dulles added, "through its Embassy in Moscow became aware of the Moscow incident and undoubtedly has a fairly good story concerning the entire situation." Forced to retire that month owing to the botch at the Bay of Pigs, Dulles immediately briefed his successor, John McCone, "concerning all pertinent details."[40]

FBI officials' possession and dissemination of information—and rumors—about homosexual activities helped sustain a homophobic climate in government, in ways that supplemented official and popular anxieties about the Communist internal security threat. Yet the FBI's actions were never confined to those individuals or situations that could compromise legitimate security interests because the individual could influence official policy or had access to classified information.

For example, in October 1957, based on a tip from the Catholic priest John Cronin, FBI officials began an intensive investigation of a prominent (name redacted) "professor at an eastern university" who allegedly had been detained by Soviet officials in Kiev who had discovered him "in a compromising position." FBI officials' concerns stemmed from this professor's prominence as a Soviet scholar and thus his ability to influence public opinion. FBI officials classified this as an espionage investigation. But this was not the peak of their obsession with homosexual activities. That involved Hollywood actor Rock Hudson. Having learned about Hudson's homosexuality from a "confidential source" in 1965, Hoover in 1966 alerted the Johnson White House to this discovery. FBI memoranda record the underlying basis for FBI officials' concern: Hudson might play an FBI agent in a movie.[41]

CHAPTER EIGHT

• • •

The Perils of Partisanship

> I told the Senator [Joseph McCarthy] that we [FBI] were worried for fear that the cause had suffered and that there was a very definite reaction setting in against Congressional Committees and he would be smart to get off on some other subject [than current hearings on the Voice of America].
>
> —FBI Assistant Director Louis Nichols, July 23, 1953

NICHOLS'S COMMENT captures both the spirit of the FBI's politics of counterintelligence and the perils of that covert politics, perils that first became apparent during the early 1950s.

Nichols's reference to "the cause" highlights the underlying purpose of FBI officials' covert alliance with selected congressmen, congressional committees, and reporters and columnists: their shared interest in promoting a militantly anti-Communist politics. By the 1950s, FBI officials had abandoned a law enforcement mission of developing evidence to indict and convict those suspected of violating the nation's espionage laws—in part because FBI information was uncovered illegally or confirmed no violation of federal law. More often, FBI director Hoover and senior FBI officials leaked derogatory personal and political information to trusted anti-Communists. They were willing to do so, having taken great care to minimize the risk that their politically motivated leaking activities might be made public. These precautions included the institution of special records procedures to ensure that no record documenting such activities could be discovered, and by conditioning their assistance, and its continuance, on the recipients' agreement not to disclose FBI involvement.

This practice, however, ran the risk of ambitious and sometimes reckless politicians. By the early 1950s, members of Congress such as Senator McCarthy, and congressional committees such as the Senate Internal Security Subcommittee, often found it politically expedient to enhance their credibility by disclosing that their charges were based on information provided by the seemingly apolitical FBI. In so doing they violated both the strict condition of FBI assistance and the bureaucratic interests of FBI officials.

Republican successes in the 1952 presidential and congressional elections proved to be both the opportunity for an expanded FBI political counterintelligence role—and then the abrupt end of this secret collaboration. Having won national power by capitalizing on public concerns that the Roosevelt and Truman administrations were "soft toward communism," conservative Republicans intended to exploit their control of key congressional committees to sustain a politics of anti-communism. They fully anticipated support of a Republican White House and attorney general. Furthering this goal required continued FBI assistance. Yet the anti-Communists' extreme partisanship eventually proved perilous to FBI director Hoover's image of apolitical professionalism. At various times between 1953 and 1955, Hoover and senior FBI officials decided they could no longer assist their anti-Communist allies.

The first such crisis involved the plans of Senator McCarthy—the Republican most identified with a politics of militant anti-communism and with the successful attacks on the Truman administration's "softness toward communism." McCarthy was at first unprepared for the Democrats' reaction to his dramatic charges of 1950 that the Truman administration had knowingly abetted communism. His rambling performance and apparent lack of hard evidence had convinced Democratic Senate leaders that year to authorize a special investigation into his allegations of eighty-one cases of "known Communists in the State Department." In response, many Republicans and reporters rallied to the senator's defense. Under the informal leadership of J. B. Matthews, former staff director of the House Committee on Un-American Activities, Republican activists and reporters George Waters, Ed Nellor, and Willard Edwards provided research and writing aid to enable the senator to rebut the Democrats on the investigating committee and Truman administration officials. McCarthy was also able to capitalize on FBI director Hoover's assistance.[1]

Given the political dimensions of McCarthy's attack on the Truman administration, any FBI assistance to the senator had to be circumspect and carefully camouflaged. Hoover urged McCarthy to hire former FBI agent Don Surine as a staff investigator. Surine not only brought with him investigative skills; he regularly and secretly exchanged information with Hoover and FBI associate director Clyde Tolson.[2] More important, FBI officials devised special records procedures to disguise the fact that McCarthy's information about the suspect political affiliations of his eighty-one cases came from FBI files. On receipt of the information from his FBI contacts in blind memorandum form, for example, Surine "would insert the information appearing in the Bureau report in the form of a summary of information appearing in the CSC [Civil Service Commission] files, thus making it appear that his office had secured a CSC file rather than a Bureau file."[3]

These procedures preclude a definitive understanding of the extent of the FBI's assistance to McCarthy from 1950 to 1952—beyond former FBI assistant director William Sullivan's general description that Hoover "had us preparing material for [McCarthy] regularly, kept furnishing it to him while [Hoover] publicly denied that we were helping him."[4] All this changed with the 1952 election.

Following his reelection that year and elevation to the chairmanship of the powerful Senate Committee on Government Operations, McCarthy was in a strong position to launch investigations of federal agencies and departments. The senator nonetheless recognized that, despite this institutional base, he would need FBI assistance. In late November 1952 he contacted Guy Hottel, head of the FBI's Washington, D.C., field office. He "anticipated closer cooperation and more extended use of the FBI and its facilities following the beginning of the new Congress," McCarthy advised Hottel, adding that "in the past, it was not always to one's advantage to be seen talking to or associating with" him, but that "all this would be changed now with his re-election and the new Congress." McCarthy told Hottel he planned to confer with Hoover "in the not too distant future relative to his obtaining suggestions for prospective investigative personnel for his investigative committee [the Permanent Investigations Subcommittee of the Senate Committee on Government Operations]."[5]

Telephoning Hoover on November 28, McCarthy emphasized that, with his new chairmanship, he now had a special need for "good staff." Responding to the senator's request for his recommendations of "a number of competent investigators that he might consider for appointment to this staff," Hoover ordered FBI associate director Clyde Tolson to give this matter "prompt attention."[6] Six weeks later, on January 12, 1953, McCarthy met personally with Hoover. After encouraging the FBI director to "feel free to contact him whenever I [Hoover] saw any activity of any member of his staff . . . which I did not feel was in the best interests of administration," the senator outlined "generally the over-all plans which he has for carrying on the work of his committee" and his intention to be "in contact" with the FBI "from time to time."[7]

Unlike the 1950–1952 period, Hoover was not acting insubordinately in servicing McCarthy's needs. McCarthy and other Republicans had won control of Congress and the White House by exploiting public doubts about the Truman administration's commitment to an effective internal security program. To sustain this political advantage, senior Eisenhower administration officials at first intended to support McCarthy's—and other congressional—investigations of Communist activities, which had the ancillary purpose of exposing the failures of the Roosevelt and Truman administrations. These twin objectives required administration officials to address the question of the FBI's relationship to the congressional McCarthyites, and whether the new attorney general should honor congressional requests for FBI assistance.

As early as February 1953, Hoover ordered the FBI's liaison to Congress and the media, FBI assistant director Nichols, to brief Deputy Attorney General William Rogers on the FBI's ongoing relationship with the Senate Internal Security Subcommittee (dating from 1951) and how the FBI in general handled congressional requests for information. In response, Rogers specifically authorized FBI officials to honor the McCarthy Committee's requests for FBI name checks for all proposed staff appointees. FBI officials should also consider, Rogers counseled, the McCarthy Committee's other requests, deciding "each case . . . on its merits" as there "might be legitimate instances wherein the Bureau should cooperate but that this should be decided in individual cases." He and

Attorney General Herbert Brownell, Rogers emphasized, "wanted to do whatever the Bureau wanted to do" and would back FBI officials whether or not they cooperated. In the specific case of the McCarthy Committee's proposed investigation of the Voice of America (VOA), Rogers authorized full cooperation. McCarthy had recently announced his intention to investigate possible "mismanagement, subversion, and kickbacks" by VOA employees. Although the McCarthy Committee's ensuing hearings on the VOA were meandering and often unfair, the publicity benefited both the publicity-conscious senator and the Eisenhower administration. Indeed, McCarthy defended the hearings as confirming how career VOA employees, who had civil service tenure, "are doing a rather effective job of sabotaging [Secretary of State John Foster] Dulles' and Eisenhower's foreign policy program."[8]

Rogers's encouraging cooperation prompted the McCarthy Committee to submit a flurry of requests to the FBI. Despite the volume of these requests, Rogers a month later reaffirmed this policy of cooperation, advising Nichols that "for the time being, when we [FBI] receive requests" from the McCarthy Committee, "we should decide each on its merits and do all we could do to slow them down."[9]

Valuing this approved relationship, Hoover ordered Nichols to maintain a "close liaison" with Senator McCarthy and his principal counsels Roy Cohn and Don Surine. Under this arrangement, McCarthy agreed to provide "transcripts of testimony of interest to us [FBI]" while the FBI in turn "perform[ed] name checks" on individuals requested by the McCarthy Committee. Between March 16 and April 16, 1953, the FBI conducted seventy-four name checks on behalf of McCarthy's committee.[10]

Rogers's and Brownell's assumption—that FBI assistance to McCarthy would promote the Eisenhower administration's political interests—proved to be partly unwarranted. McCarthy's different political agenda surfaced as early as March 1953, triggered by the president's controversial nomination of Charles Bohlen as U.S. ambassador to the Soviet Union.

Since the late 1940s, and more pointedly during the 1952 election campaign, Republicans in Congress—and the party in its 1952 platform—had assailed the Roosevelt administration's policies at the 1945 Yalta Conference. Claiming that the Yalta agreements on Eastern Europe and the Far East had been responsible for the expansion of Soviet influence in Eastern Europe and the Communist conquest of China, Republican candidates in 1952 pledged to initiate a more militant anti-Soviet policy, which would include purging all "Yalta men" from key policymaking positions in the State Department. Eisenhower's nomination of Bohlen contradicted that stance, since Bohlen had served as a translator for the U.S. delegation at the Yalta Conference and thereafter continued to defend the Yalta agreements as being in the national interest. During Senate confirmation hearings and debate, conservative Republican senators questioned Bohlen's loyalty, character, and the wisdom of his appointment to this sensitive diplomatic post. Indeed, rumors circulated in early March that Bohlen was homosexual and that the State Department's chief security official was unwilling to grant him a security clearance.[11]

Senator McCarthy assumed a leadership role in this unsuccessful effort to submarine the Bohlen nomination. Capitalizing on his recently established "close liaison" with the FBI, McCarthy telephoned Hoover later that month, before the start of Senate debate, to convey his concern about the Bohlen nomination and his more general belief that "there was presently no change" from Truman's appointees "and everything was running about the same as it was a year ago." The senator solicited Hoover's assessment of "how bad [Bohlen] actually was." Hoover evaded a direct answer, saying that the FBI had not yet conducted a security clearance investigation of Bohlen, having only recently been given this assignment. McCarthy immediately raised a new line of inquiry, asking whether Bohlen "was a homosexual." "He did not know," Hoover replied, adding that "was a very hard thing to prove and the only way you could prove it was either by admission or by arrest and forfeiture of collateral. I [Hoover] stated this had not occurred in [Bohlen's] case at all as far as we [FBI] knew, but it is a fact, and I believed very well known that he is associating with individuals of that type." The FBI director admitted that his agency had uncovered "no evidence to show any overt act, but he [Bohlen] had certainly used very bad judgment in associating with homosexuals." Owing to the lack of hard evidence, Hoover and McCarthy concurred, such associations and rumors could not be used to discredit Bohlen. When McCarthy specifically asked Hoover to provide him with a public source or other information for his use during floor debate on Bohlen's confirmation, Hoover pleaded an inability to help. The FBI had investigated Bohlen "from the security and morals angle," Hoover stated, but "frankly most of the information we got was from the State Department. I indicated we did not go into the analysis of political speeches and so forth, as that was supposed to be handled by the State Department."[12]

Refusing to be drawn into an intramural Republican conflict between McCarthyite senators and the Eisenhower administration, Hoover nonetheless remained committed to influencing McCarthy's anti-Communist crusade. On the one hand he endorsed McCarthy's proposed plan to look into the Ford Foundation's funding of academic studies that questioned the purpose and consequences of anti-Communist initiatives by state legislatures and the Hollywood blacklist. On the other hand Hoover sought to dissuade McCarthy from launching an investigation into the noted atomic scientist J. Robert Oppenheimer. McCarthy should realize, Hoover warned, that any inquiry into Oppenheimer's loyalty would be opposed by the scientific community and would also impinge on the responsibilities of other congressional committees, notably the Joint Committee on Atomic Energy. He urged McCarthy instead to ensure that any such investigation "be done with a great deal of preliminary spade work so that if and when the Committee moved into the open it would have substantive facts upon which to predicate its actions." McCarthy promised to follow this advice.[13]

Hoover's sensible suggestions went to the essence of McCarthy's problems. After surging to national prominence, the senator invariably made sweeping allegations without having done the necessary homework to document them. It was one thing for McCarthy to employ such tactics during speeches in the Senate or before sympathetic political or social groups. It was quite another to launch highly publicized hearings where other senators and Democratic staff counsel could challenge his contentions and expose his lack of evidence. In addition, McCarthy's publicized forays suffered from a lack of consistency and purpose, in part the result of bitter infighting among his staff. By June 1953 the senator had concluded that at minimum these staff conflicts required the replacement of Francis Flanagan as chief counsel of the Permanent Investigations Subcommittee by J. B. Matthews, whom he had relied on in 1950 when preparing for the Tydings Committee investigation.

McCarthy, however, had not cleared the Matthews appointment with senior FBI officials. Apologizing to FBI assistant director Nichols for his failure to have "call[ed] the Director" to brief him on the Matthews appointment, McCarthy nonetheless praised Matthews's "dominant personality" as essential "to control the situation so far as the Committee is concerned, and he knows this will be highly pleasing to the Director." Nichols quickly disabused McCarthy of this notion, stressing that "quite frankly" the FBI director would have opposed Matthews's appointment in light of his activities during the 1930s as a member of the staff of the House Committee on Un-American Activities. Nichols cited instances "wherein we [FBI] had contacted Matthews and thereafter seen items in the paper." A surprised McCarthy said he had been led to believe that Matthews "was close to the Bureau and the Bureau held Matthews in high regard." While conceding that FBI officials had failed to convey their negative feelings about Matthews to the senator, Nichols remarked that "naturally we would subordinate our feelings on those fighting Communism" but that McCarthy "should be cautious about Matthews issuing press releases."

Responsible for briefing Hoover on congressional matters, Nichols anticipated that the FBI director might decide to sever the FBI's "close liaison" with the senator over the Matthews appointment. The diplomatic Nichols was eager to avert a break, and he assured his boss that McCarthy intended to be "very cautious." Matthews should be given "a chance," Nichols recommended, though FBI officials would have to "keep our guard up but at the same time see if he [Matthews] has changed his ways." A skeptical Hoover ordered Nichols to let him "see what we have on Matthews first."[14]

Hoover's reservations proved to be well founded, though not because of Matthews's actions as the McCarthy Committee's staff director. Almost concurrent with his appointment, in an article titled "Reds and Our Churches" that he wrote for the right-wing *American Mercury,* Matthews described Protestant clergymen as the "largest single group supporting the Communist apparatus in the United States today." Given McCarthy's prominence as a Catholic and the militant anti-communism of the Catholic church hierarchy, Matthews's sweeping aspersion provoked a bitter backlash. Democratic senators on the Permanent Investigations Subcommittee—who had not been consulted on the Matthews appointment—prominent Protestant clergy, and even Southern Democratic senators Harry Byrd and John Stennis immediately condemned Matthews's charges, forcing McCarthy to seek Matthews's resignation.[15]

McCarthy again needed an effective staff director, but this time he asked his aide, Jean Kerr, to contact Hoover. Her approach would allow McCarthy to deny having "been in touch with the Director." Kerr's mission was to obtain Hoover's agreement to the appointment of a current FBI employee, Frank Carr, as the subcommittee's new chief of staff. At the outset of her meeting with Hoover, Kerr placed the Carr appointment in the context of the situation "growing out of the recent Matthews incident." Hoover replied that he could not "accede to" Carr's appointment, emphasizing that it was not his role to "concur or not concur." McCarthy and Committee Counsel Roy Cohen had already been told, the FBI director reiterated, that "I would not ask Mr. Carr to take the position . . . and that I would neither approve nor disapprove if he took the position." Hoover then pointed out the perils of this proposed appointment: appointing a current FBI employee "engaged upon work dealing with subversive activities would, no doubt, be seized upon by critics of the Senator and of the FBI as a deliberate effort to effect a direct 'pipe line' into the FBI and that it would make it necessary for the Bureau to be far more circumspect in all of its dealings with the McCarthy Committee should Mr. Carr be appointed." Asked by Kerr whether he would "publicly" object to the Carr appointment, Hoover replied that he would not. When Kerr solicited Hoover's recommendations of "some name or names" whom the senator should consider for this post, the FBI director agreed to think about it but advised that this should not be construed as counseling the senator as to "what he should do or as to whom he should appoint."[16]

Kerr did not tell McCarthy about Hoover's reservations that appointing Carr would inevitably affect their "close liaison." As a result, McCarthy appointed Carr chief counsel. The Wisconsin senator soon learned of Hoover's displeasure and its consequences the next week, during a meeting with FBI assistant director Nichols about matters of interest to the committee. At the outset, McCarthy expressed his pleasure at having resolved the committee's staff problem, noting that he "was very glad the Director finally approved Carr's coming with the staff." Nichols informed a surprised McCarthy that the senator had been misled. Hoover had told Kerr he "would not give Carr a leave of absence, we [FBI] would not release him, we would not ask him to go to the Committee, we would not approve him going to the Committee, that obviously if Carr resigned [from the FBI] and wanted to go with the Committee that was his business." In fact, Nichols informed McCarthy, "the Director would literally and figuratively 'give him hell' " at their next meeting. Nichols then spelled out the consequences of the Carr appointment: "it now placed a very tight restriction upon the Bureau, that we would have to lean over backwards because if at any time the Committee came up with something having an FBI angle, the charge would be made that Carr was a pipeline and that it would have been so much better to have had an outsider."[17]

Because Carr's appointment compromised what was to have been a covert relationship, FBI officials severed their "close liaison" with McCarthy. An October 1953 FBI memorandum blandly describes this change: "We have furnished information to the Senate Permanent Investigative [sic] Committee (McCarthy) up until the late summer [1953] when the Committee appointed former Special Agent Carr as Staff Director. Since then no information has been furnished to this Committee."[18]

In covertly assisting McCarthy, FBI officials were not simply promoting "the cause" of anti-communism. They understood that McCarthy's immediate purpose was to discredit the Truman administration and its predecessor as having knowingly abetted Communist subversion. In ending the relationship, Hoover did so not because of Senator McCarthy's evolving conflict with the new Republican administration—previewed in McCarthy's unsuccessful attempt to thwart the Bohlen nomination, and fully exposed during his investigation of army security procedures and the 1954

Army-McCarthy hearings. The catalyst instead was the reckless exposure by McCarthy and his key staff of the FBI's covert role in promoting the senator's anti-Communist politics. Having to choose between promoting "the cause" and preserving the FBI's bureaucratic interests, Hoover chose the latter.

FBI officials' covert relationship with another anti-Communist congressional committee, the Senate Internal Security Subcommittee (SISS), soon encountered the same dilemma.

In 1951, Senator Pat McCarran, the arch-conservative Democratic chairman of the Senate Judiciary Committee, had created SISS as a permanent subcommittee. SISS's specific responsibility was to monitor the enforcement of the nation's internal security laws and to recommend further legislative measures. McCarran's decision to create SISS illustrated his doubts about the Truman administration's commitment to an effective internal security program, symbolized by President Truman's September 1950 veto of the Internal Security (or McCarran) Act. McCarran had drafted this stringent internal security law and had steered it through congressional passage, including the overriding of Truman's veto.

McCarran immediately sounded out Hoover about his interest in FBI assistance to this new subcommittee, and the FBI director agreed to cooperate with the SISS chairman on "a personal basis"—much as he had with HUAC in 1947 and Senator McCarthy in 1950. In March 1951, however, the FBI-SISS relationship blossomed, the result of a crucial decision by Attorney General J. Howard McGrath. During a meeting with SISS members to discuss the subcommittee's plans and objectives, McGrath privately confided that "he was delegating complete responsibility to the Director to do whatever the Director felt should be done." SISS counsel Jay Sourwine immediately initiated discussions with FBI assistant director Nichols about this arrangement, observing that other Justice Department officials were unaware of McGrath's decision and would have been dissatisfied had they learned of it, but that what they "did not know would not hurt them." SISS "will play ball with the Bureau," Sourwine pledged, and "in the event we [FBI] have the information [sought by SISS], they [SISS] would like to secure the information from us." Sourwine further extolled McCarran's "very high personal regard for the Director and would do just about anything the Director asked him to do." Should Hoover require "any help on the Hill" in the future, Sourwine proferred, he should contact McCarran directly or indirectly through Sourwine, who would then "take care of any matter."[19]

Nichols worked out the general terms of this covert relationship—but only after having FBI agents investigate SISS staff members to be sure of their discretion and unimpeachable character.[20] At a later meeting, McCarran assured Nichols that "there was little likelihood of anybody ever knowing exactly what cooperation was extended by the FBI because the Senator would certainly respect the Bureau's position on anything." Nichols and McCarran agreed that SISS would focus on matters "of current internal security significance, that the Senator was not interested in going into any situation which had been corrected or wherein the individual was no longer involved, that the Senator wanted to use the Committee to not only strengthen internal security for the good of the United States but to help the Bureau in every possible manner." In return, FBI officials agreed to process all SISS name check requests after being provided the subcommittee's reasons for them and provide "suggestive leads and/or information to be used in questioning witnesses." FBI reports would fall into two categories and had to be handled accordingly: the first would consist of public source information, and the second, information that could have been obtained only from FBI files. McCarran moreover agreed not to subpoena FBI records.[21]

Because released FBI records on this covert liaison are massively redacted, the scope and effect of the FBI's assistance cannot be definitively established. The names of the individuals submitted for investigation by SISS staff are invariably redacted in the released FBI records, and some FBI communications with SISS are redacted altogether. The released records do, however, describe the subjects of SISS interest. For 1951–1952, these include the Institute of Pacific Relations, the subject of controversial, highly publicized hearings conducted by SISS;[22] individuals who had been subjects of FBI loyalty investigations;[23] employees of the Federal Communications Commission;[24] individuals employed in the radio, television, and "show business" industries, including Richard Rodgers, Oscar Hammerstein, Moss Hart, and unnamed CBS employees;[25] the prominent American Civil Liberties Union attorney Arthur Garfield Hays;[26] employees of the New York book publisher W. W. Norton—triggered by publication of a critical book about the Ellen Knauff alien deportation case;[27] and "Communist infiltration in education." FBI assistant director Nichols characterized this last request as "an excellent opportunity for a real service to be rendered" and recommended that the FBI "furnish any information as it occurs from time to time on college Professors and teachers who are members of the Communist Party." Such assistance to SISS, Nichols emphasized, would supplement the FBI's Responsibilities Program,* adding that the FBI could readily identify "a few of these cases which the Committee staff could then investigate."[28]

Nichols's recommendation that the FBI promote an SISS investigation of higher education was not immediately acted upon, owing to the fact that it had been proposed in the waning weeks of the 1952 election campaign. Republican election victories resulted in Senator William Jenner's replacement of McCarran as chairman of SISS.

Because Attorney General McGrath had on his own secretly

*Described later in this chapter.

approved the SISS-FBI liaison program, the new Republican administration could have discontinued this arrangement. But this seemed unlikely since the Republican congressional leadership had pointedly portrayed the Truman administration's unwillingness to produce subpoenaed FBI and other executive-branch records to congressional committees as a partisan cover-up that served to undermine the nation's internal security interests.

Eisenhower's appointee as attorney general, Herbert Brownell, immediately tackled this delicate issue of executive-legislative relations and executive secrecy. He specifically solicited Hoover's assessment of the FBI's "present arrangement" with SISS. The FBI director informed the attorney general that the FBI had provided "summaries of any pertinent information" to SISS and that this liaison was "highly satisfactory." Brownell thereupon concurred that there was no need to "change existing procedures or practices of the Bureau."

Armed with this charge, Hoover met personally with Senator Jenner and the new SISS counsel, Robert Morris, to discuss the general terms of this reauthorized relationship. The FBI director began by affirming his willingness to adhere to any arrangement that SISS worked out with the attorney general. Hoover, however, outlined his own preferences: that SISS maintain "in confidence information from our files," designate a specific individual to work as liaison with the FBI, and hold "to a minimum" requests for FBI assistance. Both Hoover and Jenner commended the absence of leaks and the value of confidentiality that had characterized the FBI-SISS relationship since 1951. Concluding the meeting, Jenner reaffirmed his willingness to "help the Bureau whenever the Bureau needs a forum for a matter we [FBI] cannot handle."

After his own conference with SISS, Deputy Attorney General Rogers informed Hoover that the attorney general "would leave up to the Bureau the scope of its cooperation" with SISS, and that he and Brownell would back up the FBI director on whatever he decided. When Hoover extolled the great value of SISS's investigation of the Institute of Pacific Relations, Rogers observed that the attorney general's permissive authorization would allow Hoover to seize any opportunity to assist SISS "if the public interest could be served through a forum such as that presented by Congress." Rogers asked only to be kept fully informed "on what our [FBI] position was so that he could keep the Attorney General posted and could support us to the fullest degree." In fact, the only reservation expressed by Justice Department and FBI officials throughout these discussions related to the volume of SISS requests and the possibility that other congressional committees might try to exploit this relationship as a precedent, which could result in the administration's loss of control over information.[29]

Brownell's and Hoover's reservations proved entirely warranted. In the ensuing months, SISS staff bombarded their FBI contacts with requests for information relating to proposed hearings on United Nations employees, labor unions, higher education, the book publishing industry, and former Treasury Department employees identified by Elizabeth Bentley in 1945 as members of a Soviet espionage ring. Because of the volume of these requests, as early as May 1953 FBI officials reassessed the "advisability of completely discontinuing the supplying of any information" to SISS. They quickly concluded that overall "we [FBI] do benefit considerably and are in a position to protect the Bureau's interests," and that the "lesser of two evils is to continue furnishing information to the Committee but to keep it to a minimum." Hoover ordered that "we must put brakes on & make certain we carefully screen all requests."[30]

FBI officials enthusiastically assisted SISS's investigation of "Communist infiltration in education," an investigation that had first been proposed during the waning days of McCarran's chairmanship. In February 1953, SISS counsel Robert Morris requested FBI assistant director Nichols's assistance in identifying "a good case at the above colleges [Sarah Lawrence, Bennington, and Harvard] for use in subsequent hearings regarding Communist infiltration in education." Hoover agreed—"Yes, help if we can"—and ordered FBI field offices to forward any information to FBI headquarters concerning suspected Communist employees at these colleges.[31]

Action on this initiative, however, was temporarily placed on hold, owing to the announced plans of HUAC also to investigate Communists in education. To prevent overlap and institutional rivalry, Vice President Richard Nixon invited HUAC and SISS members and staff to meet with him, at which time he urged them to "work as a joint committee." But SISS opposed this idea as impinging on Senate prerogatives.* After the rejection of joint collaboration, FBI officials provided SISS with the names of two alleged Communists employed at Sarah Lawrence and six at Harvard. Unable to identify any Communists at Bennington, the FBI informed SISS of two individuals employed at Duke University. This information was to be used at SISS hearings in March 1953.[32]

This secret FBI-SISS relationship ended in 1954, but not because of the volume of SISS requests or the prospect that SISS inquiries might compromise ongoing FBI investigations. Instead the catalyst stemmed from Attorney General Brownell's and FBI director Hoover's actions in the Harry Dexter White matter, actions that threatened to expose how Eisenhower administration officials and the Republican congressional leadership had politicized the FBI.

As Eisenhower's campaign manager in the 1952 presidential campaign, Brownell had pursued a strategy that capitalized on public doubts about the Truman administration's commitment to internal security. Brownell aimed to sustain this political advantage

*In the interim, FBI officials learned that White House aide Wilton Persons "has been able to stop" a proposal that the Eisenhower administration intercede to foreclose any such congressional investigation.

after the election, and for a time he regularly cited statistics on the number of "security" risks that had been dismissed under Eisenhower's stringent security program. But the attorney general inadvertently created a political firestorm in November 1953, one that raised questions about his leadership of the Department of Justice. Speaking to a sympathetic businessmen's group in Chicago that month, Brownell cited the case of former Treasury Department official Harry Dexter White as an example of the Truman administration's loose internal security program in contrast to the new Republican administration's greater vigilance.*

The former Democratic president bitterly denounced Brownell's speech, accusing the attorney general of McCarthyism. Defending his own actions as president, Truman declared that he had read the FBI reports but had effected an arrangement with the FBI director to allow White's nomination to go forward. Otherwise, Truman claimed, White and other individuals would have been forewarned that they were being monitored by the FBI.

To rebut Truman and the underlying questions about his own impartiality, Brownell secured the sympathetic forum of an SISS hearing on November 17, 1953. Accompanied by Hoover, Brownell maintained that Truman had in fact willfully ignored FBI warnings and that there had been no Truman-Hoover arrangement. In preparing for the hearing, Brownell asked Hoover to review his (Brownell's) proposed testimony while the FBI director in turn identified the dates of his reports to the Truman administration in 1945–1946 and had his aides prepare a chart detailing the FBI's "distribution of investigative information" to Truman and senior administration officials about White and others named by Elizabeth Bentley as members of a Soviet espionage ring. Brownell im-

*In 1946, Truman had nominated White as executive director of the International Monetary Fund, despite having received a flurry of FBI reports based on Elizabeth Bentley's FBI interviews questioning White's loyalty. See pages 41–42 and 106–108.

mediately declassified Hoover's reports to the Truman White House and senior administration officials, and these were both cited and reprinted in the records of the SISS hearings. Furthermore, in his own testimony before SISS, Hoover denied having effected any arrangement to allow the White nomination to go forward. Truman's withdrawal of White's name, Hoover emphasized, would not have compromised the FBI's ongoing investigation into Bentley's allegations.[33]

Because of Hoover's public and private assistance, Brownell successfully rebutted Truman's charge of McCarthyism and the related question of whether he had the temperament to oversee the Justice Department impartially. Brownell later confided that Truman's criticisms had threatened to end his tenure as attorney general "and that he would not now [1955] be Attorney General except for the Director's very forthright statement before the Senate Subcommittee on Internal Security."[34]

If Brownell welcomed Hoover's willingness to testify in this politically charged setting, even conservative Southern Democrats bitterly resented the FBI director's action. They may have been militant anti-Communists, but such Southern Democrats as Mississippi congressmen Jamie Whitten and William Winstead and Mississippi senator James Eastland were disturbed that Hoover willingly interjected himself into a partisan dispute. The FBI director, they pointed out, "has avoided appearing on Capitol Hill on many occasions in the past and . . . could have avoided that particular appearance." Whitten threatened, through one of his aides, that "when the Democrats regain control of Cong[ress] that efforts would be made, on part of Democrats, to remove Director from his position." Southern Democrats continued to be troubled by Hoover's SISS testimony. During the late 1950s they even tried to use it as leverage to pressure the FBI director not to expand FBI investigations into civil rights matters.[35]

The joint Hoover-Brownell appearance was followed by another potentially embarrassing development later that month, one that also threatened to compromise FBI covert assistance to congressional McCarthyites. In an informal address before a men's social club in Bonneville, Utah, Republican senator Karl Mundt, who had served on the House Committee on Un-American Activities as a congressman, responded to the question of an editorial writer for the *Salt Lake Tribune* by stating that FBI officials had regularly leaked information to congressional committees investigating Communist activities. Such "tipping off" occurred, the senator explained, when the FBI lacked information sufficient to secure an indictment. The writer in attendance thereupon praised this arrangement in an editorial. Disturbed on reading this account of the FBI's "connivance in substituting Congressional Committees for the courts," University of Utah political scientist J. D. Williams protested to Senator J. William Fulbright, who in a March 1954 Senate speech pointedly called attention to Mundt's "tipping off" remark. Seeking to contain this potentially damaging disclosure, Hoover dismissed this characterization of the FBI's covert actions as "an absolute lie." Attorney General Brownell, in turn, affirmed his intention to keep "inviolate the confidential nature of F.B.I. files" and denied that FBI information had been given to Senator McCarthy or to HUAC.[36]

The combination of the White and Mundt incidents, and Brownell's categorical denial, threatened the continuance of the covert FBI-SISS relationship, which was already threatened by SISS's crude partisanship and its dependence on FBI officials for direction and assistance.

In 1954, SISS launched an investigation into whether the Roosevelt administration had in 1944 destroyed files of the Office of Naval Intelligence. Seeking confirmation, SISS investigators demanded direct access to Navy Department files. Before honoring this request, Under Secretary of the Navy Thomas Gates solicited Hoover's advice on the "proper" response, emphasizing that the navy's review of these files showed that no record destruction had occurred beyond the normal practice of destroying duplicate files. Hoover urged Gates to raise this matter with the White House, since a precedent could be established should a congressional committee be granted direct access to the records of a federal agency or department.[37]

SISS's request had posed a serious threat to the executive branch's control over information; in addition, honoring the request could lead to the public disclosure of controversial executive decisions. By 1954, senior Eisenhower administration officials no longer welcomed McCarthyite inquiries that would inevitably lead to public disclosure of executive branch information. This reassessment coincided with the heightened concerns of FBI officials that SISS, though it had never subpoenaed FBI records, had come to consider the FBI as a ready reference resource to be tapped. Indeed, in February 1954, SISS counsel Charles Grimes solicited FBI assistant director Nichols's "suggestions" for future SISS investigations, the subcommittee having recently completed its highly publicized and contentious hearings into "interlocking subversion" in the executive branch during the Truman and Roosevelt administrations.*

At first Nichols unhesitatingly responded to this request. He urged Grimes to complete "unfinished business" and specifically to "tie up loose ends, particularly in the Communists in government, and that no one as yet had assayed the danger done by Communists in government." SISS, Nichols emphasized, should consider "dramatizing the role of secret Communists, particularly of those individuals on whom there was no proven record of Communist Party activity." When Nichols briefed Hoover on his response to Grimes, a cautious FBI director expressed his serious

*These hearings revisited Bentley's charges and examined why some of those she had named continued to hold appointments in the federal government.

reservations that "we don't get jockeyed into counseling this Committee. We want to cooperate but that doesn't mean guiding." Nichols then advised Grimes that the FBI "would assist in every possible way we could within the framework of our responsibilities."[38]

Grimes's report proved to be the catalyst for a Justice Department reassessment of the FBI-SISS relationship, a reassessment motivated by the continuing furor over Mundt's "tipping off" revelation. Following this review, Deputy Attorney General Rogers ordered Nichols to "be exceedingly careful" when responding to this and future SISS requests. FBI officials should limit their responses to SISS name check requests to "public source material" and then only after Grimes's assurances to "maintain confidence." Senior FBI officials were therefore ordered that "Nothing is to be given to Grimes nor Jenner Com[mittee] unless specifically cleared by Rogers."[39]

For a time, FBI officials limited their assistance to SISS to "background and public source material only." But Rogers later stipulated that no FBI document should be given to a congressional committee that "might be inaccurately and unfairly portrayed as an FBI report." Hoover thereupon requested a personal meeting with Rogers and Attorney General Brownell to reach a definitive resolution of the FBI's dissemination role. In the interim, Hoover ordered that any SISS request "will not be favorably acted upon," including even the forwarding of public source information. In the event SISS members or staff inquired about this changed policy, FBI officials were to attribute this as the decision of the attorney general. The meeting between Hoover, Brownell, and Rogers resulted in an agreement to make permanent this policy of noncooperation.[40]

In March–April 1954, when the FBI-SISS relationship was under review, an SISS inquiry resulted in greater restrictions on access to executive-branch records. As part of their general interest in documenting former Treasury Department official Harry Dexter White's subversive influence during the Roosevelt administration, SISS staff in early 1954 had become aware of the so-called Morgenthau Diaries. Secretary of the treasury during the Roosevelt administration, Henry Morgenthau had not in fact created a daily diary of his activities. His diaries instead contained copies of his correspondence, transcripts of his telephone conversations, and notes on the deliberations of senior department officials on important policy matters—transcribed by the treasury secretary's personal secretary. Morgenthau took these diaries with him on leaving office, claiming them to be his personal property. He later deeded them to the Roosevelt presidential library but on the condition that no one could review them without his permission. Morgenthau's detailed documentation made the diaries an invaluable research source, one that could offer insights into White's influence on Treasury Department policy.

When SISS staff learned from FBI officials that the Morgenthau Diaries had been deposited at the Roosevelt presidential library, they immediately sought the former treasury secretary's permission to review them. By this time a number of historians—including John Morton Blum, Arthur Schlesinger, Jr., William Langer, and J. Everett Gleason—had secured Morgenthau's permission to review the diaries.[41]

Morgenthau granted permission to SISS—then had second thoughts. In July 1955 he advised SISS of his decision "to turn over" to the General Services Administration, which administered the National Archives and presidential libraries, the responsibility to decide whether to allow any researcher to review and cite the contents of the diaries. SISS would have to negotiate with the Eisenhower administration to obtain continuing access or approval to cite specific documents during planned hearings.[42]

SISS formally subpoenaed the General Services Administration in October 1955 for the right to cite from three hundred documents in the Morgenthau Diaries. Eisenhower administration officials might have had no political interest in denying SISS access to these records, but the SISS subpoena posed a different institutional problem. It challenged the president's exclusive control over executive-branch information. In this instance the administration chose not to claim "executive privilege," since Morgenthau had already allowed historians to review the diaries. Instead the administration fought on the narrower ground of its right to classify information. And, after consulting with State, Defense, and Treasury Department officials and the CIA, the administration released 80 percent of the requested documents to SISS.[43]

At the same time SISS sought access to other documents, maintained by the Treasury Department itself, that recorded White's decisions as assistant secretary. This request starkly posed the issue—could executive officials deny a congressional committee access to executive-branch documents? (Truman had made the very claim in 1948 and 1950 in rejecting congressional subpoenas for FBI loyalty reports, triggering criticisms of a cover-up.) Hoping to avoid having to address this issue directly, Treasury Department officials at first approached Hoover to convey their concern over SISS's request and further to see whether the FBI wanted to review the White documents. Hoover was keenly interested in this offer but nonetheless insisted that Treasury Department officials not exploit the FBI's interest in reviewing the documents as "an excuse to withhold" them from SISS. FBI assistant director Nichols "confidentially advised" SISS counsel Jay Sourwine that the FBI was reviewing the White documents and that should administration officials deny SISS access to them, "it was not at our direction." And to ensure that Treasury Department officials could not evade this matter, Hoover ordered the FBI's Washington, D.C., field office to review the White documents "expeditiously" and to advise him as soon as possible of the "contemplated date of completion."[44]

Allowing the FBI to review the documents simply delayed the administration's decision. Unwilling to relinquish control over executive-branch records, Under Secretary of the Treasury H. Chapman Rose solicited Hoover's views on the effects of granting SISS access to the White documents "upon the security of the country." Privately dismissing this as a Treasury Department strategy to "find a way to 'pass the buck,'" Hoover personally informed Rose that the release of the White documents to SISS "is up to the Treasury" as these records pertained to day-to-day Treasury Department operations. Rose thereupon concurred with Hoover's suggestion that an experienced Treasury Department official should review the records and decide whether their release would affect the nation's security interests.[45]

Although he was unwilling to provide cover to the Eisenhower administration, Hoover was keenly interested in limiting access to FBI records. Through SISS's review of the Morgenthau Diaries, Hoover and senior FBI officials had learned that their contents included Hoover's reports and the transcripts of his telephone conversations with Morgenthau as well as transcripts of meetings among senior Treasury Department officials at which Hoover's reports were discussed. Disturbed by this discovery of the availability of records of FBI activities—to historians or members of Congress—in October 1956, Hoover pressured the National Archives to allow FBI agents to review the Morgenthau Diaries. Based on this review, FBI officials prepared—and National Archives officials agreed to—a seven-page list "of material to be excised" from 11 of the Morgenthau Diaries' 864 volumes. The FBI-identified documents were not physically excised from the bound volumes; instead, access to these volumes was denied.[46]

The situations that led to the abrupt termination of the FBI's secret liaisons with Senator McCarthy and SISS also affected another covert FBI dissemination program which Hoover had instituted in February 1951, the code-named Responsibilities Program.

A January 26, 1951, meeting of the executive committee of the National Governors' Conference was the catalyst to this FBI program. Just as congressional leaders like Senator McCarthy had tapped into widespread concerns about Communist influence in the federal bureaucracy, state legislators had assailed "subversive" influence at the local and state levels, though there they concentrated on higher education. The highly publicized nature of their charges, and those of state anti-subversive committees modeled after HUAC, threatened the administrative authority of state governors while also exposing them to charges of failing to address the "Communist threat." Frustrated particularly by local FBI officials' unwillingness to provide them with information they considered essential to an effective civil defense program, and specifically to the security of defense plants in their states, the governors appointed a delegation to meet with Hoover to discuss the general matter of FBI assistance.[47]

When Hoover was briefed on the purpose of this meeting, he ordered his aides to summarize whatever information the FBI had already compiled on the members of the gubernatorial delegation, the other governors on the executive committee, and the executive director of the National Governors' Conference.[48] This background information would not only provide him with insights into the political views of the governors but would enable him to weigh whether he could trust the governors not to leak the fact of FBI assistance, which was sure to raise serious constitutional questions. As a federal law enforcement agency, the FBI had no authority to investigate state or private employees who had violated no federal law, and, more important, no authority to share that information with state governors, given the constitutional division of powers between state and federal governments.

Hoover did meet with the gubernatorial delegation on February 2, 1951. The FBI director welcomed this opportunity to rebut some of the governors' criticisms of federal surveillance activities and to deter them from compiling and maintaining their own files on subversives.[49]

The meeting went unexpectedly well. Hoover deflected the delegation's request for information about security at defense plants by warning the governors that disseminating such information might risk disclosing the identities of FBI informers. The governors then asked for FBI information that would identify subversives employed in state universities or public utilities. Hoover readily agreed to this request, but on the condition that the FBI's assistance would be held in the "strictest confidence." A formal arrangement was effected whereby such information would be conveyed verbally to the governors (or designated officials) by the heads of FBI field offices—under the code-named Responsibilities Program. Hoover's rationale for such covert assistance captures how the FBI's role had now shifted from law enforcement to political counterintelligence: "the Bureau is responsible for the internal security of the country as a whole and [in view of the fact that] the public utilities, public organizations and semi-public organizations are serving large portions of the people, it is plain we have an obligation for the protection of the facilities when we have information of a subversive nature concerning them."[50]

At this time it is impossible to evaluate definitively the scope and impact of the FBI's Responsibilities Program. First, Hoover's requirement that SACs convey any information verbally ensured that no comprehensive record would be created of all FBI dissemination activities. Second, released records of the FBI's Responsibilities Program have been heavily redacted. The exceptional snippets of unredacted information nonetheless provide insights into the general contours and underlying political purpose of a program intended to purge "subversives" from teaching or public service appointments at the local and state levels.

For example, under the Responsibilities Program, information was provided to Chicago, Seattle, Cleveland, and New York police officials; to state attorneys general; to the mayor of Detroit; to the New York City Housing Authority; to the heads of private charitable organizations, such as the Damon Runyon Cancer Fund, the March of Dimes, and the Boy Scouts of America; and to the president of the New York Telephone Company. The largest volume of such information related to elementary and secondary school and university teachers, including those at Temple University, Harvard, MIT, the University of California at Berkeley, and the University of Wisconsin at Madison. In one case, forewarned about the radical background of Pete Seeger, Ohio governor Frank Lausche interceded to cancel the folk singer's appearance at the Ohio State Fair.[51]

FBI officials did not blindly assist all governors and other designated officials, only those they considered reliable. In some cases, FBI agents launched investigations to determine a governor's reliability. None was required for New Mexico governor and former FBI agent Edwin Mechem. A report describing Louisiana governor Robert Kennon as "very political minded, and was given to doing those things which were politically expedient for him to do," led senior FBI officials to decide not to provide information to him. FBI officials also decided not to leak information to California governor Goodwin Knight, in light of a report characterizing him as a person who "perhaps does not discriminate among the people he becomes acquainted with, and that perhaps he is somewhat gullible in these respects." Assistance to Pennsylvania governor John Fine and to Texas governor Allen Shivers was terminated following their criticisms of the FBI, and to Arkansas governor Frank Cherry when it was learned that he had disclosed his source as the FBI.[52]

Throughout the term of the Responsibilities Program, FBI officials' principal concern was that their assistance never become known. For this reason alone, FBI officials had initially been reluctant to disseminate information to governors and state officials about primary and secondary teachers. Awareness of this practice, they feared, "could be twisted by the Communist Party and its sympathizers into an endeavor by the FBI to control the thinking in the educational field." After weighing this risk, they soon concluded that "the public has now [May 1951] become educated to the dangers of Communism and that public opinion will now back up the dissemination of such information by the FBI." FBI officials, furthermore, were confident that "the risks would be minimized by careful selection of the responsible officials to whom this information would be given."[53]

This decision to expand FBI dissemination, however, quickly bedeviled FBI officials owing to the recipients' public use of the leaked information. Thus in April 1953 a California legislative committee claimed that six hundred public school teachers in Los Angeles were or had been Communist party members. The report cited the FBI as its source. A New York City school official made a similar disclosure. Then, when local school board officials fired five teachers because of their alleged Communist affiliations (based on information provided by Colorado governor Dan Thornton to state school board officials), the Colorado Federation of Teachers insisted upon examining the evidence. In a news article about this firing, the *Denver Post* quoted the executive secretary of the teachers union as stating that the school board had admitted that the source of the information about these teachers was the Justice Department and the FBI. In a follow-up series of interviews, Governor Thornton first denied any knowledge of the source but later admitted that he and other governors regularly received information from the FBI. Thornton's admission followed rumors widely circulated in California that California governor Earl Warren regularly received similar information from the FBI and circulated this information to California state officials. In another publicized incident, in November 1953, Cincinnati city manager William Kellogg defended his characterization of the director of the City Planning

Commission, Sydney Williams, as a Communist sympathizer, and said he had relied on information provided by the FBI.[54]

Responding to these recurring disclosures of FBI assistance, senior FBI officials in October 1953 debated whether to continue the Responsibilities Program. They recommended to Hoover that "the advantages of disseminating information under the program outweighed the disadvantages." While concurring, the FBI director demanded more restrictive guidelines and for the first time briefed the attorney general, Herbert Brownell, about this ongoing program. In response, Brownell informed Hoover that he had "no objection to your continuing practice . . . of disseminating information to the Governors of the various states."[55]

The confidentiality issue arose again in March 1954 when Assistant Attorney General Warren Olney, during a trip to California, learned that it was common knowledge among University of California faculty members that the FBI regularly provided information to California state officials. Briefed on Olney's discovery, Hoover ordered the head of the FBI's San Francisco office to determine whether the FBI's California recipient could keep the bureau's assistance secret. Learning that the recipient had widely disseminated FBI-provided information, Hoover banned further FBI leaks to this person "in view of the bad impression it is creating." Again senior FBI officials met to evaluate the continuation of the Responsibilities Program. Despite recurring disclosure problems, they concluded, the program was "an effective weapon of harassment of the Communist Party." Hoover reluctantly endorsed this recommendation, anticipating that "we are going to have more and more headaches with it."[56]

Hoover's reservations proved to be prescient. Triggered by Colorado governor Thornton's admissions, the *Denver Post* in an editorial criticized the FBI's dissemination practices as "extremely questionable," emphasizing that FBI information should be released only "as required to conduct prosecution of federal law."[57]

Colorado Commissioner of Education H. Grant Vest shared the concerns of the *Post*'s editors and wrote U.S. Commissioner of Education Samuel Brownell to protest the FBI's practice of disseminating information to Thornton and other governors. Brownell forwarded Vest's letter to his brother, the attorney general, who in turn urged Hoover to consider modifying the Responsibilities Program "at least as to educational officers."[58]

FBI officials rejected the attorney general's suggestion. FBI assistant director Leland Boardman summarized their reasoning: "Communist infiltration of the education system" was extremely "dangerous"—it could "slant the attitudes of many . . . students toward a tolerance of Communistic ideals." Hoover concurred.[59]

But Thornton's admission soon posed an additional public relations problem when *Denver Post* editor Lawrence Martin decided to investigate teacher dismissal practices. The *Post* published his findings in a series of articles titled "Faceless Informers." Martin's series sharply criticized the practice whereby school officials dismissed teachers without having independently evaluated information leaked by the FBI. Hoover called Attorney General Brownell's attention to this series.[60]

Still unwilling to abort the program, Hoover extolled the FBI's "definite responsibility to the public interest." Teachers, the FBI director counseled his boss, posed a particularly serious threat since they were "in an excellent position to mold the minds of our youth." Unwilling to challenge the FBI director, Brownell demurred making any decision but did inquire about how the program could be quietly ended. Hoover thereupon temporarily discontinued the program until the attorney general reached a final decision on its future.[61]

Meeting with Brownell on November 8, 1954, Hoover championed the program's value in fighting communism and expressed bewilderment that "the Board of Education . . . had not given as much attention to finding out who the Communists were as they were giving to finding out who furnished the information to the Governor of Colorado." Brownell agreed to continue the Responsibilities Program but insisted on new safeguards to ensure its confidentiality. He would reconsider this decision, the attorney general warned Hoover, should there be future leaks. On November 16 the program was thus reinstituted.[62]

Three months later, in February 1955, Hoover was alerted to the publication of the *Denver Post* series, now titled "Faceless Informers and Our Schools," in pamphlet form that would be sent to school boards around the country. Hoover and Brownell then decided to terminate the Responsibilities Program.[63]

The FBI's secret relationships with Senator McCarthy, SISS, and state governors had all been compromised because ambitious politicians had purposefully or unwittingly violated Hoover's condition that the FBI's assistance was not to be disclosed. As it happened, the FBI's most politically sensitive—and crudely partisan—action of the 1950s, the wiretapping of Henry Grunewald, was never vulnerable to this risk of disclosure.

A private investigator, Grunewald had been hired by insurance executive Henry Marsh during the 1930s to report to him on administrative and legislative initiatives in New Deal Washington. Over the ensuing decade Grunewald developed excellent contacts with isolationist Republicans in Congress and also with the former aide to President Franklin Roosevelt, Thomas Corcoran. Grunewald's political connections led to his being investigated and wiretapped by the FBI, first in 1940 and then again in 1945–1946.[64]

A colorful character, Grunewald acquired a well-founded reputation as a "fixer" and "influence peddler." Indeed, his shady activities and mercenary interests soon brought him to national prominence in 1951–1952 during congressional investigations into allegations of corruption by appointees of the Truman administration. Subpoenaed to testify during hearings into tax fraud conducted by a House Ways and Means subcommittee chaired by

Cecil King, Grunewald was an uncooperative witness. His refusal to answer the committee's questions led to his indictment on October 23, 1952, on twenty-two counts of contempt of Congress.

The so-called Truman "scandals" emerged as a powerful political issue that Republican congressional and presidential candidates successfully exploited during the 1952 elections—supplementing their criticisms of Truman's "softness toward communism." Buoyed by the success of this tactic that resulted in Republican control of both the White House and Congress, congressional Republicans and Attorney General Brownell intended to continue to indict Democratic corruption. The House Ways and Means subcommittee, now chaired by the Republican Robert Kean, revisited the Grunewald matter. And Justice Department officials sought to pressure Grunewald into cooperating by threatening a harsh sentence and further prosecution. These complementary objectives were promoted by Grunewald's pre-hearings discussions with and public testimony before the Kean Committee in March–April 1953, coincident with his trial and sentencing on the contempt of Congress charges.

Grunewald's trial on the contempt charges was to have begun on March 16, but it was delayed until March 17 owing to the heavy court docket of presiding judge Alexander Holtzoff. Although Grunewald pleaded guilty to the contempt charges, his sentencing was delayed pending his testimony before the Kean Committee. Pressured to cooperate, Grunewald continued to evade answering the committee's questions. Indeed, during sentencing hearings on June 4, Justice Department attorneys advised the court that Grunewald had not been fully cooperative. Nonetheless Judge Holtzoff handed down a fairly lenient sentence—a $1,000 fine and one year in prison, suspended to ninety days' parole.

Grunewald's legal difficulties had not ended. On July 22, 1954, a grand jury indicted him on ten counts of perjury for his testimony before the Kean Committee. And another grand jury indicted Grunewald and others on October 25 for his role in a tax fraud conspiracy during 1946–1951. Justice Department officials later dropped the perjury indictment, claiming that new evidence would preclude a successful conviction. But Grunewald was convicted of the tax fraud conspiracy charges on March 28, 1955. The Supreme Court overturned this conviction, ordering a new trial. Grunewald's second trial ended in a hung jury.

The FBI wiretapped Grunewald during the critical period dating from the start of his contempt of Congress trial through his discussions and testimony before the Kean Committee and then his sentencing hearing. Installed on March 16, 1953, the FBI's wiretap was first confined to Grunewald's Washington residence. Upon discovering that he was spending a "considerable amount of time" at his daughter's residence, and based on Attorney General Brownell's authorization of "any other residence or office space which he might occupy in the future," the FBI wiretapped her phone on April 9. FBI officials also considered wiretapping Grunewald's vacation residence in Spring Lake, New Jersey, but concluded that this wiretap might be discovered. Both the March 16 and April 9 wiretaps were terminated on June 18. FBI officials also obtained Grunewald's income tax files after ensuring that Treasury Department officials could not uncover their "reason for seeking this information." Such files, FBI officials concluded, could identify "any business ventures he might be affiliated with" as other wiretap possibilities.[65]

Wiretapping Grunewald was not Hoover's idea. Instead, "The Attorney General on February 3, 1953 requested that we [FBI] cover the activities of Grunewald and asked that a technical surveillance [wiretap] be instituted in his residence." But Hoover did pressure the FBI's Washington, D.C., field office to install the wiretap "as soon as possible so that this can be utilized as a lead." Hoover relayed the intercepted conversations daily to Brownell. At first Hoover's reports merely "digested" the contents of the intercepted conversations. On March 18, however, FBI assistant director D. Milton Ladd ordered FBI agents preparing these reports to include as well a chronological summary. Ladd explained "that there are many political ramifications to Grunewald's activities and, consequently, the chronological summary may contain isolated items to which significance might be attached." Deputy Attorney General William Rogers personally reviewed the FBI reports and, on one occasion, requested an FBI investigation of "four items of testimony of Grunewald before the Kean Committee." A May 29, 1953, request of the head of the FBI's Washington, D.C., field office further confirms the underlying political purpose of the Grunewald wiretapping operation. Should the Grunewald tap "be continued" after Grunewald's June 4 sentencing hearing, the Washington SAC inquired of Hoover, or should the tap be discontinued "immediately following the sentencing"?[66]

Hoover's reports provided the attorney general with invaluable intelligence about Grunewald's plans—useful to the Kean Committee in questioning him, useful in persuading Judge Holtzoff to hand down a harsh sentence, and useful in providing information leading to an indictment on criminal charges. Thus FBI officials learned from these wiretaps, and duly reported, Grunewald's trial strategy in the contempt case, his specific concerns that his subpoenaed testimony before the Kean Committee could influence his sentencing hearing, his specific conversations with his attorneys (one of whom was also being investigated by the Kean Committee), his specific responses to the Kean Committee's subpoena, his specific reactions to the Committee's questions, and his comments on the various tax fraud and other activities that were central to both the Kean Committee hearings and Justice Department prosecution. Consistent with his own judgmental moralism, Hoover's reports to the attorney general also detailed Grunewald's obscenity-laden conversations and womanizing.[67]

Grunewald was not a Soviet spy. Nor did he have access to

classified information. Nonetheless FBI officials classified this wiretap operation as an espionage investigation. Hoover's wiretap authorization request to Brownell was captioned "Security Information—Secret," and its purpose was misleadingly justified as "In connection with a possible unauthorized leak of official Government information."[68] Intended to minimize the risk that the FBI director's witting assistance of a partisan Republican initiative might be discovered, Hoover's subterfuge underscores how easily FBI officials could shift from promoting partisan anti-communism to partisan Republicanism.

The decision to wiretap Grunewald was potentially explosive. Had it been known at the time, it would have raised serious questions about FBI methods and purposes—the willingness of FBI officials to employ illegal investigative techniques and to do so to further the partisan objectives of a Republican administration. Yet this wiretapping operation proved to be far less risky than the FBI's covert assistance to Senators McCarthy, Jenner, and Mundt, to Father John Cronin, and to Governors Cherry and Thornton.* Hoover never worried that Attorney General Brownell would inadvertently or purposefully disclose the FBI's role. In fact, although in July 1954 Justice Department officials had sought and obtained Grunewald's perjury indictment in the friendly forum of a federal grand jury, they dropped prosecution in October 1955—ostensibly because of "new evidence"—rather than risk the possibility that the Grunewald wiretap might be disclosed during the adversary proceeding of a trial.

*This recalls President Warren G. Harding's lament to the journalist William Allen White in 1923: "I have no trouble with my enemies . . I can take care of my enemies all right. But my damn friends . . . they're the ones that keep me walking the floor nights."

CHAPTER NINE

• • •

The Lessons of History

ARE THE lessons of history that there are no secrets? The released KGB, Venona, and FBI records would seem to suggest that there are few. Soviet agents did steal some of the more sensitive U.S. military, technological, and diplomatic secrets, and U.S. counterintelligence agents in turn did learn about Soviet espionage operations and successfully identify some Soviet agents and their American sources.

But the unredacted FBI records document that the bureau uncovered only some of the Soviet Union's espionage operations while the accessible KGB and Venona records provide at best an incomplete picture of the scope of Soviet espionage activities. All relevant FBI and KGB records have not been released; only a portion of the Soviet consular messages transmitted during the years 1940–1948 were successfully deciphered, and most of the released FBI counterintelligence records are heavily redacted. The deciphered Venona messages and the KGB records confirm that Soviet agents obtained sensitive U.S. secrets relating to the Manhattan

Project and the development of the atomic bomb. They also learned of the negotiating strategies of U.S. and British officials on the status of postwar Europe and the Balkans, drafted in preparation for the Yalta Conference. Released FBI records do not explain why Soviet agents and their American recruits were not apprehended and prosecuted.

Other KGB and Venona records document not espionage but political intelligence operations: reports on the plans and objectives of Democratic and Republican officials; operations directed against Communist political adversaries—Trotskyites, Russian monarchists, Social Democrats, Russian Orthodox prelates, and anti-Russian Polish Americans; relations between the Soviet Union and other foreign governments, notably Nazi Germany; information uncovered through normal investigative reporting by American reporters and columnists; and statistical information about U.S. industrial production and military strength during World War II. The latter reports, however, were not necessarily damaging to U.S. security interests because they pertained to the military capabilities of a wartime ally, or because U.S. officials already shared similar information with Soviet officials under the lend-lease program.

The Venona Project findings document a U.S. counterintelligence success in first intercepting and then deciphering coded Soviet consular messages. This intelligence breakthrough might not have shut down Soviet espionage operations during World War II, but it did belatedly identify Soviet agents Klaus Fuchs, Donald Maclean, Kim Philby, Harry Gold, David Greenglass, Julius Rosenberg, Theodore Hall, and Judith Coplon, and apparently disabled potentially far more harmful espionage operations during the post-1945 period. U.S. intelligence officials also learned that KGB recruits William Weisband and Kim Philby had already briefed their Soviet contacts of the Venona Project breakthrough, and that this had undoubtedly triggered Soviet corrective measures to preserve the confidentiality of future coded communications. Yet the disabling of Soviet espionage owed little to the effectiveness of FBI counterintelligence.

The Venona and KGB records confirm that leaders of the American Communist party had served either as couriers or had recruited individuals to steal U.S. secrets for the Soviet Union. But as early as the late 1930s, FBI officials already knew that the Soviet Union was funding the American Communist party, and that Communist officials in 1939 had formed an underground operation to preclude discovery of their activities, and in 1943 had arranged for a meeting between Soviet agent Vassili Zubilin and the American Communist Steve Nelson to fund the placement "of Communist Party members and Comintern agents in industries engaged in secret war production for the United States Government so this information could be obtained for transmittal to the Soviet Union."[1] While the discovery of proposed espionage led to the massive code-named CINRAD and COMRAP investigations, it remains unclear whether the FBI uncovered or contained specific Soviet espionage operations.

The fact that the Soviets spied on the United States and that the United States counterspied is in itself not a startling revelation. The recently opened records confirm only what presidents, most people in the intelligence community, and sophisticated political commentators already suspected. These records do not demand a reassessment of the conventional wisdom, adding at best helpful detail or documenting the perversity of both U.S. and Soviet intelligence and counterintelligence operations. Nor was it particularly unusual that Soviet agents operating in the United States during World War II recruited ideologically driven sources. Both U.S. and Soviet intelligence operatives paid the sources they recruited, and both also looked for recruits who for ideological reasons were willing to betray their country's secrets—whether they were committed American Communists and Communist sympathizers (for the Soviets) or disaffected Soviet Communists (for the United States).

Furthermore, it is debatable whether Soviet espionage or American counterintelligence operations changed the course of history in any important way. Would the Soviets have adopted a more moderate negotiating stance at the Yalta and Potsdam conferences, pursued a different military or diplomatic strategy during World War II, or have been unable to develop atomic and nuclear weapons were it not for their successful recruitment of American and British Communists to spy on their behalf? The released FBI records do, however, document another, more disturbing consequence: the politicization of intelligence and a successful covert effort to influence public opinion.

Perhaps the best available, if indirect, evidence of the limited value of espionage and counterintelligence operations is the differing results of U.S. covert operations in postwar Europe.

The sharp deterioration in U.S.-Soviet relations from 1945 to 1947, with the onset of the cold war, led U.S. policymakers to authorize a series of covert operations during the years 1947–1952 to contain Communist influence in Western and Eastern Europe. These included the funding of the Christian Democrats in the 1948 Italian elections; an anti-Communist trade union movement in France; and propaganda, psychological warfare, sabotage, and guerrilla operations in Eastern Europe, the Balkans, and the Soviet Union. The Italian and French covert operations succeeded while those in Eastern Europe, the Balkans, and the Soviet Union were abysmal failures.[2] Public programs such as the Marshall Plan and the NATO alliance, which promoted economic and political stability in Italy and France, were far more important to the containment of communism than the CIA's covert operations. The absence of such aid programs helps explain why similar covert operations had little chance of success in Eastern Europe, the Balkans, and the Soviet Union.

Until recently, historians and other analysts of cold war internal security policy have focused narrowly on the alleged "softness toward communism" of the Roosevelt and Truman administrations. In the process they have not asked why FBI counterintelligence operations failed to apprehend and convict Soviet agents and their American recruits. And while Senator McCarthy's and HUAC's activities have commanded intensive interest, far less attention has been devoted to the FBI's politics of counterintelligence. Recently released—though heavily redacted—FBI records offer insights into both this counterintelligence failure and FBI officials' broader political purposes. They also raise disturbing questions about how secrecy, ostensibly for counterintelligence reasons, undermined limited, constitutional government based on the rule of law and accountability.

We should have known that the FBI's use of illegal investigative techniques during counterintelligence investigations had sometimes precluded the prosecution of suspected spies. But we did not know until recently another by-product of this counterintelligence dilemma: the creation of a culture of lawlessness. This is indirectly illustrated by one of the most emotionally debated developments of the early cold war years, the defection of Elizabeth Bentley.

In the aftermath of Bentley's confessions in 1945, FBI officials launched an intensive investigation to determine whether individuals whom she identified were Soviet spies. To do so, FBI agents illegally wiretapped twenty of the persons she named, beginning in November–December 1945, with some taps continuing until 1947. Had they intended to prosecute these individuals, FBI officials should not have used wiretaps. Under prevailing court rulings, any indictment based on evidence obtained through wiretaps would be dismissed. Nonetheless Justice Department officials convened a grand jury in 1947–1948. No indictments, however, were then obtained against anyone whom Bentley had named. A 1946 FBI report to the Truman White House apparently confirms that the FBI's intensive investigation—which included other illegal investigative techniques besides wiretaps, namely break-ins and mail openings—uncovered no evidence that these individuals committed espionage. In the case of at least one of the targets of these FBI wiretaps, Harry Dexter White, U.S. attorneys unsuccessfully tried to exploit the intercepted conversations to entrap White and to impugn his credibility with the grand jurors. These actions raise disturbing questions as to why FBI officials would request and attorneys general authorize wiretaps of individuals subject to a criminal inquiry, and, further, why Justice Department attorneys would then seek to launder intercepted information during the questioning of witnesses in grand jury proceedings. Recently released FBI records confirm another dimension of the practice—how secrecy itself became an all-consuming objective.

By 1966, FBI wiretapping and bugging practices had provoked critical congressional and media investigations, triggered by disclosures during the so-called Fred Black Case (in which the conviction of a Washington lobbyist for tax evasion was overturned by the Supreme Court when it was learned that the FBI had bugged his residence and office).[3] The resulting controversy caused FBI officials to assess whether to continue employing such illegal investigative techniques during criminal and national security investigations. At the same time they reconsidered their long-established policy of retaining wiretap logs that were more than twenty years old. Indeed, the head of the FBI's Washington, D.C., field office recommended destroying the wiretap logs of the twenty individuals who had been wiretapped during the Bentley investigation, owing to "the unsettled position the courts were taking on information emanating from, or connected with, technical surveillance." Because of the Supreme Court's ruling in the Black case, senior FBI officials rejected this record destruction proposal, though they urged the Washington SAC to resubmit it "If, at a later date, you feel the original information in the logs . . . will not be subject of court inquiry in the future."

The Washington SAC resubmitted this request in 1970, emphasizing that "all" subsequent FBI investigations had "failed to break the apparent conspiracy of silence" of those named by Bentley, and that there "appears to be no possibility of any prosecution or court inquiry at any time." Hoover again rejected the recommendation. Conceding that it was "well reasoned," the FBI director stressed that one of the twenty, Alger Hiss, had a pending suit challenging the special law that Congress had enacted in 1950 denying him a government pension. "It is not believed to be an opportune time," Hoover counseled, "to destroy the technical surveillance logs of Hiss and [the other 19] listed" by the Washington SAC. But he should resubmit this request whenever a court decision was "reached" on Hiss's suit.

This confirmation of the FBI's wiretapping of individuals currently under investigation and of FBI officials' interest in destroying the logs of these wiretaps was discoverable because they were recorded in memoranda in the FBI's Record Destruction File. Had the Washington SAC's recommendation been approved in 1970, not only the wiretap logs would have been destroyed; the memorandum recommending this record destruction would also have been done away with. Inadvertently, these records confirm that the FBI's Record Destruction File does not constitute a complete record of all FBI record destruction decisions and practices.[4]

The proposal to destroy both the wiretap logs and the memorandum recommending this destruction was not an atypical practice. Another sensitive FBI program became discoverable owing to a recorded decision to destroy records.

Dating at least from the 1940s, FBI officials compiled "summary" memoranda on prominent politicians—members of Congress, governors, and presidential and vice presidential candidates and their key advisers. In his secret office file FBI director Hoover maintained some of the more sensitive "summary" memoranda. These records related to Democratic senator and 1960 Democratic presidential nominee John Kennedy, Republican senator and 1960 Republican vice presidential nominee Henry Cabot Lodge, and Illinois governor and 1952 and 1956 Democratic presidential nominee Adlai Stevenson.[5]

By the 1950s this informal, ad hoc practice had been refined to ensure that "summary memoranda" would be prepared on all candidates for election to Congress. FBI assistant director Louis Nichols verbally instructed senior officials at FBI headquarters to institute "a systematic review of data" maintained at FBI headquarters and to incorporate in summary memoranda "any information" forwarded by the heads of FBI field offices. In 1960 all SACs were first instructed in writing to review their office's files and then forward to FBI headquarters in Washington any information on congressional candidates "by routing slip, not letter" or in "sealed envelopes addressed to the Crime Records Division." "This matter was to be handled discreetly and the information submitted in an informal [non record] basis," and no "formal [i.e., recorded and indexed in the FBI central records system] communication" was to be created. Furthermore, when SACs on "rare occasions" submitted data "in formal communications," they were "orally instructed to remove from the files all copies of the material, and the communications were treated here [FBI headquarters] as informal ones with no record being created in Bureau files." On receipt of this information from SACs, FBI officials in Washington incorporated it with whatever information had already been filed at FBI headquarters to comprise the "summary" memorandum on the congressional candidate.

To ensure that the retention of such records could never be discovered, these memoranda were maintained in the FBI's Administrative Review Unit, separate from official FBI records, where they were filed alphabetically and "updated on a continuing basis." They included the attitude of the candidate (and then member of Congress) toward law enforcement, but also information on his personal background, "allegations of criminal or corrupt practices, subversive activities, and immoral conduct." Should the candidate be defeated, the prepared memorandum was destroyed. Similarly, should an elected member of Congress be defeated, the memorandum was to be kept for six years in the event he was later reelected. After that, the memorandum was destroyed.[6]

The "summary" memorandum procedure was an ingenious system which allowed senior FBI officials to deny that "files" or "dossiers" were maintained on members of Congress. No such files or dossiers could be uncovered through a search of the FBI's central records system—nor could it have been discovered that a system had been established whereby officials at FBI headquarters, assisted by SACs, purposefully compiled and maintained derogatory information on members of Congress.

Despite the care taken to prevent discovery of this practice, in October 1972 the "summary memorandum" procedure was inadvertently compromised. A zealous FBI agent in Ohio, "contrary to specific instructions," contacted the local newspaper that month to request information about a Democratic congressional candidate. Having become acting FBI director just six months earlier, and unaware of this Hoover-era policy, L. Patrick Gray III demanded a briefing. To allay congressional and press concerns raised by the Ohio incident, Gray ordered that the practice be discontinued and that all summary memoranda were to be immediately destroyed.

Officials in the FBI's Files and Communications Division did not automatically comply with Gray's order. They informed him that under provisions of the Federal Records Act of 1950, the FBI "cannot destroy materials in our files without specific authority from the Archivist of the United States."

The FBI's Office of Legal Counsel dissented from the Files and

Communications Division's conclusion about the need to obtain the Archivist's approval. The 1950 Act "can reasonably be interpreted," the Office of Legal Counsel argued, to exclude the summary memoranda "in that such information was not received by the FBI under any provision of Federal law or in any necessary connection with the transaction of public business." The Office of Legal Counsel identified a further consequence of any such request: the "definite possibility that the Congress can get into the act," since the administrator of General Services, who supervised the National Archives, was authorized under this legislation to seek the "advice and counsel" of Congress—which "conceivably will be the opening by which members of Congress could get their hands on this raw material." The Office of Legal Counsel accordingly urged Gray to take this matter up with the attorney general, since the Department of Justice might concur "with our conclusion that . . . [this material] is not an official FBI record, and never was, and hence can be destroyed without permission of the Archivist." Gray thereupon solicited the attorney general's guidance as to whether the FBI could destroy the summary memoranda "without the Archivist's knowledge or permission." When the department concluded that the Archivist's approval was required, Gray decided to "take the position that summary memoranda are a part of FBI official files; will not be disclosed to unauthorized persons; and permission will not be requested from Archives to destroy."[7] They may or may not be extant.

These were not the sole instances in which FBI officials tried to sanitize the record.[8] Dating from 1940, and refined in succeeding years, Hoover authorized a series of separate records procedures to ensure the undiscoverable destruction of especially sensitive records.

The first of these records procedures—"blue," revised to "pink" and then to "informal" memoranda—were intended to ensure the undiscoverable destruction of informal (nonrecord) communications among senior FBI officials. Written on specially colored paper, these memoranda contained the following printed notation on the bottom: "This Memorandum Is for Administrative Purposes. To Be Destroyed After Action Is Taken and Not Sent to Files." In 1942, Hoover extended this procedure to all SAC requests for his required approval to conduct break-ins. Such memoranda were to be captioned "Do Not File" to ensure that they would not be indexed and serialized in the FBI's central records system. This notation enabled FBI officials, when processing communications from field offices, to route these submissions immediately to FBI assistant directors to be filed in their office files. The SAC submitting such requests simultaneously created "informal" memoranda "showing he obtained Bureau [FBI headquarters] authority, and this memorandum is filed in his [office] safe until the next inspection by Bureau inspectors at which time it is destroyed." The intent of the blue/pink/informal and the Do Not File procedures was to ensure the undiscoverable destruction of especially sensitive records. Even this fail-safe system had its drawbacks when senior FBI officials at FBI headquarters failed to destroy the contents of their office files regularly. Accordingly, in March 1953 Hoover ordered them "periodically [to] review their [office] memoranda and destroy them as promptly as possible but in no case shall they be retained in excess of six months."[9]

FBI officials were not alone in sanitizing records. Upon leaving office in 1973, CIA director Richard Helms ordered his secretary to destroy the contents of his office file, including transcripts of his office conversations. Senior CIA officials during the 1960s destroyed virtually all agency records pertaining to the covert operation to overthrow the Mossadeq government in Iran and restore the Shah to the throne; in 1991 destroyed the agency's file on Chilean secret police chief Manuel Contreras, a CIA informer who was later convicted for ordering a car bombing in Washington, D.C., that resulted in the death of Chilean exile Orlando Letelier and an American associate; and in 1973 destroyed the records of the agency's drug testing programs. "Precautions" must be taken, the CIA's inspector general wrote in 1957, to preclude the discovery of the CIA's drug testing program "not only to protect operations from exposure to enemy forces but also to conceal these activities from the American public in general. The knowledge that the agency is engaging in unethical and illicit activities would have serious consequences in political and diplomatic circles and would be detrimental to the accomplishment of [the CIA's] mission."[10]

The interest in secrecy was not intended to safeguard sensitive information from foreign spies. Classified information was maintained in safes and restricted to individuals with the required security clearance. The purpose behind record destruction procedures was to ensure that specific records would never see the light of day. The Do Not File procedure particularly underscores this political purpose to avert public, judicial, or congressional scrutiny.

The only extant FBI memorandum that unwittingly describes in detail the nature and purpose of this records procedure was prepared by FBI assistant director William Sullivan. He began by conceding that break-ins were "clearly illegal," a rather stark admission for a law enforcement official. The Do Not File system ensured that no record of a request to conduct a break-in would be indexed or filed in the FBI's central records system, thereby precluding the possible discovery of "clearly illegal" investigative activities in those instances when FBI officials had to respond to court-ordered discovery motions or congressional subpoenas. FBI assistant director Charles Brennan conceded that advantage during 1975 congressional testimony, in responding to a series of pointed questions posed by Republican senator Richard Schweiker. In framing his queries, Schweiker aptly characterized the Do Not File procedure as the "perfect coverup" and "really total deception." FBI officials' assertions that the FBI central records system contained no record of illegal conduct, Schweiker observed, "would be technically" truthful "because of the way that wording is constructed."[11]

The lessons of history, then, are that there *are* secrets. In the case of the FBI, these secrets undermined a system of government based on accountability and the rule of law. Secrecy also subverted the ability of the attorney general to oversee FBI operations* and meet his responsibility to ensure that constitutional limitations were honored.

Recognizing that break-ins, for example, were "clearly illegal," FBI officials did "not obtain authorization . . . from outside the Bureau [i.e., the attorney general]. Such a technique involves trespass and is clearly illegal; therefore, it would be impossible to obtain any legal sanction for it." But FBI officials' willingness to authorize break-ins was not their sole approval of "clearly illegal" activity conducted without the attorney general's knowledge. From the early 1940s to 1951, FBI officials did not inform the attorney general of FBI microphone surveillances, the installation of which normally required trespass. In October 1951, FBI director Hoover briefed Attorney General J. Howard McGrath about such installations. He had no problem, McGrath responded, when microphones were installed without trespass—that is, spike microphones installed in the wall of an adjoining room. But those installed by means of trespass "are in the area of the Fourth Amendment, and evidence so obtained and from leads so obtained is inadmissible." McGrath continued, "The records [of the attorney general's office] do not indicate that this question dealing with microphones has ever been presented before; therefore,

*Seemingly a frequent FBI practice, as highlighted by FBI officials' insubordination when leaking information to Senator McCarthy in 1950; covertly collaborating with Congressman Nixon in August–December 1948 during the HUAC hearings and the Hiss grand jury proceedings; and blackmailing Justice Department officials—re the Corcoran wiretap—to influence their 1950 testimony relating to the *Amerasia* case plea-bargain decision.

please be advised that I cannot authorize the installation of a microphone *involving a trespass* under existing law."

McGrath knew that such installations were illegal, but he did not explicitly ban this FBI practice. And despite the attorney general's conclusion, FBI officials did not abandon their practice. They simply scaled back microphone installations and monitored them more closely. Because they continued to contravene a written (if secret) conclusion of the attorney general, FBI officials recognized their vulnerability unless this formal position was either rescinded or modified. The opportunity came in 1952 with the election of the more security-minded Eisenhower administration and the appointment of Herbert Brownell as attorney general. Ostensibly seeking guidance about a recent Supreme Court decision in *Irvine v. California,* FBI officials in 1954 advised Brownell that "in a few instances" microphones had been installed "on our own" and yet "we [FBI] should have more backing of the [Justice] Department to utilize microphone surveillance where the intelligence to be gained was a necessary adjunct to security matters and important investigations, in instances where prosecution is not contemplated." They urged Brownell to institute the same procedures as those governing wiretaps: namely, that the attorney general review and authorize each FBI microphone installation. Unwilling to accept responsibility for formally authorizing such practices, Brownell instead issued a generally worded secret order that ceded broad latitude to FBI officials, with no need to obtain his approval. As justification, Brownell urged, "the Attorney General would be in a much better position to defend the Bureau in the event there should be a technical trespass if he had not heretofore approved it."

Brownell's decision to defer to Hoover ensured that the FBI director alone would decide whether to install microphones and whether to brief the attorney general on the scope and targets of such practices.

This arrangement continued until 1965 when Attorney General Nicholas Katzenbach required his own advance approval of each microphone installation, and further directed that ongoing approved microphones must be reauthorized every six months. Under Katzenbach's rules, Justice Department officials regularly briefed the courts whenever an FBI microphone had been employed in cases that went to trial.

Katzenbach's new rules and procedures infuriated FBI officials. FBI assistant director James Gale succinctly summarized the mindset of FBI officials toward the attorney general, the courts, and Congress. In a May 1966 memorandum, Gale starkly admitted that, of the 738 microphones installed by the FBI between 1960 and 1966, Justice Department officials or U.S. attorneys prosecuting a case had been notified of only 158 of these "sources." Should FBI officials notify the Justice Department about all FBI microphones, Gale contended—adding that his view was shared by the FBI's "three investigative divisions"—department officials would likely inform "the courts with resultant adverse publicity to the Bureau which could give rise in the present climate to a demand for a Congressional inquiry of the Bureau." FBI officials, Gale continued, should not have "to rely on the internal security of the Department's operations" since "the Department in its zeal to be all things to all men in law enforcement is frequently working with such groups as the President's Crime Commission, special committees in Congress inquiring into matters of a criminal nature and with numerous local, state and Federal investigators seeking information which they feel they cannot obtain elsewhere." Such advance notification, Gale observed, could encourage Justice Department officials to drop the prosecution of organized crime cases, admitting that "the Department has successfully prosecuted 15 hoodlums of whom we are aware, but of whom the Department had no knowledge of our microphone coverage."[12]

The FBI's interest in secrecy and in minimizing the attorney general's oversight role was not predicated on national security considerations or even the possibility that leaks might compromise legitimate security interests. Gale's memorandum conveys the sense of righteousness and injured innocence and the culture of lawlessness that shaped FBI policies. His memorandum further confirms how secrecy encouraged FBI officials to act independently, even insubordinately.

The ideological considerations that underlay the FBI's secret politics of counterintelligence bring to mind the ideologically motivated actions of other federal employees. Ideology led American Communists and Communist sympathizers to deliver classified documents to Soviet agents during the 1930s and World War II. These individuals made a conscious decision to convey such information to individuals whom they knew to be agents of a foreign power, even if they were temporary military allies. While not in every case treasonous, their actions violated the public trust and their responsibilities as federal employees to comply with the law and adhere to official policies.

The motivations of FBI officials may have been sincerely patriotic, based on their own political views of the nation's security interests. Their decisions to leak information to ideologically supportive members of Congress and journalists nonetheless damaged a democratic system of limited government. They were not disinterested professionals; they exploited secrecy to shroud their insubordination and their efforts to influence the political culture and promote, in the words of FBI assistant director Louis Nichols, "the cause." One by-product of this culture of secrecy was that it prevented a critical examination of the FBI's failure to apprehend and help convict Soviet spies. For, in a final irony that even George Orwell would have deemed Orwellian, the special Do Not File procedure devised by the nation's chief law enforcement official precluded the discovery of his authorization of "clearly illegal" activities.

Notes

PREFACE: THE HAZARDS OF RESEARCH INTO SOVIET AND AMERICAN SECRETS

1. Allen Weinstein and Alexander Vassiliev, *The Haunted Wood: Soviet Espionage in America—the Stalin Era* (New York, 1999), pp. xi, xv–xvii.
2. Harvey Klehr, John Earl Haynes, and Kyrill M. Anderson, *The Soviet World of American Communism* (New Haven, 1998), pp. xiii–xvi.
3. Robert Louis Benson and Michael Warner, eds., *Venona: Soviet Espionage and the American Response, 1939–1957* (Washington, D.C., 1996), pp. v, vii–viii, xii–xvi, xxx–xxxi; David Alvarez, *Secret Messages: Codebreaking and American Diplomacy, 1930–1945* (Lawrence, Kans., 2000), pp. 110, 112, 157, 202–205, 207–213, 218, 223; John Earl Haynes and Harvey Klehr, *Venona: Decoding Soviet Espionage in America* (New Haven, 1999), pp. ix, 6, 8–9, 23–36, 339; and Alexander Stephan, *"Communazis": FBI Surveillance of German Emigre Writers* (New Haven, 2000), p. 34. On the military's role in intercepting Soviet (and Axis) consular messages, see U.S. Senate, Select Committee to Study Governmental Operations with Respect to Intelligence Activities, *Special Detailed Staff Reports on Intelligence Activities and the Rights of Americans,* Book III, pp. 423, 767, and *Intelligence Activities and the Rights of Americans,* Book II, p. 58 (both 94th Cong., 2d. Sess., 1976); and *Hearings on Intelligence Activities,* Vol. 5, *The National Security Agency and Fourth Amendment Rights,* 94th Cong., 1st sess., 1975, pp. 6, 17, 58; U.S. House, Subcommittee of the Committee on Government Operations, *Hearings on the Interception of Nonverbal Communications by Federal Intelligence Agencies,* 94th Cong., 1st and 2d sess., 1975–1976, pp. 241, 249.

4. Benson and Warner, *Venona,* p. xxiv; Haynes and Klehr, *Venona,* p. 15; Daniel P. Moynihan, *Secrecy: The American Experience* (New Haven, 1998), pp. 70–71.
5. Moynihan, *Secrecy,* pp. 70–71 (a photocopy of the October 1949 FBI memorandum is reprinted on p. 72); Michael Warner, "Did Truman Know About Venona?" *Center for the Study of Intelligence Bulletin,* 11 (Summer 2000), pp. 2–4.
6. Roosevelt's orders were reaffirmed and expanded by Truman. Athan Theoharis, *Spying on Americans: Political Surveillance from Hoover to the Huston Plan* (Philadelphia, 1978), pp. 41–53, 67–80, 97–100, 105–106, 125–126, 130, 197–208; Athan Theoharis, ed., *From the Secret Files of J. Edgar Hoover* (Chicago, 1991), pp. 129–130, 133–139, 180–182, 184–194; Athan Theoharis and John Stuart Cox, *The Boss: J. Edgar Hoover and the Great American Inquisition* (Philadelphia, 1988), pp. 11–15, 150–154, 169–174, 178–185. These initiatives either lacked specific legislative authorization (preventive detention, "intelligence" investigations, investigations of federal employees) or were illegal (wiretapping, bugging, mail opening, break-ins).
7. Statistics compiled and provided by the Research/Communications Unit of the FBI, reprinted with annual breakdowns in Athan Theoharis, "A Brief History of the FBI's Role and Powers," in Athan Theoharis, ed., *The FBI: A Comprehensive Reference Guide* (Phoenix, 1999), pp. 4–5.
8. For a brief discussion of the FBI Executives' Conference, see Susan Rosenfeld, "Organization and Day-to-Day Activities," in Theoharis, *FBI Reference Guide,* p. 214. The following citations are a random sample of the FBI's "national security" redactions covering some of the memoranda of these meetings for the 1945–1951 period in the FBI Executives' Conference file. See Memos, FBI Executives Conference to FBI Director, February 17, 1945 (FBI 66-2554-3518); October 3, 1947 (FBI 66-2554-6371); November 4, 1947 (FBI 66-2554-6544); April 16, 1948 (FBI 66-2554-6764); May 22, 1948 (FBI 66-2554-6823); April 27, 1949 (FBI 66-2554-7216); and June 22, 1949 (FBI 66-2554-7288). See also Memo, Waikart to Nichols, June 15, 1951, FBI 66-2554–Not Recorded.

9. On the SAC Letters procedure, see Theoharis, "Brief History" and "Chronology of Key Events," in Theoharis, *FBI Reference Guide,* pp. 12, 362. The following citations of FBI "national security" redactions are from a random sampling of the SAC Letters file (66-04) for the 1939–1945 period. All were serialized Not Recorded. Some of the letters were captioned "Personal and Confidential," others "Strictly Confidential," and still others contained no caption. In some cases the context confirms that the redacted material pertained to Axis activities, others to Communist activities, while in other cases it is impossible to understand the targeted group or purpose. The following list identifies merely the date of the various redacted letters: December 22, 1939; October 24, 1940 (2); October 29, 1940; February 6, 1941; April 22, 1941; July 1, 1941; July 22, 1941; July 28, 1941; August 14, 1941; October 21, 1941; October 28, 1941; November 24, 1941; December 18, 1941; December 24, 1941; February 16, 1942; April 1, 1942; April 3, 1942; April 30, 1942; May 20, 1942; June 17, 1942; October 2, 1942; October 22, 1942; October 29, 1942; November 12, 1942; December 5, 1942; February 25, 1943; No. 152, Series 1943; No. 177, Series 1943; No. 282, Series 1943; No. 286, Series 1943; No. 351, Series 1943 (August 23, 1943); No. 491, Series 1943; May 10, 1944; October 18, 1944. See also Letter, Hoover to SAC, New York, March 14, 1940; Letter, Hoover to SAC, Boston, and enclosure, April 19, 1943; and Letter, Hoover to All SACs and Memo re CLOG Case, June 24, 1943.

CHAPTER ONE. THE SOVIET ESPIONAGE THREAT

1. Benson and Warner, in *Venona,* reprint selected Venona messages that document Soviet intelligence operations. See pp. 199–450.
2. *Ibid.,* pp. xxiv–xxviii.
3. *Ibid.,* p. xxxii.
4. Weinstein and Vassiliev, *The Haunted Wood,* pp. 50–71, 110–150. Indeed, KGB agents assigned Dickstein the code name Crook and in their reports described him as "an unscrupulous type, greedy for money."

5. *Ibid.*, pp. 38–49.
6. *Ibid.*, p. 44n.
7. *Ibid.*, p. 34.
8. *Ibid.*, pp. 34–35.
9. *Ibid.*, pp. xxi–xxiv, 36–37.
10. *Ibid.*, pp. 25, 29.
11. Haynes and Klehr, *Venona,* p. 47.
12. Alvarez, *Secret Messages,* pp. 204–213, 218, 223; Benson and Warner, *Venona,* pp. xiii, xxii, xxxiii.
13. Contrast Haynes and Klehr's account and citation with Benson and Warner, *Venona,* p. xiv.
14. Haynes and Klehr, *Venona,* p. 48.
15. Benson and Warner, *Venona,* pp. xviii, 43–48, 59. Robert Lamphere and Tom Shachtman, *The FBI–KGB War: A Special Agent's Story* (New York, 1986), p. 84.
16. Haynes and Klehr, *Venona,* pp. 114, 167, 173, 249. The authors' penchant to indict, despite having uncovered no evidence confirming accusations that specific individuals were involved in espionage, is repeated in their treatment of the atomic scientist and head of the Manhattan Project, J. Robert Oppenheimer. After asking, "What do the Venona cables have to say about J. Robert Oppenheimer?" they respond, "Directly very little, but indirectly perhaps a bit more." They then note that Venona offers no evidence that Oppenheimer spied or compromised the atomic bomb project. Nonetheless they conclude: "While the preponderance of the evidence argues against Oppenheimer having been an active Soviet source, one matter cannot be ruled out. The possibility exists that up to [August 1944] . . . he may have overlooked the conduct of others whom he had reasonable grounds to question, a passivity motivated by his personal and political ties to those persons." *Ibid.*, pp. 329–330.
17. New York to Moscow, No. 1579, September 28, 1943, Venona messages.
18. Washington to Moscow, No. 1822, March 30, 1945, Venona messages.

CHAPTER TWO. THE FAILURE OF U.S. COUNTERINTELLIGENCE

1. The above quote is from McCarthy's February 1950 speech in Wheeling, West Virginia, which brought him national prominence. The speech is reprinted in Ellen Schrecker, *The Age of McCarthyism: A Brief History with Documents* (Boston, 1994), pp. 211–214.
2. Richard Gid Powers, *Secrecy and Power: The Life of J. Edgar Hoover* (New York, 1987), p. 239.
3. The FBI memoranda on the Lore interviews are reprinted in Tiger, *In Re Alger Hiss,* Volume II, pp. 208–209.
4. Memo, name-redacted agent to name-redacted agent, December 10, 1948, FBI file on Alger Hiss, serial #198.
5. Memo, Hoover to Tolson, Tamm, Ladd, and Carson, October 11, 1945, FBI 62-116606-1. Memo, name-redacted agent to name-redacted agent, December 10, 1948, FBI file on Alger Hiss, serial #198. Letter, Hoover to Vaughan, October 19, 1945, and Report, Soviet Espionage Activities, PSF FBI, Truman presidential library. FBI Report, Underground Soviet Espionage Organization (NKVD) in Agencies of the United States Government, October 21, 1946, p. 108, Truman presidential library. Tiger, *In Re Alger Hiss,* Volume II, pp. 249–282. Memo, Ladd to Hoover, November 13, 1953, FBI 101-2668-52. Athan Theoharis, "Unanswered Questions: Chambers, Nixon, the FBI, and the Hiss Case," in Athan Theoharis, ed., *Beyond the Hiss Case: The FBI, Congress, and the Cold War* (Philadelphia, 1982), pp. 268–270.
6. Letter, Conroy to FBI Director, March 28, 1946, FBI 66-6766 (reprinted in Tiger, *In Re Alger Hiss,* Volume I, pp. 253–257).
7. Haynes and Klehr, *Venona,* p. 13.
8. Gary May, *Un-American Activities: The Trials of William Remington* (New York, 1994), pp. 87–88; Theoharis, "Unanswered Questions," p. 269.
9. This number is confirmed both by a 1970 FBI report recommending the destruction of the wiretap logs relating to the Bentley-inspired inves-

tigation—see Memo, SAC Washington to FBI Director, March 6, 1970, FBI 66-3286-53—and by an FBI report on this investigation sent to the Truman White House—see FBI Report, Underground Soviet Espionage Organization (NKVD) in Agencies of the United States Government, October 21, 1946, pp. 24, 25, 26, 28–41, 44, 59, 63–64, 67, 73, 85–87, 93, 95, 100, 110, 125, 136, 142, 145, 148, 154–155, 159, 168–172, 182–183, 186–187, 190, 195, 258, 260–262, 269, 271–272, Truman presidential library.

10. FBI Report, Underground Soviet Espionage Organization, pp. 28, 30, 33–34, 37, 46–47, 49, 70, 74, 77, 96, 138, 142, 146, 150, 190, 216–217, 229, 231–232, 249–250, 254, 258, 260, 262.
11. *Ibid.*, pp. 75, 279, 282; Haynes and Klehr, *Venona,* p. 179. The targets of the break-ins were Nathan Silvermaster, Ursula Wasserman, and Jane Keeney.
12. FBI Report, Underground Soviet Espionage Organization, p. 1.
13. May, *Un-American Activities,* pp. 88–89.
14. *Ibid.*, pp. 89–94.
15. *Ibid.*, pp. 94–96.
16. Memo, SAC Washington to FBI Director, March 6, 1970, FBI 66-3286-53.
17. Benson and Warner, *Venona,* p. xv.
18. New York to Moscow, No. 1014, July 20, 1944; New York to Moscow, No. 1385, October 1, 1944; New York to Moscow, No. 1845, December 31, 1944; New York to Moscow, No. 27, January 8, 1945; New York to Moscow, Nos. 284 and 286, March 28, 1945; New York to Moscow, No. 992, June 26, 1945; Venona messages.
19. New York to Moscow, No. 1340, September 21, 1944; New York to Moscow, No. 1600, November 14, 1944; New York to Moscow, No. 1657, November 27, 1944; New York to Moscow, No. 1773, December 16, 1944; Venona messages.
20. New York to Moscow, No. 1332, September 18, 1944; New York to Moscow, No. 1004, June 25, 1943; New York to Moscow, No. 1033, July 1, 1943; New York to Moscow, No. 1047, July 2, 1943; New York to

Moscow, No. 1431, September 2, 1943; New York to Moscow, No. 586, April 29, 1944; New York to Moscow, Nos. 613–614, May 3, 1944; New York to Moscow, No. 826, June 7, 1944; New York to Moscow, No. 982, July 12, 1944; New York to Moscow, No. 1022, July 20, 1944; New York to Moscow, No. 1043, July 25, 1944; New York to Moscow, No. 1220, August 26, 1944; New York to Moscow, No. 1266, September 6, 1944; New York to Moscow, Nos. 1325–1326, September 15, 1944; New York to Moscow, No. 1328, September 15, 1944; New York to Moscow, No. 1354, September 22, 1944; New York to Moscow, No. 1385, October 1, 1944; New York to Moscow, Nos. 1388–1389, October 1, 1944; New York to Moscow, Nos. 1433–1435, October 10, 1944; New York to Moscow, No. 1516, October 25, 1944; New York to Moscow, No. 1524, October 27, 1944; New York to Moscow, No. 1582, November 12, 1944; New York to Moscow, No. 1755, December 14, 1944; New York to Moscow, No. 1791, December 20, 1944; New York to Moscow, Nos. 12–13, 15–16, January 4, 1945; New York to Moscow, No. 50, January 11, 1945; New York to Moscow, No. 275, March 25, 1945; Venona messages.

21. New York to Moscow, No. 27, January 8, 1945, and New York to Moscow, No. 992, June 26, 1945, Venona messages.
22. Moscow to Canberra (copies to New York, San Francisco, Ottawa), No. 142(a), September 12, 1943, Venona messages.
23. Moscow to Canberra (copies to Havana, Mexico City, Ottawa, San Francisco, New York), Nos. 233, 232, December 2, 1944, Venona messages.
24. New York to Moscow, No. 595, May 1, 1944; New York to Moscow, No. 1022, July 20, 1944; New York to Moscow, No. 1524, October 27, 1944; New York to Moscow, No. 1755, December 14, 1944; New York to Moscow, No. 50, January 11, 1945; New York to Moscow, No. 1328, September 15, 1944; Venona messages.
25. Benson and Warner, *Venona*, pp. xvii, 49–50, 55–58, 106–108, 113. Report, name-redacted agent, April 22, 1947, FBI 100-203581-5421. Draft Statement, J. Edgar Hoover on FBI Wiretap Uses, March 26, 1955, pp. 14–15, Wiretapping Use of in FBI Folder #164, Official and Confidential File of FBI Director J. Edgar Hoover (henceforth Hoover O&C). Letter,

Hoover to Hopkins, May 7, 1943, reprinted in Benson and Warner, *Venona,* pp. 49–50.

26. New York to Moscow, No. 594, May 1, 1944; New York to Moscow, No. 600, May 2, 1944; New York to Moscow, Nos. 613–614, May 3, 1944; New York to Moscow, No. 654, May 9, 1944; New York to Moscow, No. 724, May 19, 1944; New York to Moscow, No. 726, May 20, 1944; New York to Moscow, No. 740, May 24, 1944; New York to Moscow, No. 799, June 3, 1944; New York to Moscow, No. 907, June 26, 1944; New York to Moscow, No. 951, July 4, 1944; New York to Moscow, No. 1145, August 10, 1944; New York to Moscow, No. 1202. August 23, 1944; New York to Moscow, No. 87, January 19, 1945; Venona messages.
27. Memo, Branigan to Sullivan, February 9, 1966, Kravchenko, Victor folder, Folder #102, Hoover O&C. Blind Memo, April 1, 1944, appended to Memo, Hoover to Attorney General, undated, both in Francis Biddle Papers, F.B.I., Roosevelt presidential library.
28. Blind Memo [initialed by FBI assistant director Edward Tamm], December 26, 1944, Kravchenko folder, Folder #102, Hoover O&C.
29. New York to Moscow, No. 1431, September 2, 1943; New York to Moscow, No. 1243, August 31, 1944; New York to Moscow, Nos. 1388–1389, October 1, 1944; New York to Moscow, Nos. 12, 13, 15, 16, January 4, 1945; New York to Moscow, No. 337, April 8, 1945; Venona messages.
30. Weinstein and Vassiliev, *The Haunted Wood,* p. 279.
31. *Ibid.,* pp. 103–109.
32. Draft Statement of J. Edgar Hoover, March 26, 1955, p. 14, Wiretapping, Use of in FBI folder, Folder #164; and Memo, Wannall to Brennan, March 29, 1971, Intelligence Coverage Domestic and Foreign folder, Folder #90; both in Hoover O&C. Benson and Warner, *Venona,* pp. 49–50, 106–108. Memo, FBI Executives Conference to FBI Director, January 9, 1952, FBI 66-2554-9337.
33. Personal and Confidential Letter, Hoover to Watson, September 28, 1940, and attached Memo re: Washington Embassies, September 27,

1940, OF 10-B, Roosevelt presidential library. FBI director Hoover periodically sent to the Roosevelt White House snippets of information gleaned from this wiretap of the Soviet embassy. See, for example, Letter, Hoover to Watson, February 21, 1941, OF 10-B, and Letter, Hoover to Secretary of the Treasury, July 23, 1940, Morgenthau Diaries, Vol. 287, pp. 252–253, both in Roosevelt presidential library. Alvarez, *Secret Messages,* p. 214. FBI agents also unsuccessfully sought entry (disguised as building inspectors) to the Soviet consulate in New York City in 1944.

34. Letter, Hoover to Watson, November 16, 1939, and accompanying memorandum of same date, OF 10-B; Letter, Morgenthau to Hoover, April 16, 1940, and Letter, Hoover to Secretary of the Treasury, August 14, 1940, Morgenthau Diaries, Vol. 294, pp. 231–232; both in Roosevelt presidential library.

35. Benson and Warner, *Venona,* pp. 49–50, 106–107. Personal and Confidential Letter, Hoover to McIntyre, December 13, 1938, OF 263; Strictly Confidential Letter, Hoover to Watson, October 25, 1940, and accompanying report, Present Status of Espionage and Counter Espionage of the Federal Bureau of Investigation, October 24, 1940, OF 10-B; Personal and Confidential Letter, Hoover to Morgenthau, November 29, 1940, Morgenthau Diaries, Vol. 334, pp. 105–107; Memo, Klaus to Morgenthau, January 13, 1941, Morgenthau Diaries, Vol. 347, p. 132; Telephone Conversation, Harrison and Morgenthau, October 23, 1940, Morgenthau Diaries, Vol. 324, pp. 236–238; Letter, Hoover to Watson, January 6, 1940, OF 10-B; Memo, Gaston to Morgenthau, March 10, 1943, Morgenthau Diaries, Vol. 615, pp. 191–192; Letter, Morgenthau to Hoover, August 7, 1940, and Memo, Cochran to Morgenthau, August 6, 1940, Morgenthau Diaries, Vol. 290, pp. 97–98; Memo, Watson to Secretary of the Treasury, January 11, 1940, OF 10-B; all in Roosevelt presidential library.

36. Stephan, "*Communazis,*" pp. 2, 20, 44, 67, 76, 117, 119–122, 125–127, 195–196, 254, 271.

37. *Ibid.,* pp. 20, 50, 119, 163, 254, 257.

38. *Ibid.*, pp. 20, 125, 127.
39. *Ibid.*, pp. 35, 36, 43, 44, 45, 67, 76, 77, 85, 89, 122, 123, 128–129, 138, 190, 192, 195, 199, 253–254, 257, 259–266, 269, 275–276.
40. Letter, Hood to FBI Director, August 9, 1943, and accompanying memo, FBI 100-138754-19; Report, name-redacted agent, February 16, 1944, FBI 100-138754-32; Letter, Hood to FBI Director, June 28, 1947, FBI 100-138754-173; Memo, Coyne to Ladd, July 9, 1947, FBI 100-138754-unclear; Memo, Ladd to FBI Director, October 2, 1947, FBI 100-138754-251x1.
41. On Leach wiretap, see Memo, Hood to FBI Director, June 8, 1944, FBI 100-138754-unclear. On Los Angeles Workers School wiretap, see Memo, SAC Los Angeles to FBI Director, June 22, 1944, FBI 100-138754-37. On Anderson wiretap, see Memo, Hottel to FBI Director, October 24, 1947, FBI 100-138754-269. On Baldwin wiretap, see Letter, Hottel to FBI Director, October 9, 1947, FBI 100-138754-258. On Lawson wiretap, see Memo, SAC Los Angeles to FBI Director, June 22, 1947, FBI 100-138754-37; Letter, Hood to FBI Director, July 5, 1947, FBI 100-138754-106; Memo, SAC Los Angeles to FBI Director, May 31, 1946, FBI 100-138754-126; Letter, Hood to FBI Director, July 11, 1946, FBI 100-138754-130; and Letter, Hood to FBI Director, October 15, 1947, FBI 100-138754-264. On Salt wiretap, see Letter, Hood to FBI Director, October 15, 1947, FBI 100-138754-264, and Letter, Hood to FBI Director, October 20, 1947, FBI 100-138754-265. On Biberman wiretap, see Report, name-redacted agent, June 4, 1945, FBI 100-138754-95x and Letter, Hood to FBI Director, October 15, 1947, FBI 100-138754-264. On Robison wiretap, see Memo, SAC Los Angeles to FBI Director, March 17, 1945, FBI 100-138754-81. On Wahl wiretap, see Memo, Hottel to FBI Director, November 1, 1947, FBI 100-138754-287; Report, name-redacted agent, November 8, 1947, FBI 100-138754-unclear; Memo, Hottel to FBI Director, November 15, 1947, FBI 100-138754-318. On Crum wiretap, see Memo, Ladd to FBI Director, October 9, 1947, FBI 100-138754-248; Memo, SAC San Francisco to FBI Director, November 13, 1947, FBI 100-138754-unclear. On Popper wiretap, see (among others) Memo,

Coyne to Ladd, November 10, 1947, FBI 100-138754-309; Memos, Hottel to FBI Director (October 18, 1947, FBI 100-138754-338; November 15, 1947, FBI 100-138754-318; and December 8, 1947, and accompanying wiretap summary, FBI 100-138754-364). On recommendation to wiretap Margolis, see Recommendation to Wiretap Margolis form, Los Angeles SAC, February 3, 1948, FBI 100-138754-397.

42. Michal Belknap, *Cold War Political Justice: The Smith Act, the Communist Party, and American Civil Liberties* (Westport, Conn., 1977), p. x.
43. Personal and Confidential Letter, Watson to Hoover, October 31, 1940; Memo, Roosevelt to Watson, October 31, 1940; Strictly Confidential Letter, Hoover to Watson, October 25, 1940; Strictly Confidential Report: Present Status of Espionage and Counter Espionage Operations of the Federal Bureau of Investigation; all in OF 10-B, Roosevelt presidential library.
44. Memo, Watson to the President, May 23, 1941; Personal and Confidential Letter, Hoover to Watson, May 22, 1941; Memo, May 15, 1941; all in OF 10-B, Roosevelt presidential library.

CHAPTER THREE. THE COMINTERN APPARATUS INVESTIGATION

1. Benson and Warner, *Venona,* pp. 49–50, 106–108, 113; Report, name-redacted agent, April 22, 1947, FBI 100-203581-5421.
2. Personal and Confidential Letter, Pieper to Hoover, April 7, 1943, FBI 100-203581-x; Report, name-redacted agent, May 7, 1943, FBI 100-203581-1; Letter, Hoover to SAC New York, May 15, 1943, FBI 100-203581-2-4; Airtel, Hoover to SAC San Francisco, date redacted, but May 1943, FBI 100-203581-47; Memo, Ladd to Welch, April 24, 1943, FBI 100-203581-64; Memo, Hoover to SAC New York, May 26, 1943, FBI 100-203581-102.
3. The text of the Russian letter and the translation are reprinted in Benson and Warner, *Venona,* pp. 52–54.

4. Report, name-redacted agent, December 15, 1944, FBI 100-203581-3702.
5. Narrative, Re: Comintern Apparatus, January 30, 1945, FBI 100-203581-3914.
6. Memorandum for the File, COMRAP, February 6, 1948, reprinted in Benson and Warner, *Venona,* pp. 105–115.
7. Report, name-redacted agent, July 5, 1946, FBI 100-203581-2816; Report, name-redacted agent, October 30, 1944, FBI 100-203581-3379; Report, name-redacted agent, December 15, 1944, FBI 100-203581-3702; Narrative report, January 30, 1945, FBI 100-203581-3914; Report, name-redacted agent, April 26, 1945, FBI 100-203581-4378; Report, name-redacted agent, August 30, 1945, FBI 100-203581-4650; Report, name-redacted agent, April 5, 1946, FBI 100-203581-5236.
8. See, for example, Personal and Confidential Memos, Hoover to Attorney General, June 2, 1943, FBI 100-203581-164; June 9, 1943, FBI 1002-3581-171; August 30, 1943, FBI 100-203581-568; September 7, 1943, FBI 100-203581-602; January 1, 1944, FBI 100-203581-1286; March 25, 1944, FBI 100-203581-1894; April 19, 1944, FBI 100-203581-2074; May 6, 1944, FBI 100-203581-2148; May 13, 1944, FBI 100-203581-2217; (2) June 5, 1944, FBI 100-203581-2470 and FBI 100-203581-2528; June 7, 1944, FBI 100-203581-2527; July 1 and July 24, 1944, FBI 100-203581-2805 and FBI-203581-2806; and October 28, 1944, FBI 100-203581-3337.
9. Personal and Confidential Memo, Hoover to Attorney General, May 22, 1943, FBI 100-203581-49.
10. Personal and Confidential Memo, Hoover to Attorney General, May 12, 1943, FBI 100-203581-88.
11. Personal and Confidential Memo, Hoover to Attorney General, September 1, 1943, FBI 100-203581-574.
12. Personal and Confidential Memo, Hoover to Attorney General, March 11, 1944, FBI 100-203581-1766.
13. Personal and Confidential Memo, Hoover to Attorney General, July 27, 1944, FBI 100-203581-2840.
14. Personal and Confidential Memo, Hoover to Attorney General, undated but July 25, 1944, FBI 100-203581-2861.

15. Personal and Confidential Memo, Hoover to Attorney General, December 6, 1944, FBI 100-203581-3530.
16. Personal and Confidential Memo, Hoover to Attorney General, December 14, 1944, FBI 100-203581-3639.
17. Memo, Strickland to Ladd, November 22, 1944, FBI 100-203581-3546.
18. Personal and Confidential Letter, Pieper to Ladd, May 22, 1944, FBI 100-203581-2405.
19. Memo, SAC Albany to FBI Director, May 31, 1943, FBI 100-203581-119; Memo, Hoover to SAC Albany, July 5, 1943, FBI 100-203581-119; Letter, Pieper to FBI Director, July 28, 1943, FBI 100-203581-432; Letter, Belmont to FBI Director, September 7, 1943, FBI 100-203581-695; Report, name-redacted agent, December 29, 1943, FBI 100-203581-1478; Personal and Confidential Letter, Conroy to FBI Director, February 17, 1944, FBI 100-203581-1647; Personal and Confidential Letter, Hood to FBI Director, April 8, 1944, FBI 100-203581-1944; Report, name-redacted agent, October 27, 1944, FBI 100-203581-3392; Personal and Confidential Memo, Pieper to FBI Director, November 11, 1944, FBI 100-203581-3407; Teletype, Conroy to FBI Director, November 15, 1944, FBI 100-203581-3425; Memo, Guerin to FBI Director, January 22, 1945, FBI 100-203581-3861.
20. Teletype, SAC New York to FBI Director, June 4, 1943, FBI 100-203581-154.
21. Memo, name-redacted agent to Ladd, June 10, 1943, FBI 100-203581-200; Report, name-redacted agent, June 15, 1943, FBI 100-203581-215; Teletype, SAC New York to FBI Director, June 19, 1943, FBI 100-203581-224.
22. Personal and Confidential Letter, Fletcher to FBI Director, June 26, 1943, FBI 100-203581-331; Personal and Confidential Letter, Vincent to FBI Director, August 10, 1943, FBI 100-203581-621; Personal and Confidential Letter, Conroy to FBI Director, August 21, 1943, FBI 100-203581-706; Report, name-redacted agent, December 17, 1943, FBI 100-203581-1237; Report, name-redacted agent, December 29, 1943, FBI 100-203581-1409; Report, name-redacted agent, January 27, 1944, FBI 100-203581-1553; Report, name-redacted agent, November 22, 1943,

FBI 100-203581-1761; Memo, Hottel to FBI Director, August 19, 1944, FBI 100-203581-2040; Report, name-redacted agent, January 10, 1944, FBI 100-203581-1396; Report, name-redacted agent, December 21, 1943, FBI 100-203581-1297.

23. Personal and Confidential Letter, Hoover to SAC New York, July 7, 1943, FBI 100-203581-332; Personal and Confidential Letter, Hoover to SAC San Francisco, September 4, 1943, FBI 100-203581-612; Letter, Suran to FBI Director, September 4, 1943, FBI 100-203581-700; Letter, Suran to FBI Director, November 15, 1943, FBI 100-203581-1086; Personal and Confidential Letter, Hoover to SAC New York, April 11, 1944, FBI 100-203581-1967; Memo, Buckley to Ladd, June 17, 1944, FBI 100-203581-2824.
24. Letter, Conroy to FBI Director, August 4, 1943, FBI 100-203581-491.
25. Teletype, Conroy to FBI Director, September 7, 1943, FBI 100-203581-623.
26. Personal and Confidential Letter, Hoover to SAC San Francisco, September 9, 1943, FBI 100-203581-641.
27. Teletype, Conroy to FBI Director, February 12, 1944, FBI 100-203581-1727; Memo, Buckley to Ladd, May 1, 1944, FBI 100-203581-2121; Personal and Confidential Memo, Hoover to SAC Chicago, May 15, 1944, FBI 100-203581-2274; Confidential Letter, Conroy to FBI Director, November 15, 1944, FBI 100-203581-3425; Memo, name-redacted agent to Ladd, November 19, 1944, FBI 100-203581-3471; Memo, Ladd to Tamm, November 30, 1944, FBI 100-203581-3511; Memo, Mumford to Ladd, November 30, 1944, FBI 100-203581-3550.
28. Personal and Confidential Memo, Hoover to SAC San Francisco, November 27, 1944, FBI 100-203581-3474.
29. Report, name-redacted agent, December 15, 1944, FBI 100-203581-3702.
30. Narrative, Re: Comintern Apparatus, January 30, 1945, FBI 100-203581-3914.
31. Report, name-redacted agent, December 15, 1944, FBI 100-203581-3702; Report, name-redacted agent, March 15, 1945, FBI 100-203581-4178. See also Narrative, Re: Comintern Apparatus, January 30, 1945, FBI 100-

203581-3914; Report, name-redacted agent, July 2, 1943, FBI 100-203581-584.

32. Benson and Warner, *Venona,* p. 51; Weinstein and Vassiliev, *The Haunted Wood,* pp. 110–117; Personal and Confidential Memo, Hoover to Attorney General, May 12, 1943, FBI 100-203581-88; Report, name-redacted agent, July 2, 1943, FBI 100-203581-584.
33. Report, name-redacted agent, June 11, 1943, FBI 100-203581-267; Report, name-redacted agent, July 2, 1943, FBI 100-203581-584; Narrative, Re: Comintern Apparatus, January 30, 1945, FBI 100-203581-3914; Report, name-redacted agent, February 26, 1947, FBI 100-203581-5404.
34. Report, name-redacted agent, December 15, 1944, FBI 100-203581-3702.

CHAPTER FOUR. THE COUNTERINTELLIGENCE DILEMMA: CONTAINMENT OR LAW ENFORCEMENT?

1. Theoharis and Cox, *The Boss,* pp. 248–250. For a detailed account of the FBI's and the Justice Department's successful prosecution of Communist party officials under the Smith Act, see Peter Steinberg, *The Great "Red Menace": United States Prosecution of American Communists, 1947–1952* (Westport, Conn., 1984); Belknap, *Cold War Political Justice;* and Arthur Sabin, *In Calmer Times: The Supreme Court and Red Monday* (Philadelphia, 1999).
2. FBI Report, Underground Soviet Espionage Organization (NKVD) in Agencies of the United States Government, October 21, 1946, pp. 24, 25, 26, 28–41, 44, 46–47, 49, 59, 63–64, 67, 70, 73–75, 77, 85–87, 93, 95–96, 100, 110, 125, 136, 138, 142, 145–146, 148, 150, 154–155, 159, 168–172, 182–183, 186–187, 190, 195, 216–217, 229, 231–232, 249–250, 254, 258, 260–262, 269, 271–272, 279, 282, Truman presidential library.
3. New York to Moscow, No. 1340, September 21, 1944; New York to Moscow, No. 1600, November 14, 1944; New York to Moscow, No. 1657, November 27, 1944; New York to Moscow, No. 1715, December 5, 1944; New York to Moscow, No. 1773, December 16, 1944; Venona messages.

4. New York to Moscow, No. 1585, November 12, 1944; New York to Moscow, Nos. 1749–1750, December 13, 1944; New York to Moscow, No. 1773, December 16, 1944; New York to Moscow, No. 298, March 31, 1945; Venona messages. Weinstein and Vassiliev, *The Haunted Wood,* pp. 196–197.
5. The Rosenberg case is discussed in Ronald Radosh and Joyce Milton, *The Rosenberg File: A Search for the Truth* (New York, 1984), and Walter and Miriam Schneir, *Invitation to an Inquest* (Garden City, N.Y., 1965). On Hall, see Benson and Warner, *Venona,* p. xxvi; Weinstein and Vassiliev, *The Haunted Wood,* pp. 196–197; Moynihan, *Secrecy,* pp. 62, 147–152.
6. Radosh and Milton, *The Rosenberg File,* pp. 247, 251, 261, 264–265, 456–463; Walter and Miriam Schneir, *Invitation to an Inquest,* pp. 129, 131, 138, 139, 143–144, 147–148, 151–152, 156, 161, 164, 181, 196–198, 378–390, 392.
7. Lamphere and Schachtman, *The FBI-KGB War,* pp. 78–86, 99–115.
8. Lamphere and Schachtman, *The FBI-KGB War,* p. 113; Theoharis, *Spying on Americans,* p. 101.
9. Weinstein and Vassiliev, *The Haunted Wood,* pp. 91, 216, 226n.
10. Theoharis, *Spying on Americans,* pp. 100–101. Memo, FBI Director to Attorney General, June 9, 1949; Undated Routing Slip, Hoover; Memo, Ladd to FBI Director, June 14, 1949; Coplon, Judith, Case folder, Folder #53, Hoover O&C. Minutes of Cabinet Meeting, June 10, 1949, Matt Connelly Papers, Cabinet Minutes, Truman presidential library.
11. Theoharis, *Spying on Americans,* p. 101.
12. Memo, Nichols to Tolson, January 12, 1950; Memo, Fletcher to Ladd, January 11, 1950; Memo, Nichols to Tolson, January 12, 1950, Judith Coplon folder, Official and Confidential File of FBI Assistant Director Louis Nichols (henceforth Nichols O&C).
13. Memo, Nichols to Tolson, January 10, 1950, Coplon folder, Nichols O&C.
14. Theoharis, *Spying on Americans,* pp. 102–103; Percival Bailey, "The Case of the National Lawyers Guild, 1939–1958," in Theoharis, *Beyond the Hiss*

Case, pp. 136–147. See also Letters, Durr to Truman, June 20, 1949, and January 19, 1950; and Letter, Truman to Durr, June 23, 1949; all in OF 10-B, Truman presidential library.

15. Strictly Confidential Bureau Bulletin No. 34, Series 1949, July 8, 1949, FBI 66-03-996.
16. Personal Attention Strictly Confidential SAC Letter No. 69, Series 1949, June 29, 1949, FBI 66-1372-1; JUNE Memo, Wannall to Sullivan, January 17, 1969, FBI 66-1372-49.
17. Athan Theoharis, "In-House Coverup: Researching FBI Files," in Theoharis, *Beyond the Hiss Case,* p. 28.
18. Draft Statement of J. Edgar Hoover, March 26, 1955, p. 14, Wiretapping, Use of in FBI folder, Folder #164, Hoover O&C. The FBI had wiretapped Communist party headquarters and based on this wiretap then bugged Nelson's residence. See also Memo, Wannall to Brennan, March 29, 1971, Intelligence Coverage Domestic and Foreign folder, Folder #90, Hoover O&C, and Memo, FBI Executives Conference to FBI Director, January 9, 1952, FBI 66-2554-9337.
19. Memo, Tamm to FBI Director, November 4, 1943, FBI 100-203581-1168.
20. Report, Underground Soviet Espionage Organization, p. 1.
21. *U.S. v. John Doe,* Harry Dexter White, March 24 and 25, 1948, pp. 2698–2699, 2726–2732; the specific question about his telephone conversation with Silverman is on pp. 2698–2699.
22. Letter, McGrath to President, undated but ca. 1950, and accompanying memos, "The Amerasia Case," and "Report of the Department of Justice in Connection with the Amerasia Case," WHCF, Confidential File, Justice Department, Truman presidential library. Klehr and Radosh, *The Amerasia Spy Case,* pp. 52–53. Summary Memorandum Re: Philip Jaffe, March 3, 1953, Philip Jaffe folder, Nichols O&C.
23. Summary Memorandum Re: Philip Jaffe, March 3, 1945, Jaffe folder, Nichols O&C; Eban Ayers Diary, June 12, 1950, Truman presidential library.
24. Summary Memorandum Re: Philip Jaffe, March 3, 1953; Memo, Gurnea to Hoover, June 2, 1945; Memo, Ladd to Hoover, June 5, 1950; Memo,

Nichols to Tolson, June 13, 1950, Jaffe folder, Nichols O&C. Memo, Ladd to Hoover, May 23, 1945, White House Correspondence, 1945 CO Technical Coverage folder, Folder #1, Hoover O&C. Strictly Personal and Confidential Memo, Gurnea to Hoover, June 2, 1945, FBI 62-63007-unclear. White House Security Survey (1945) folder, Folder #160, Hoover O&C.

25. Personal and Confidential Letter, Hoover to Vardaman, August 17, 1945, and accompanying Summary Memorandum, PSF FBI, Truman presidential library. Although the original copy of this FBI memorandum was declassified and accessible at the Truman library since October 1976, FBI officials redacted the copy of this memorandum maintained in the White House Security Survey file when releasing this file to me in 1996 in response to my fourth appeal of redactions to Hoover's Official and Confidential File. On the Corcoran transcripts, see Technical Summaries to the White House folder, Folder #2, Hoover O&C. I have not cited specific transcripts, for the volume of such citations would have resulted in a note pages long. In 1945, at least, the Corcoran wiretap proved to be an invaluable source of intelligence for the Truman White House about the plans of its liberal New Deal critics in Congress, the Democratic National Committee, and even the U.S. Supreme Court.
26. Theoharis and Cox, *The Boss,* pp. 240–241; "Report of the Department of Justice," WHCF, Confidential File, Justice Department, Truman presidential library.
27. Summary Memorandum Re: Philip Jaffe, March 3, 1953; Unsigned Memo to Nichols, undated; Blind Memo Re: Amerasia Case, May 25, 1950; all in Jaffe folder, Nichols O&C.
28. Memos, Hoover to Tolson, Nichols, and Ladd, May 30 and 31 (2), 1950; Summary Memorandum Re: Philip Jaffe, March 3, 1953; Memo, Nichols to Hoover, June 27, 1950; Blind Memo, May 29, 1950; all in Jaffe folder, Nichols O&C. Correlation Summary Re: Thomas Corcoran, January 26, 1956, FBI 62-63007-36.
29. "The Amerasia Case," WHCF, Confidential File, Justice Department, Truman presidential library.

30. Memo, Nichols to Hoover, November 8, 1953; Memo, Ladd to Hoover, June 5, 1950; Memo, Gurnea to Hoover, June 2, 1945; Memo, Nichols to Tolson, June 13, 1950; all in Jaffe folder, Nichols O&C.

CHAPTER FIVE. POLITICIZING JUSTICE: THE HISS AND REMINGTON INDICTMENTS

1. Memo, Tamm to FBI Director, December 17, 1940, and Memo, Hoover to Smith, December 20, 1940, FBI 100-7321-1.
2. Do Not File Memo, Tamm to FBI Director, November 5, 1945, Wiretapping folder, Nichols O&C.
3. See the various cards in the FBI's National Security Electronic Surveillance Card File listing the dates of the inception and discontinuance of the taps and bugs installed by the FBI on these various unions.
4. Confidential Informant card; Memo, Foxworth to FBI Director, May 9, 1941; Personal and Confidential Memo, Hoover to McGuire, May 13, 1941; Memo, Tamm to FBI Director, May 31, 1944; Justice Department folder, Nichols O&C. Memo, name deleted to name deleted, December 10, 1948, FBI file on Alger Hiss, serial #198.
5. Memo, FBI Executives Conference to FBI Director, August 2, 1949, FBI 66-2554-7344; Memo, FBI Executives Conference to FBI Director, April 16, 1948, FBI 66-2554-6845x.
6. Jessica Wang, *American Science in an Age of Anxiety: Scientists, Anti-Communism, and the Cold War* (Chapel Hill, 1999), pp. 58–84; see also pp. 96–97, 110, 125, 128, 150, 161, 166, 169, 221, 327 n29.
7. In 1999 the transcripts of the grand jury pertaining to the Hiss-Chambers case were publicly released. Volume 7 of the grand jury transcripts (which covered Chambers's October 1948 grand jury testimony), however, was missing. The quoted excerpt came from Hiss's 1949 trial since Hiss's attorneys had been granted access to those portions of Chambers's October grand jury testimony to challenge his credibility. The quoted

exchange is cited in Allen Weinstein, *Perjury: The Hiss-Chambers Case* (New York, 1978), p. 177.

8. *Ibid.*, p. 271.
9. Grand Jury Transcripts, *U.S. v. John Doe,* Jay David Whittaker Chambers, December 9, 1948, pp. 3825–3873.
10. Grand Jury Transcripts, *U.S. v. John Doe,* Robert E. Stripling, December 9, 1948, pp. 3767–3769.
11. Grand Jury Transcripts, *U.S. v. John Doe,* Alger Hiss, March 16, 1948, pp. 2633–2669.
12. Grand Jury Transcripts, *U.S. v. John Doe,* Alger Hiss, December 6, 7, 8, 10, 11, 13, 14, and 15, 1948, pp. 3546–3568, 3719–3723, 3938–3950, 4044–4046, 4144–4154, 4382–4433, 4486–4496.
13. Richard Nixon, *RN: The Memoirs of Richard Nixon* (New York, 1978), p. 58; Garry Wills, *Nixon Agonistes* (New York, 1971), pp. 36–37; Allen Weinstein, "Nixon vs. Hiss: The Story Nixon Tells and the Other Story," *Esquire* (November 1975), p. 77.
14. Grand Jury Transcripts, *U.S. v. John Doe,* Karl E. Mundt, May 17, 1949, pp. 7369–7370.
15. Grand Jury Transcripts, *U.S. v. John Doe,* Karl E. Mundt, May 17, 1949, pp. 7380–7383; Grand Jury Transcripts, *U.S. v. John Doe,* Robert E. Stripling, December 9, 1948, pp. 3764–3767, 3770–3774.
16. Memo, Nichols to Tolson, December 2, 1948, FBI files on Alger Hiss, Serial #101.
17. Grand Jury Transcripts, *U.S. v. John Doe,* Robert E. Stripling, December 9, 1948, pp. 3781–3783, 3790–3791; Grand Jury Transcripts, *U.S. v. John Doe,* Richard M. Nixon, December 13, 1948, pp. 4168, 4175–4176, 4178–4181; Memo, Nichols to Tolson, December 3, 1948, FBI 74-1333-647.
18. Grand Jury Transcripts, *U.S. v. John Doe,* Karl E. Mundt, May 17, 1949, p. 7390; Weinstein, *Perjury,* pp. 271–275; John Chabot Smith, *Alger Hiss: The True Story* (New York, 1976), pp. 264–265.
19. Memo, Ladd to FBI Director, December 9, 1948, FBI files on Alger Hiss, Serial #157.

20. Grand Jury Transcripts, *U.S. v. John Doe,* Richard M. Nixon, December 13, 1948, pp. 4155–4202.
21. Grand Jury Transcripts, *U.S. v. John Doe,* Samuel J. Pelovitz, December 10, 1948, pp. 3982–4008; Grand Jury Transcripts, *U.S. v. John Doe,* Jay David Whittaker Chambers, December 10 and 21, 1948, pp. 4008–4018, 4745; Grand Jury Transcripts, *U.S. v. John Doe,* Jay David Whittaker Chambers, January 18, 1949, pp. 5386–5391, 5395–5406, 5415–5418, 5422–5425.
22. Grand Jury Transcripts, *U.S. v. John Doe,* Felix August Inslerman, January 3, 4, 5, 6, 13, 18, and 19, 1949, pp. 4902–4918, 4988–4999, 5000–5060, 5122–5159, 5288–5334, 5354–5385, 5426–5430, 5459–5545.
23. Grand Jury Transcripts, *U.S. v. John Doe,* Felix August Inslerman, January 5 and 19, 1949, pp. 5624–5626, 5462–5490, 5591–5593.
24. Grand Jury Transcripts, *U.S. v. John Doe,* Elizabeth Inslerman, January 11, 12, 13, and 19, 1949, pp. 5218–5222, 5223–5287, 5335–5353, 5431–5458.
25. Grand Jury Transcripts, *U.S. v. John Doe,* Felix August Inslerman, January 13 and 18, 1949, pp. 5292–5300, 5364–5365. Elizabeth Inslerman was also questioned about her husband's employment status in 1935. Grand Jury Transcripts, *U.S. v. John Doe,* Elizabeth Inslerman, January 13, 1949, pp. 5335–5353.
26. May, *Un-American Activities,* pp. 59, 68–110.
27. *Ibid.*, pp. 111–144.
28. *Ibid.*, pp. 157–167.
29. *Ibid.*, pp. 156, 234–236; see also pp. 227–229.
30. *Ibid.*, pp. 203–204.
31. *Ibid.*, pp. 177–179, 232.

CHAPTER SIX. THE POLITICS OF COUNTERINTELLIGENCE

1. Memo, FBI Director to Attorney General, April 1, 1941, Jackson, Robert H. Folder, Folder #91, Hoover O&C.
2. Airtel, FBI Director to SACs, July 18, 1963, FBI 100-3-116. This program

and FBI monitoring of civil rights activities are discussed in detail in Kenneth O'Reilly, *"Racial Matters": The FBI's Secret War on Black America, 1960–1972* (New York, 1989).

3. Athan Theoharis, *Spying on Americans: Political Surveillance from Hoover to the Huston Plan* (Philadelphia, 1978), pp. 166, 172; Frank Donner, *The Age of Surveillance* (New York, 1980), pp. 5, 139–144.
4. This vast literature is summarized in two annotated bibliographies: Athan Theoharis, ed., *The FBI: An Annotated Bibliography and Research Guide* (New York, 1994), and "Annotated Bibliography," in Theoharis, *FBI Reference Guide,* pp. 385–396.
5. John Donovan's thoughtful and well-researched Ph.D. dissertation, "Crusader in the Cold War: A Biography of Fr. John F. Cronin, S.S., 1908–1994" (Marquette University, 2000), surveys Cronin's prominent role within the Catholic Church in advancing social justice and anti-Communist objectives. His study also offers fascinating insights into Cronin's covert relationship with Richard Nixon.
6. Memo, Mumford to Ladd, October 18, 1943, FBI 94-35404-x.
7. Donovan, "Crusader in the Cold War," pp. 39–54.
8. Memo, Ladd to FBI Director, March 11, 1946, FBI 94-35404-3. Memo, Tyler to Tamm, June 28, 1947, and attached blind memoranda "furnished to" Cronin, dated June 13 and August 3, 6, 7, 25, and 30, 1945, FBI 94-35404-55. Donovan, "Crusader in the Cold War," pp. 81–95. Donovan's Appendix I details the specific pages in Cronin's reports derived from the FBI reports; see pp. 226–228.
9. Memo, Tamm to FBI Director, April 18, 1947, and accompanying "Report on Communism, April 1947," FBI 94-35404-53x; Letter, Cronin to Tamm, undated but early November 1946, and accompanying draft "Report on Communist Activities . . . November 1946," FBI 94-35404-46; Memo, Tamm to FBI Director, November 5, 1946, FBI 94-35404-51; Memo, Ladd to Tamm, November 7, 1946, FBI 94-35404-52; Memo, Nichols to Tolson, March 21, 1946, FBI 94-35404-2.
10. Memo, Tamm to Ladd, April 15, 1946, FBI 94-35404-22.
11. Memo, Tamm to FBI Director, January 2, 1946, FBI 94-35404-46x; Let-

ter, Cronin to Tamm, November 13, 1946, FBI 94-35404-45; Memo, Tamm to FBI Director, November 15, 1946, FBI 94-35404-45; Letter, Tamm to Cronin, November 15, 1946, FBI 94-35404-45; Memo, Ladd to FBI Director, October 30, 1946, FBI 94-35404-43; Letter, Cronin to Hoover, January 23, 1947, FBI 94-35404-48. Peter Irons, "American Business and the Origins of McCarthyism: The Cold War Crusade of the United States Chamber of Commerce," in Robert Griffith and Athan Theoharis, eds., *The Specter: Original Essays on the Cold War and the Origins of McCarthyism* (New York, 1974), pp. 78–82.

12. Memo, Ladd to FBI Director, October 30, 1946, FBI 94-35404-43.
13. Memo, Ladd to FBI Director, March 11, 1946, FBI 94-35404-3; Donovan, "Crusader in the Cold War," p. 55.
14. Letter, Cronin to Hoover, February 9, 1946, and reply, February 15, 1946, FBI 94-35404-1.
15. Memo, Ladd to Tamm, March 13, 1946, FBI 94-35404-5; Memo, Ladd to FBI Director, March 13, 1946, FBI 94-35404-4; Memo, McGuire to Nichols, March 15, 1946, FBI 94-35404-7; Memo, Tamm to FBI Director, April 18, 1946, FBI 94-35404-23; Memo, Tamm to FBI Director, April 30, 1946, FBI 94-35404-25; Memo, name-deleted agent, June 25, 1946, FBI 94-35404-21.
16. Memo, Tamm to FBI Director, June 27, 1946, FBI 94-35404-28; Memo, FBI Director to SAC, Washington, July 25, 1946, FBI 94-35404-29; Memo, Tamm to FBI Director, September 24, 1946, FBI 94-35404-35; Memo, Tamm to FBI Director, April 15, 1947, FBI 94-35404-51; Memo, Hottel to FBI Director, June 8, 1949, FBI 94-35404-Not Recorded.
17. The FBI's massive COMPIC file does not contain a copy of Hoover's August 1942 directive, which however is cited and quoted from in subsequent documents in this file. See, Letter, Hoover to SAC, Los Angeles, September 6, 1942, and accompanying list of radical activists, FBI 100-138754-1; Teletype, Hoover to SAC, Los Angeles, November 9, 1942, FBI 100-138754-2; Report, name-deleted agent, February 18, 1943, FBI 100-138754-4. The order discontinuing this investigation is Memo, Belmont to Boardman, January 3, 1956, FBI 100-138754-1103.

18. Letter, Hoover to SAC, Los Angeles, November 21, 1942, FBI 100-138754-3; Report, name-deleted agent, February 18, 1943, FBI 100-138754-4.
19. Letter, Hoover to SAC, Los Angeles, June 21, 1943, FBI 100-138754-5; Teletypes, Hoover to SAC, Los Angeles, July 3 and 9, 1943, FBI 100-138754-7 and FBI 100-138754-10. The referenced films either portrayed the Soviet Union sympathetically (*Mission to Moscow, Our Russian Front*) or were anti-fascist (*Hangmen Also Die, This Land Is Mine*).
20. Report, name-deleted agent, July 10, 1943, FBI 100-138754-9; Letter, Hood to FBI Director, July 8, 1943, and accompanying memo re: *Mission to Moscow,* July 2, 1943, FBI 100-138754-13; Letter, Hood to FBI Director, May 27, 1943, and accompanying memo re: *Mission to Moscow,* May 14, 1943, FBI 100-138754-14.
21. Letter, Hood to FBI Director, August 9, 1943, and accompanying memo identifying Communists employed in Hollywood, FBI 100-138754-19; undated and unserialized Memo, Hoover to Tamm and Ladd; see also pp. 46–47 of Report, name-deleted agent, February 16, 1944, FBI 100-138754-32.
22. Report, name-deleted agent, August 25, 1943, FBI 100-138754-21.
23. Report, name-deleted agent, October 11, 1943, FBI 100-138754-22.
24. Letter, Hoover to SAC, Los Angeles, April 29, 1944, FBI 100-138754-27.
25. Letter, Hood to FBI Director, June 28, 1947, FBI 100-138754-173; Memo, Coyne to Ladd, July 9, 1947, FBI 100-138754-unclear; Memo, Ladd to FBI Director, October 2, 1947, FBI 100-138754-251X1.
26. Report, name-deleted agent, April 20, 1944, FBI 100-138754-26.
27. Letter, Hoover to SAC, Los Angeles, May 8, 1944, FBI 100-138754-29. The Los Angeles office prepared this list in June 1944 and thereafter submitted monthly reports identifying Communist employees and the films with which they were affiliated. See Letter, Hood to FBI Director, June 3, 1944, FBI 100-138754-35.
28. Personal and Confidential Memo, Hoover to Attorney General, October 31, 1944, and accompanying report re: Communist Infiltration of the

Motion Picture Industry, FBI 100-138754-59. An undaunted Hoover sought to exploit the changed situation following Truman's accession to the presidency, submitting the same report to White House aide Harry Vaughan. Memo, Hoover to Vaughan, May 4, 1945, and accompany report re: Communist Infiltration of the Motion Picture Industry, FBI 100-138754-94.

29. Memos, Nichols to Tolson, July 2, 1945, FBI 100-138754-96, and July 3, 1945, FBI 100-138754-97; Memo, Ladd to Tamm, July 3, 1945, FBI 100-138754-98; Memo, Hoover to Tolson and Ladd, July 4, 1945, FBI 100-138754-99.
30. Memo, Hoover to Attorney General, March 13, 1947, FBI 61-7582-1455.
31. Memo, Tolson to Hoover, May 12, 1947, FBI 61-7582-1462.
32. Letter, Hood to FBI Director, May 12, 1947, FBI 61-7582-1465; Teletype, Los Angeles to FBI Director, May 13, 1947, FBI 61-7582-1463; Memo, Nichols to Tolson, May 13, 1947, FBI 61-7582-1465.
33. Memo, Coyne to Ladd, July 11, 1947, FBI 100-138754-185; Teletype, Hoover to SAC, Los Angeles, May 13, 1947, FBI 61-7582-1464; Teletype, Hood to FBI Director, May 13, 1947, FBI 61-7582-1466; Letter, Hood to FBI Director, May 14, 1947, and copy of Memo Re: Communist Activities in Hollywood, FBI 61-7582-1468. The eleven were Bertolt Brecht, Edward Dmytryk, Hanns Eisler, Paul Henreid, Lisa Henreid, Regina Kaus, Fritz Kortner, Johanna Kortner, Peter Lorre, Adrian Scott, and Salka Viertel.
34. Memo, Hoover to Tolson, Tamm, Ladd, and Nichols, June 24, 1947, FBI 100-138754-165.
35. Memo, Coyne to Ladd, July 11, 1947, FBI 100-138754-185; Memo, FBI Director to SAC, New York, July 25, 1947, FBI 138754-unclear; Memos, FBI Director to SAC, Los Angeles, July 2, 1947, FBI 100-138754-unclear, and July 11, 1947, FBI 100-138754-176; Letters, Hood to FBI Director, June 28, 1947, FBI 100-138754-137, July 15, 1947, FBI 100-138754-unclear, July 25, 1947, FBI 100-138754-x175, and August 5, 1947, with accompanying Report, name-deleted agent, August 4, 1947, FBI 100-138754-188; Letter, Scheidt to FBI Director, July 25, 1947, FBI 100-138754-174; Tele-

types, Hoover to SAC, Los Angeles, June 24, 1947, FBI 100-138754-166, and August 21, 1947, FBI 100-138754-192.

36. Letter, Smith to Hoover, June 26, 1947, and reply, July 8, 1947, FBI 100-138754-unclear; Memos, Mohr to Tolson, July 18, 1947 (2), FBI 100-138754-184 and FBI 100-138754-unclear; Memo, FBI Director to SAC, Los Angeles, July 21, 1947, FBI 100-138754-unclear; Letters, Hood to FBI Director, June 30, 1947, FBI 100-138754-172, August 22, 1947, FBI 100-138754-220, September 13, 1947, FBI 61-7582-1476, and October 13, 1947, FBI 61-7582-1478; Memo, SAC, Los Angeles to FBI Director, August 12, 1947, FBI 61-7582-1471.
37. Memos, Nichols to Tolson, August 21, 1947, FBI 100-138754-219, August 27, 1947, FBI 100-138754-219, August 29, 1947, FBI 100-138754-211, September 2, 1947, FBI 100-138754-unclear, and September 10, 1947, FBI 100-138754-224; Memo, Coyne to Ladd, undated and unserialized, captioned "Request of House Committee on Un-American Activities for a Check of Bureau Files on 40 Individuals Identified with Motion Picture Industry," included in FBI 100-138754.
38. Memo, Tolson to FBI Director, September 11, 1947, FBI 100-138754-218; Memo, Ladd to FBI Director, September 3, 1947, FBI 100-138754-122; Memo, Tamm to FBI Director, September 12, 1947, FBI 100-138754-225; Memo, Coyne to Ladd, September 17, 1947, FBI 100-138754-251X.
39. Victor Navasky, *Naming Names* (New York, 1980), p. 317n. None of the forty blind memoranda are included in the 100-138754 file. Navasky, however, located the FBI's blind memorandum on Larry Parks (one of the forty) in Parks's FBI file.
40. Letters, Hood to FBI Director, September 13, 1947, FBI 100-138754-230, and September 17, 1947, FBI 100-138754-unclear.
41. Richard Freeland, *The Truman Doctrine and the Origins of McCarthyism: Foreign Policy, Domestic Politics, and Internal Security, 1946–1948* (New York, 1972), p. 240; Memo, Nichols to Tolson, October 28, 1947, FBI 100-138754-286; Memo, Coyne to Ladd, October 28, 1947, FBI 100-138754-305; Report, name-deleted agent, November 8, 1947, FBI 100-138754-308.

42. Memo, Nichols to Tolson, October 28, 1947, FBI 100-138754-286.
43. On the Crum wiretap, see Memo, Ladd to FBI Director, October 9, 1947, FBI 100-138754-248; Memo, SAC, San Francisco to FBI Director, November 13, 1947, FBI 100-138754-unclear. On the Wahl wiretap, see Memo, Hottel to FBI Director, November 1, 1947, FBI 100-138754-287; Report, name-redacted agent, November 8, 1947, FBI 100-138754-unclear; Memo, Hottel to FBI Director, November 15, 1947, FBI 100-138754-318. On the Popper wiretap as well as transcripts of some of the intercepted conversations, see Memo, Coyne to Ladd, November 10, 1947, FBI 100-138754-309; Memos, Hottel to FBI Director, October 18, 1947, FBI 100-138754-338, November 15, 1947, FBI 100-138754-318, December 8, 1947, and accompanying wiretap summary, FBI 100-138754-364, December 29, 1947, FBI 100-138754-373, and January 14, 1948, and accompanying wiretap summary, FBI 100-138754-386.
44. Memos, FBI Director to Attorney General, November 26, 1947 (2), FBI 100-138754-322 and FBI 100-138754-323, December 30, 1947, FBI 100-138754-372, April 2, 1947 (2), FBI 100-138754-427 and FBI 100-138754-438, April 8, 1948, FBI 100-138754-441, April 10, 1948 (2), FBI 100-138754-437 and FBI 100-138754-450, and April 26, 1948, FBI 100-138754-451; Memos, FBI Director to Quinn, March 23, 1948, FBI 100-138754-419, April 23, 1948, FBI 100-138754-452, and May 7, 1948 (2), FBI 100-138754-457 and FBI 100-138754-458.
45. Memo, Quinn to FBI Director, April 12, 1948, FBI 100-138754-446.
46. Walter Goodman, *The Committee: The Extraordinary Career of the House Committee on Un-American Activities* (New York, 1968), p. 218.
47. U.S. Senate, Select Committee to Study Governmental Operations with respect to Intelligence Activities, *Supplementary Detailed Staff Reports on Intelligence Activities and the Rights of Americans,* Book III, 94th Cong., 2d sess., 1976, pp. 430, 437; Theoharis and Cox, *The Boss,* pp. 203–219, 279–300.
48. Memo, Ladd to FBI Director, May 21, 1948, FBI 100-138754-465.

CHAPTER SEVEN. THE POLITICS OF MORALITY

1. David Oshinsky, *A Conspiracy So Immense: The World of Joe McCarthy* (New York, 1983), pp. 114, 133.
2. *New York Times,* March 1, 1950, p. 2; March 9, 1950, p. 5; March 12, 1950, p. 36; March 15, 1950, p. 5.
3. *New York Times,* April 19, 1950, p. 25; April 25, 1950, p. 5; April 26, 1950, p. 1; May 5, 1950, p. 15.
4. *New York Times,* May 20, 1950, p. 8.
5. *New York Times,* May 21, 1950, p. 43; May 22, 1950, p. 8; May 25, 1950, p. 19; June 8, 1950, p. 8; June 15, 1950, p. 6.
6. Memorandum of Conversation (John Finlator, Department of State Personnel Division; Fred Traband, Department of State Security Division; Lt. Roy Blick), March 29, 1950 and Memo, Fletcher to Nicholson, May 3, 1950, White House Central File, Confidential File, Sex Perversion, Truman presidential library. Letter, Hoover to Souers, and enclosed list, April 10, 1950, PSF, FBI, Truman presidential library.
7. Memo, Jean to Peurifoy, June 20, 1950; Memo, Humelsine to Webb, and accompanying memoranda, June 24, 1950; Memo, Humelsine to Webb, undated; Memo, Flanagan (Hoey Committee counsel), June 27, 1950; Memo, Spingarn to Dawson, June 29, 1950; Memo, Spingarn re Hoey Subcommittee, June 29, 1950; Memo, Spingarn to Hechler, June 30, 1950; Memo, Dawson to Snyder, July 1, 1950; Memo, Maletz to Spingarn, July 3, 1950; Memo, Spingarn re Hoey Subcommittee, July 5, 1950; Memo, Nash to Spingarn, July 7, 1950; Memo, Spingarn re Hoey Subcommittee, July 10, 1950; Memo, Spingarn to Dawson, July 21, 1950; Memo, Spingarn for Files, July 24, 1950; White House Central Files, Confidential File, Sex Perversion, Truman presidential library.
8. Memo, ld to Dawson, June 30, 1950 and Memo, Lloyd to Spingarn, July 3, 1950, White House Central Files, Confidential File, Sex Perversion, Truman presidential library.
9. *New York Times,* December 16, 1950, p. 3.

10. *New York Times,* April 28, 1951, p. 7.
11. Memo, FBI Executives Conference to FBI Director, October 14, 1953, FBI 62-93875-Not Recorded; Memo, Boardman to FBI Director, October 28, 1954, FBI 62-93875-2503; Memo, name-withheld FBI agent to Rosen, October 22, 1954, FBI 62-93875-Not Recorded.
12. See preceding note's citations.
13. Memo, Wolfinger (head of Disposition Division) to Directors (NCD and NNF) re Disposition Job No. NO1-65-78-5, December 27, 1977, and Request for Record Disposition Authority, James Awe, January 15, 1978 (copies in author's possession). The author thanks *San Francisco Examiner* reporter Seth Rosenfeld for sharing these memos and his correspondence with FBI officials on this matter. See also *San Francisco Examiner,* January 13, 1991, p. 1.
14. Memo, Scheidt to Hoover, April 17, 1952; Sex Deviate index card on Stevenson, Adali [sic] Ewing; Memo, Ladd to FBI Director and accompanying blind memorandum, June 24, 1952; Memo, Jones to Nichols, July 24, 1952; Stevenson, Adlai E. folder, Folder #143, Hoover O&C.
15. Letter, Love to Hoover, November 12, 1952, and reply, November 17, 1952, Stevenson folder, Folder #17, Hoover O&C.
16. Memo, SAC, Springfield to FBI Director, February 9, 1953, and Memo, Belmont to Ladd, March 3, 1953, Stevenson folder, Folder #17, Hoover O&C.
17. Memo, Belmont to Ladd, December 2, 1952, Stevenson folder, Folder #143, Hoover O&C.
18. Memo, Belmont to Ladd, January 6, 1953; Memo, Belmont to Ladd, March 3, 1953; Memo, Scatterday to Belmont, April 12, 1960; Memo, Cleveland to Evans, October 31, 1964; Stevenson folder, Folder #143, Hoover O&C. Memo, SAC, Springfield to FBI Director, February 9, 1953, and Memo, Belmont to Ladd, March 3, 1953; Stevenson folder, Folder #17, Hoover O&C.
19. Memo, Jones to Nichols, July 24, 1952, and accompanying detailed summary memorandum on Stevenson; Memo, Jones to Nichols, July 23,

1952, Stevenson folder, Folder #143, Hoover O&C. Correlation Summary on Stevenson, March 22, 1956, Stevenson folder, Folder #17, Hoover O&C.

20. Personal and Confidential Memo, Nichols to FBI Director, August 29, 1952, Stevenson folder, Folder #143, Hoover O&C.
21. Memo, Hottel to Ladd, August 13, 1952; Memo, Ladd to FBI Director, August 15, 1952; (Two) Blind Memos re Adlai Stevenson, August 14, 1952; Memo, Rosen to Ladd, August 22, 1952; Memo, Rosen to Ladd, August 25, 1952; Blind Memo re Adlai Stevenson, August 25, 1952; Stevenson folder, Folder #17, Hoover O&C.
22. Memo, Belmont to Ladd, January 19, 1953, Stevenson folder, Folder #17, Hoover O&C.
23. Memo, Cleveland to Evans, October 31, 1964, Stevenson folder, Folder #143, Hoover O&C.
24. Letter, Hoover to Watson, July 2, 1965, Stevenson folder, Folder #17, Hoover O&C.
25. Memo, Nichols to Tolson, December 9, 1952, Eisenhower, Dwight David folder, Nichols O&C.
26. Memo, Nichols to FBI Director, December 16, 1952, Eisenhower folder, Nichols O&C. The original copy of this Nichols memo was filed in Vandenberg, Arthur folder, Folder #150, Hoover O&C, and contains Hoover's handwritten notation arranging the December 20 interview.
27. Memo, Nichols to FBI Director, December 23, 1952, Eisenhower folder, Nichols O&C.
28. Memo, Hoover to Tolson, Nichols, and Ladd, January 5, 1953, Eisenhower folder, Nichols O&C. Memo, Hoover to Tolson, DeLoach, and Gale, November 25, 1968, Personal File of FBI Associate Director Clyde Tolson.
29. Routing Slip, Belmont to Gandy, April 19, 1957; withheld five-page Secret Service Report, April 18, 1957; Memo, Hoover to Tolson, Boardman, and Belmont, April 17, 1957; Memos (2), Hoover to Tolson, Boardman, Belmont, and Nichols, April 17, 1957; Memo, Hoover to Tolson, Boardman, Belmont, and Nichols, April 18, 1957; Memo, Hoover to Tolson, Board-

man, and Belmont, April 19, 1957; Memo, Hoover to Tolson, Boardman, Belmont, and Nichols, May 10, 1957; White House Employees—Homosexuals folder, Folder #159, Hoover O&C.

30. Memo, Hoover to Tolson, Boardman, Belmont, and Nichols, April 17, 1957, Alsop, Joseph folder, Folder #26, Hoover O&C. Memo, Hoover to Tolson, Boardman, and Belmont, April 19, 1957, White House Homosexuals folder, Folder #159, Hoover O&C.
31. Letter, Dulles to Hoover, April 1, 1957, and accompanying Memorandum signed by Alsop, undated but February 23, 1957, Alsop folder, Folder #26, Hoover O&C. See also Memo, Roach to Belmont, April 26, 1957, and accompanying "A" and "B" enclosures, Alsop folder, Folder #26, Hoover O&C.
32. Letter, Dulles to Hoover, March 27, 1957, and attached memorandum; Memo, Hoover to Tolson, Boardman, and Belmont, March 28, 1957; and Memo, Hoover to Tolson, Boardman, and Belmont, April 1, 1957; Alsop folder, Folder #26, Hoover O&C.
33. Summary Memorandum, Joseph and Stewart Alsop, March 29, 1957; Memo, Hoover to Tolson, Boardman, Belmont, and Nichols, April 2, 1957; Alsop folder, Folder #26, Hoover O&C.
34. Memo Hoover to Tolson, Boardman, and Belmont, April 1, 1957; Memo, Hoover to Tolson, Boardman, Belmont, and Nichols, April 3, 1957; Memo, Hoover to Tolson, Boardman, Belmont, and Nichols, April 4, 1957; Letter, Hoover to Dulles, April 5, 1957; Letter, Dulles to Hoover, April 1, 1957; Alsop folder, Folder #26, Hoover O&C.
35. Letter, Dulles to Hoover, April 5, 1957; Letter, Hoover to Dulles, April 9, 1957; Letter, Dulles to Hoover, April 16, 1957; Letter, Hoover to Dulles, April 19, 1957; Memo, Scatterday to Belmont, October 28, 1958; Alsop folder, Folder #26, Hoover O&C.
36. Memo, Hoover to Tolson, Boardman, and Belmont, April 17, 1957; Memo, Hoover to Tolson, Boardman, Belmont, and Nichols, April 17, 1957; Memo, FBI Director to Attorney General, May 2, 1957; Memo, Hoover to Tolson, Boardman, Belmont, and Nichols, May 10, 1957; Alsop folder, Folder #26, Hoover O&C.

37. The Gaither Commission report, "Deterrence and Survival in the Nuclear Age," was reprinted by the Joint Committee on Defense Production, 94th Cong., 2d sess., 1976. See also Richard Crockett, *The Fifty Years War: The United States and the Soviet Union in World Politics, 1941–1991* (London, 1995), pp. 143–145. David Streitfeld cites examples of Alsop's criticisms in his biographical sketch of Alsop, *Washington Post,* April 13, 1995, p. C1. Alsop's criticisms that the Eisenhower administration's fiscal conservatism endangered national security were consistent with his earlier criticisms of the Truman administration. For example, see Michael Hogan, *A Cross of Iron: Harry S. Truman and the Origins of the National Security State, 1945–1954* (New York, 1998), pp. 177–178, 286–287, 307.
38. Memo, Hoover for Personal Files, April 14, 1959, Alsop folder, Folder #26, Hoover O&C.
39. Memo, Hoover for Personal Files, April 23, 1959, Alsop folder, Folder #26, Hoover O&C.
40. Memo, L'Allier to Sullivan, October 13, 1961, Kennedy, John F. folder, Folder #13, Hoover O&C.
41. Memo, SAC, Washington to FBI Director, October 15, 1957, FBI 65-7570-1; Memo, name-deleted FBI Supervisor to SAC, Washington, October 16, 1957, FBI 65-7570-2; Airtel, SAC, Washington to FBI Director, October 21, 1957, FBI 65-7570-3. *Milwaukee Sentinel,* May 19, 1986, p. 3.

CHAPTER EIGHT. THE PERILS OF PARTISANSHIP

1. Thomas Reeves, *The Life and Times of Joe McCarthy* (New York, 1982), pp. 223–227, 247–249, 267, 339; Oshinsky, *A Conspiracy So Immense,* p. 118; Kenneth O'Reilly, *Hoover and the Un-Americans: The FBI, HUAC, and the Red Menace* (Philadelphia, 1983), pp. 126, 337 n56; William Sullivan, *The Bureau: My Thirty Years in Hoover's FBI* (New York, 1979), pp. 45–167.

2. Reeves, *Life and Times,* pp. 126–127, 245–246, 312–314, 548; Oshinsky, *A Conspiracy So Immense,* pp. 117, 257–258, 324.
3. Memo, Hottel to FBI Director, September 19, 1950, FBI 121-41668-28; Memo, Ladd to FBI Director, October 5, 1950, FBI 121-41668-Not Recorded.
4. Sullivan, *The Bureau,* pp. 45, 267. See also Ovid Demaris, *The Director* (New York, 1975), pp. 162–163.
5. Memo, Hottel to FBI Director, November 28, 1952, FBI 94-37708-76x.
6. Memo, Hoover to Tolson, December 1, 1952, FBI 94-37708-77.
7. Memo, Hoover to Tolson, January 13, 1953, FBI 94-37708-79x.
8. Memo, Nichols to Tolson, February 4, 1953, FBI 62-88217-Not Recorded; Oshinsky, *A Conspiracy So Immense,* pp. 266–276; Reeves, *Life and Times,* pp. 477–491.
9. Memo, Nichols to Tolson, March 9, 1953, FBI 62-88217-Not Recorded.
10. Memos, Keay to Belmont, March 20 and 27, April 5, 13, and 20, 1953, all FBI 62-88217-Not Recorded; Memo, FBI Executives' Conference to Tolson, June 2, 1953, FBI 62-88217-Not Recorded.
11. Athan Theoharis, *The Yalta Myths: An Issue in U.S. Politics, 1945–1955* (Columbia, Mo., 1970), pp. 44–175; on the Bohlen nomination, see pp. 165–175; Jeff Broadwater, *Eisenhower and the Anti-Communist Crusade* (Chapel Hill, 1992), pp. 63–65.
12. Memo, Hoover to Tolson, Ladd, and Nichols, March 18, 1953, McCarthy, Senator Joseph folder, Folder #105, Hoover O&C.
13. *Ibid.;* Memo, Hoover to Tolson, Ladd, Belmont, and Nichols, May 19, 1953, FBI 62-96332-Not Recorded.
14. Memo, Pennington to Ladd, June 25, 1953, FBI 62-96332-50; Memo, Nichols to Tolson, June 24, 1953, FBI 94-37708-Not Recorded.
15. Reeves, *Life and Times,* pp. 498–502; Oshinsky, *A Conspiracy So Immense,* pp. 252–253, 318–321.
16. Memo, Nichols to Tolson, July 23, 1953, Miscellaneous A–Z folder, Nichols O&C; Memo, Hoover to Tolson and Nichols, July 14, 1953, McCarthy folder, Folder #105, Hoover O&C.

17. Memo, Nichols to Tolson, July 23, 1953, Miscellaneous A–Z folder, Nichols O&C.
18. Memo, FBI Executives' Conference to FBI Director, October 14, 1953, FBI 121-23278-Not Recorded.
19. Memo, Nichols to Tolson, March 22, 1951, FBI 62-88217-24.
20. Memo, Belmont to Ladd, March 22, 1951, FBI 62-88217-24x; Memo, Laughlin to Belmont, March 31, 1951, FBI 62-88217-25.
21. Memo, Nichols to Tolson, March 30, 1951, FBI 62-88217-29; Memo, Nichols to Tolson, April 3, 1951, FBI 62-88217-31; Memo, Belmont to Ladd, November 15, 1951, FBI 62-88217-339.
22. Memo, Nichols to Tolson, March 30, 1951, FBI 62-88217-28; Memo, Nichols to Tolson, January 22, 1952, FBI 62-88217-460.
23. Memo, Belmont to Ladd, April 14, 1951, FBI 62-88217-31.
24. Memo, Nichols to Tolson, April 11, 1951, FBI 62-88217-33.
25. Memo, name-redacted SISS staff to Nichols, undated and unserialized but FBI 62-88217-74; Memo, Belmont to Ladd, June 29, 1951, FBI 62-88217-Not Recorded; Blind Memo, July 16, 1951, FBI 62-88217-113; Memo, Belmont to Ladd, June 27, 1951, FBI 62-88217-118; Memo, Sourwine to Laughlin, September 4, 1951, unserialized but FBI 62-88217-189; Memo, Laughlin to Ladd, September 13, 1951, FBI 62-88217-Not Recorded; Memo, Belmont to Ladd, March 20, 1952, FBI 62-88217-555.
26. Memo, Belmont to Ladd, August 2, 1951, FBI 62-88217-Not Recorded.
27. Memo, Belmont to Ladd, March 31, 1952, FBI 62-88217-596.
28. Memo, Nichols to Tolson, October 3, 1952, FBI 62-882178-793.
29. Memo, Hoover to Tolson, Ladd, and Nichols, November 25, 1952, FBI 62-88217-854; Memo, Belmont to Ladd, January 30, 1953, FBI 62-88217-898; Memo, Rosen to Ladd, February 6, 1953, FBI 62-88217-unclear; Memo, Nichols to Tolson, January 26, 1953, FBI 62-88217-901; Memo, FBI Director to Attorney General, January 28, 1953, FBI 62-88217-901; Memo, FBI Director to Attorney General, March 4, 1953, FBI 62-88217-919; Memo, Nichols to Tolson, February 4, 1953, FBI 62-88217-Not Recorded; Memo, Nichols to Tolson, March 9, 1953, FBI

62-88217-947; Memo, Nichols to Tolson, March 4, 1953, FBI 62-88217-Not Recorded.

30. Airtel, FBI Director to SAC Albany, February 18, 1953, FBI 62-88217-909; Memo, FBI Executives' Conference to Tolson, May 8, 1953, FBI 62-88217-1061; Memo, Nichols to Tolson, February 27, 1953, FBI 62-88217-943; Memo, Nichols to Tolson, September 2, 1953, FBI 62-88217-Not Recorded; Memo, Nichols to Tolson, September 10, 1953, FBI 62-88217-1208; Memos, Keay to Belmont, March 23 and 30, April 5 and 10, 1953, all in FBI 62-88217-Not Recorded; Memo, Nichols to Tolson, March 7, 1953, FBI 62-88217-1885; Memo, Baumgardner to Belmont, March 3, 1953, FBI 62-88217-Not Recorded; Memo, Hoover to Tolson, Nichols, Boardman, and Belmont, March 31, 1954, FBI 62-88217-1438.
31. Airtel, FBI Director to SAC Albany, February 18, 1953, FBI 62-88217-909.
32. Memo, Nichols to Tolson, March 7, 1953, FBI 62-88217-1885; Memo, Baumgardner to Belmont, March 3, 1953, FBI 62-88217-Not Recorded.
33. Theoharis and Cox, *The Boss,* pp. 271–272; Memo, Hoover to Tolson, Nichols, and Ladd, November 13, 1953, FBI 62-88217-Not Recorded; Routing Slip, Gandy (checked "see me") accompanying thirty pages of charts titled "Distribution of Investigative Information by the FBI to the White House, Attorney General and Employing Government Agencies," Bentley, Elizabeth folder, Folder #34, Hoover O&C.
34. Memo, Nichols to Tolson, December 14, 1955, FBI 62-88217-1810.
35. Memo, Holloman to Hoover, February 3, 1954, Director folder, Nichols O&C; Memo, Tracy to Hoover, April 1, 1954, and Memo, Nease to Tolson, January 22, 1958, Hoover, J. Edgar Director folder, Folder #85, Hoover O&C.
36. O'Reilly, *Hoover and the Un-Americans,* pp. 128–129.
37. Memo, Hoover to Tolson, Boardman, and Nichols, March 11, 1954, FBI 62-88217-Not Recorded; Memo, Hoover to Tolson, Boardman, Belmont, and Nichols, March 15, 1954, FBI 62-88217-Not Recorded.
38. Memo, Nichols to Tolson, March 1, 1954, FBI 62-88217-1405; Memo, Nichols to Tolson, February 23, 1954, FBI 62-88217-1404.

39. Memo, Nichols to Tolson, March 19, 1954, FBI 62-88217-1433.
40. Memo, Sizoo to Belmont, March 30, 1954, FBI 62-88217-Not Recorded; Memo, FBI Director to Attorney General, April 1, 1954, FBI 62-88217-Not Recorded; Memo, FBI Director to Deputy Attorney General Rogers, April 9, 1954, FBI 62-88217-1479; Memo, Hoover to Tolson, Nichols, Boardman, and Belmont, June 14, 1954, FBI 62-88217-Not Recorded; Memo, Belmont to Boardman, June 17, 1954, FBI 62-88217-Not Recorded; Memo, Nichols to Tolson, July 20, 1954, FBI 62-88217-Not Recorded.
41. Memo, Newton to Fawcett, September 13, 1991 (copy in author's possession), and Letter, Newton to Theoharis, September 23, 1992. I thank Verne Newton, director of the Franklin D. Roosevelt presidential library, for providing me with a copy of his report to the head of the presidential library system concerning the disposition and handling of the Morgenthau Diaries.
42. Memo, Nichols to Tolson, April 5, 1954, FBI 62-88217-Not Recorded; Memo, Nichols to Tolson, July 6, 1955, FBI 62-88217-Not Recorded.
43. Memo, Nichols to Tolson, October 13, 1955, FBI 62-88217-1765; Memo, Nichols to Tolson, October 8, 1955, FBI 62-88217-1775; Memo, Belmont to Boardman, November 9, 1955, FBI 62-88217-1795; Memo, FBI Director to Attorney General, November 10, 1955, FBI 62-88217-1795.
44. Memo, Belmont to Boardman, October 12, 1955, FBI 62-88217-Not Recorded; Memo, Nichols to Tolson, October (day unclear) 1955, FBI 62-88217-Not Recorded; Airtel, FBI Director to SAC Washington, October 21, 1955, FBI 62-88217-Not Recorded.
45. Memo, Roach to Belmont, January 13, 1956, FBI 62-88217-1834; Memo, Roach to Belmont, January 6, 1956, FBI 62-88217-1835; Memo, Hoover to Tolson, Boardman, Belmont, and Nichols, January 13, 1956, FBI 62-88217-1836.
46. Memo, Newton to Fawcett, September 13, 1991, and "List of material to be excised for F.B.I." containing handwritten notation "This job done in Aug. 1957." The removal from the National Archives of these FBI-related documents was not exceptional, FBI director Hoover having consistently

acted to ensure that no FBI record, dating from the bureau's creation in 1908, would be accessible at the National Archives. Theoharis and Cox, *The Boss,* pp. 68n, 267–268.

47. Memo, Belmont to Ladd, February 5, 1951, FBI 62-93875-7; Memo, Nichols to Tolson, February 2, 1951, FBI 62-93875-9; Memo, Nichols to Tolson, February 5, 1951, FBI 62-93875-16; Memo, Belmont to Ladd, February 9, 1951, FBI 62-93875-21; Memo, Ladd to FBI Director, February 12, 1951, FBI 62-93875-22; Memo, Belmont to Boardman (with attached summary of Responsibilities Program), March 31, 1955, FBI 62-93875-2663.
48. Memo, Nichols to Tolson, February 2, 1951, FBI 62-93875-9; Memo, Jones to Nichols, February 2, 1951, FBI 62-93875-13; Memo, Jones to Nichols, February 8, 1951, FBI 62-93875-58; Memo, Jones to Tolson, February 10, 1951, FBI 62-93875-47x.
49. Memo, Nichols to Tolson, February 2, 1951, FBI 62-93875-14x; Memo, Hoover to Tolson, Ladd, and Nichols, February 6, 1951, FBI 62-93875-6.
50. Memo, FBI Executives' Conference to FBI Director, October 14, 1953, FBI 62-93875-Not Recorded; Memo, Nichols to Tolson, February 12, 1951, FBI 62-93875-4; SAC Letter #17, February 13, 1951, FBI 62-93875-Not Recorded; Memo, Belmont to Ladd, February 13, 1951, FBI 62-93875-86; SAC Letter #19, February 17, 1951, FBI 62-93875-Not Recorded; Memo, Belmont to Ladd, May 15, 1951, FBI 62-93875-271.
51. O'Reilly, *Hoover and the Un-Americans,* pp. 207–208. Memo, Belmont to Ladd, May 7, 1951, FBI 62-93875-229; Letter, SAC Chicago to FBI Director, August 17, 1951, FBI 62-93875-535; Letter, FBI Director to SAC Chicago, September 13, 1951, FBI 62-93875-535; Memo, SAC Chicago to FBI Director, December 22, 1954, FBI 62-93875-9-3; Letter, SAC Seattle to FBI Director, May 4, 1951, FBI 62-93875-Not Recorded; Memos (2), Belmont to Ladd, May 21, 1951, FBI 62-93875-333 and FBI 62-93875-342; Letter, SAC New York to FBI Director, November 29, 1954, FBI 62-93875-2535; Letter, FBI Director to SAC New York, December 6, 1954, FBI 62-93875-2535; Memo, Belmont to Ladd, September 10, 1951, FBI 62-93875-534; Memo, SAC Cleveland to FBI Director, April 4, 1955, FBI

62-93875-2661; Memo, Belmont to Boardman, April 7, 1954, FBI 62-93875-2168; Memo, SAC Philadelphia to FBI Director, March 23, 1953, FBI 62-93875-1361; Memo, Nichols to Tolson, July 9, 1953, FBI 62-93875-1478; Letter, SAC New York to FBI Director, February 16, 1954, FBI 62-93875-2073; Letter, FBI Director to SAC New York, March 2, 1954, FBI 62-93875-2073; Memo, SAC New York to FBI Director, February 15, 1954, FBI 62-93875-2418; Memo, Belmont to Boardman, October 14, 1954, FBI 62-93875-2453; Letter, SAC Philadelphia to FBI Director, May 25, 1951, FBI 62-93875-372; Memo, Hoover to Tolson, Boardman, and Nichols, March 30, 1954, FBI 62-93875-Not Recorded; Letter, SAC Milwaukee to FBI Director, FBI 62-93875-1544; Letter, FBI Director to SAC Milwaukee, August 13, 1953, FBI 62-93875-1544.

52. Letter, FBI Director to SAC Philadelphia, October 29, 1953, FBI 62-93875-1747; Teletype, SAC Portland to FBI Director, February 6, 1951, FBI 62-93875-40; Memo, Belmont to Ladd, September 21, 1953, FBI 62-93875-1650; Letter, SAC Mobile to FBI Director, October 15, 1953, FBI 62-93875-1751; Letter, FBI Director to SAC Mobile, October 30, 1953, FBI 62-93875-1751; Memo, SAC New Orleans to FBI Director, October 8, 1953, FBI 62-93875-1744; Letter, FBI Director to SAC New Orleans, October 28, 1953, FBI 62-93875-1744; Letter, SAC San Francisco to FBI Director, November 18, 1953, FBI 62-93875-1829; Letter, FBI Director to SAC San Francisco, December 4, 1953, FBI 62-93875-1829; Memo, Belmont to Boardman, December 3, 1954, FBI 62-93875-2529; Memo, Belmont to Ladd, December 8, 1953, FBI 62-93875-1843; Memo, Baumgardner to Belmont, March 4, 1954, FBI 62-93875-2087; Memo, Belmont to Ladd, February 23, 1954, FBI 62-93875-2033; Letter, FBI Director to SAC Little Rock, February 23, 1954, FBI 62-93875-2045.

53. Memo, FBI Executives' Conference to FBI Director, April 30, 1951, FBI 62-93875-204; SAC Letter #47, May 12, 1951, FBI 62-93875-Not Recorded.

54. Letter, SAC Los Angeles to FBI Director, April 15, 1953, FBI 62-93875-Not Recorded; Memo, Belmont to Ladd, April 17, 1953, FBI 62-93875-1278; Memo, Belmont to Boardman, May 13, 1954, FBI 62-93875-2278;

Letter, SAC Denver to FBI Director, July 14, 1954, FBI 62-93875-2358; Teletype, SAC Denver to FBI Director, May 11, 1954, FBI 62-93875-2282; Memo, Martin to Belmont, May 11, 1954, FBI 62-93875-2326; Memo, SAC Denver to Belmont, May 12, 1954, FBI 62-93875-2326; Memo, Belmont to Boardman, March 13, 1954, FBI 62-93875-2278; Memo, Belmont to Boardman, March 31, 1955, FBI 62-93875-2663; Letter, SAC Los Angeles to FBI Director, February 20, 1953, FBI 62-93875-1142; Memo, Belmont to Ladd, October 15, 1953; FBI 62-93875-1704; Memo, Jones to Nichols, December 3, 1953, FBI 62-93875-1845.

55. Memo, Belmont to Ladd, October 20, 1953, FBI 62-93875-Not Recorded; SAC Letter #53–72, October 27, 1953, FBI 62-93875-Not Recorded; Memo, FBI Executives' Conference to FBI Director, October 14, 1953, FBI 62-93875-Not Recorded; Memo, FBI Executives' Conference to Tolson, November 24, 1953, FBI 62-93875-1848; Memo, FBI Director to Attorney General, December 2, 1953, FBI 62-93875-1848; Memo, FBI Director to Attorney General, December 23, 1953, FBI 62-93875-1892; Memo, FBI Director to Attorney General, February 4, 1954, FBI 62-93875-2007.
56. Memo, Hoover to Tolson, Boardman, and Nichols, March 30, 1954, FBI 62-93875-Not Recorded; Memo, Hoover to Tolson, Boardman, Belmont, and Nichols, March 30, 1954, FBI 62-93875-Not Recorded; Teletype, SAC San Francisco to FBI Director, FBI 62-93875-2172; Memo, Belmont to Boardman, May 31, 1954, FBI 62-93875-2172; Memo, Belmont to Boardman, April 6, 1954, FBI 62-93875-2164; Memo, Belmont to Boardman, March 31, 1954, FBI 62-93875-2663; Memo, Baumgardner to Belmont, March 4, 1954, FBI 62-93875-2087; Memo, FBI Executives' Conference to Tolson, April 7, 1954, FBI 62-93875-2257.
57. *Denver Post,* May 11, 1954 (copy in FBI 62-93875).
58. Memo, Hoover to Tolson, Boardman, Belmont, and Nichols, July 19, 1954, FBI 62-93875-2360; Memo, Boardman to FBI Director, July 22, 1954, FBI 62-93875-2377.
59. Memo, Boardman to FBI Director, July 22, 1954, FBI 62-93875-2377.
60. Martin's *Denver Post* series is included in the FBI's 62-93875 file. For FBI

officials' reactions to this series and briefing of Attorney General Brownell, see Memo, Belmont to Boardman, March 31, 1955, FBI 62-93875-2663; Memo, FBI Director to Attorney General, September 28, 1954, FBI 62-93875-2462; Memo, FBI Director to Attorney General, September 29, 1954, FBI 62-93875-2414.

61. Memo, FBI Director to Attorney General, October 13, 1954, FBI 62-93875-2465; Airtel, FBI Director to All SACs, October 21, 1954, FBI 62-93875-2461.
62. Memo, Hoover to Tolson, Boardman, Belmont, and Nichols, November 9, 1954, FBI 62-93875-Not Recorded; Memo, Attorney General to FBI Director, November 10, 1954, FBI 62-93875-2499; Memo, FBI Director to Attorney General, November 15, 1954, FBI 62-93875-2510; SAC Letter #54–65, November 16, 1954, FBI 62-93875-Not Recorded.
63. Memo, SAC Buffalo to FBI Director, February 14, 1955, FBI 62-93875-Not Recorded; Memo, FBI Director to Attorney General, March 3, 1955, FBI 62-93875-2657; Memo, Attorney General to FBI Director, March 7, 1955, FBI 62-93975-2656; Memo, Hoover to Tolson, Boardman, and Nichols, March 7, 1955, FBI 62-93875-2653; SAC Letter #55–21, March 10, 1955, FBI 62-93875-Not Recorded.
64. Athan Theoharis, "FBI Wiretapping: A Case Study of Bureaucratic Autonomy," *Political Science Quarterly,* 107 (Spring 1992), pp. 107, 112–114.
65. Memo, SAC Washington to FBI Director, May 29, 1953, FBI 65-6165-164; Memo, Rosen to Ladd, June 19, 1953, FBI 65-6165-166; Memo, SAC Washington to FBI Director, March 16, 1953, FBI 65-6165-123; Wiretap subject card: Henry William Grunewald, March 16, 1953, FBI 65-6165-124; Memo, Rosen to Ladd, March 17, 1953, FBI 65-6165-127; Memo, FBI Director to SAC Washington, March 20, 1953, FBI 65-6165-129; Memo, Rosen to Ladd, March 18, 1953, FBI 65-6165-127; Memo, Rosen to Ladd, March 19, 1953, FBI 65-6165-137; Memo, Rosen to Ladd, April 3, 1953, FBI 65-6165-1-148; Memo, Ladd to FBI Director, March 13, 1953, FBI 65-6165-118; Personal and Confidential Memo, Hoover to Attorney General, March 16, 1953, FBI 65-6165-119; Memo, Rosen to Ladd, March 13, 1953, FBI 65-6165-121.

66. Personal and Confidential Memo, Hoover to Attorney General, March 16, 1953, FBI 65-6165-119; Memo, Rosen to Ladd, March 13, 1953, FBI 65-6165-121; Memo, Ladd to Rosen, March 18, 1953, FBI 65-6165-126; Memo, SAC Washington to FBI Director, May 29, 1953, FBI 65-6165-164; Memo, Rosen to Ladd, May 1, 1953, FBI 62-994444-6.
67. I have not cited all the reports prepared on the Grunewald wiretap and then sent to Attorney General Brownell. These were prepared daily between March 18 and June 6, 1953. For examples, see Memo, SAC Washington to FBI Director, March 17, 1953, FBI 65-6165-1-124; Memo, FBI Director to Attorney General, March 18, 1953, FBI 65-6165-1-124; Memo, SAC Washington to FBI Director, March 19, 1953, FBI 65-6165-1-125; Memo, FBI Director to Attorney General, March 20, 1953, FBI 65-6165-1-125; Memo, SAC Washington to FBI Director, March 18, 1953, FBI 65-6165-1-126; Memo, FBI Director to Attorney General, March 19, 1953, FBI 65-6165-1-128; Memo, FBI Director to Attorney General, March 25, 1953, FBI 65-6165-1-129; Memo, FBI Director to Attorney General, March 30, 1953, FBI 65-6165-1-134; Memo, FBI Director to Attorney General, March 31, 1953, FBI 65-6165-1-136; Memo, FBI Director to Attorney General, April 28, 1953, FBI 65-6165-1-168; Memo, FBI Director to Attorney General, May 25, 1953, FBI 65-6165-1-191.
68. Personal and Confidential Memo, Hoover to Attorney General, March 16, 1953, FBI 65-6165-119.

CHAPTER NINE. THE LESSONS OF HISTORY

1. The quote describing the Zubilin-Nelson arrangement is from a May 1943 report of FBI director Hoover to the Roosevelt White House, reprinted in Benson and Warner, *Venona,* pp. 49–50.
2. The failure of U.S. covert operations in Eastern Europe, the Balkans, and the Soviet Union is chronicled in Peter Grose, *Operation Rollback: America's Secret War Behind the Iron Curtain* (Boston, 2000). On the Italian and French covert operations, see U.S. Senate, Select Committee

to Study Governmental Operations with Respect to Intelligence Activities, *Supplementary Detailed Staff Reports on Foreign and Military Intelligence,* Book IV, 94th Cong., 2d sess., 1976, pp. 12–40.

3. For a brief history of the Black case, see Theoharis and Cox, *The Boss,* pp. 368–393. FBI documents recording the responses of FBI officials to this case are reprinted in Theoharis, *From the Secret Files of J. Edgar Hoover,* pp. 153–176, 267–275.
4. Memo, SAC, Washington to FBI Director, March 6, 1970, and Memo, FBI Director to SAC, Washington, March 11, 1970, both FBI 66-3286-Not Recorded.
5. These memoranda are reprinted in Theoharis, *From the Secret Files,* pp. 31–33, 77–80, 282–286. Similar memoranda on President Dwight Eisenhower and his key advisers in his 1952 campaign for the presidency are also reprinted in *ibid.,* pp. 52–56.
6. Memo, Jones to Bishop, November 4, 1972, FBI 66-3286-Not Recorded.
7. Memo, Jones to Bishop, November 4, 1972, FBI 66-3286-Not Recorded; Memo, Jones to Bishop, November 9, 1972, FBI 66-3286-1120; Memo, Gray to Attorney General, November 13, 1972, FBI 66-3286-1118; Memo, Erickson to Gray, November 21, 1972, FBI 66-3286-1121; Memo, Kelley to Attorney General, July 5, 1973, FBI 66-3286-1136.
8. The contrast between Gray's decision to seek counsel and Hoover's unilateral decision to destroy summary memoranda once they were no longer useful indirectly highlight Hoover's independence and indifference to the law. During his directorship, FBI operations were Hoover's exclusive domain, and FBI officials never formally deliberated whether their decisions to destroy "informal" records conformed to the provisions of the 1950 Federal Records Act.
9. On the pink-blue memoranda procedure, see Memo, Hoover to Tolson et al., April 11, 1940, FBI 66-3665-544; Memo, Tolson to Hoover, March 21, 1944, FBI 66-A-2670x; Memo, Hoover to FBI Assistant Directors and Supervisors, November 15, 1944, FBI 66-3365-759; Memo, Hoover to All FBI Supervisors, March 1, 1942, FBI 66-3475-29x; Memo, McIntire to Mumford, August 20, 1942, FBI 62-116758. On Do Not File memoranda,

see Memo, Sullivan to DeLoach, July 19, 1966, "Black Bag" Jobs folder, Folder #36, Hoover O&C. On regular destruction of office files, see Memo, Hoover to Tolson et al., March 19, 1953, FBI 66-2095-100.

10. These and other CIA separate records and record destruction practices are more fully discussed in Athan Theoharis, "In-House Cover-Up: Researching FBI Files," pp. 39–40, 43; *New York Times,* May 29, 1997, p. A11, and November 14, 2000, p. A8. Other CIA record destruction practices, employed during the Iran-Contra affair, are described in *Final Report of the Independent Counsel for Iran/Contra Matter, Vol. 1, Investigations and Prosecutions* (Washington, D.C., 1993), pp. 255–259.
11. Senate Select on Intelligence Activities, *Hearings on Intelligence Activities, Vol. 2, Huston Plan,* pp. 130–131.
12. Relevant documents pertaining to FBI microphone surveillance policy and notification of the attorney general and the Justice Department are reprinted in Theoharis, *From the Secret Files,* pp. 136–152.

Index

Acheson, Dean, 38
Action in the North Atlantic, 153n
Adams, Arthur, 27–28, 27n, 73n; FBI wiretapping, 69
Adams, Sherman: Alsop matter, 191, 194
Administrative pages, 91–92, 142
Allen, George, 42; FBI reports, 108
Alsop, Joseph: homosexuality, 191–197; "missile gap" columns, 195, 282n37
Alsop, Stewart, 192, 193
Altschuler, Lydia, 86
Altschuler case, 67
Amerasia: case, 31n, 41, 97–109, 247n; FBI break-ins, 98; FBI bugging, 99; FBI wiretapping, 98
American Civil Liberties Union, 111
American Mercury, 207
American Peace Mobilization: FBI break-in, 112
Ames, Aldrich, 10
Amtorg, 63
Anderson, Marguerite, 59
Anonymous letter, 63, 65
Arlen, Richard, 159
Armed Forces Security Agency, 18
Army Security Agency, 7, 9
Army-McCarthy hearings, 210
Arnett, Peter, 144
Aronoff, Jacob, 73n
Association of Retired Intelligence (KGB) Officers, 4
AT&T: FBI wiretapping, 89

Baldwin, C. B.: 59
Barr, Joel, 82
Barry, Frank, 183–184
Becker, Samuel, 73n, 74
Belmont, Alan, 181
Bennington College, 215
Benson, Robert, 24, 25
Bentley, Elizabeth, 26, 29, 36, 39, 55, 86; espionage activities, 41–43, 56, 77, 80, 84, 214, 239–240; Remington case, 114, 131–138
Berlau, Ruth, 58
Berle, Adolf, 35, 36, 116; COMRAP, 94–95
Bernay, Eric, 73n Bessie, Alvah, 159n
Biberman, Herbert, 159n; FBI wiretapping, 59
Biddle, Francis: FBI reports, 156; FBI wiretapping, 61, 68, 68n, 94; Kravchenko defection, 51–53
Bittleman, Alexander, 73n; FBI wiretapping, 68
Black, Fred: case, 240–241
Blick, Roy, 173, 174
Blind memoranda, 142, 145–146, 159–160, 162, 162n, 163, 180, 200, 276n39

Index

Blum, John Morton, 221
Boardman, Leland, 229
Bohlen, Charles, 192, 204–205, 209
Bowman, Ralph, 73n
Boy from Stalingrad, 153n
Boy Scouts of America, 226
Bradley, Omar, 9
Bransten, Louise, 73n, 77
Break-ins, 11, 34, 43, 56, 57–59, 64, 69, 80, 84, 95, 98–99, 100, 103–104, 105, 112, 131, 154, 155, 163, 245–247
Brecht, Bertolt, 58
Brennan, Charles, 246
Bridges, Styles, 171–172
Browder, Earl, 62, 73n; espionage activities, 32, 74, 74n, 77, 95, 136
Brownell, Herbert, 192–194; allegations regarding Harry Dexter White appointment, 107, 215–217; FBI bugging, 248; FBI covert relations, 203, 213–223; Grunewald wiretap, 232–234, 291n67
Brownell, Samuel, 229
Brunini, John: Hiss grand jury, 128; Remington grand jury, 131, 134–138
Bugging, 11, 34, 56–58, 64, 70, 74–75, 84, 99, 112, 145, 240, 247–250
Bullitt, William, 22, 51
Byrd, Harry, 207
Byrnes, James, 39, 41

Callahan, Nicholas, 188
Campbell, Alexander, 123, 124; Hiss grand jury, 115
Cannon, Al, 145
Capell, Frank, 186
Carr, Frank, 208–209
Carsman, Eveline, 73n
Catholic Church: FBI relations with, 145–150
Central Intelligence Agency (CIA), 172; Alsop matter, 192–197; COMRAP, 66; record destruction, 245–246; records restriction, 8; Venona Project, 8
Chambers, Whittaker, 19–21, 21n, 132; allegations regarding Hiss, 35–40, 45, 56, 114–131, 269n7
Chanler, William, 137
Cherry, Frank, 226, 234
Chevalier, Haakon, 73n; FBI wiretapping, 69
Church Committee, 144
Churchill, Winston, 15, 17
CINRAD, 63, 237
CIO Council, 112
CIO Maritime Committee, 112
Civil rights activists: FBI surveillance, 110, 111, 139, 140, 154
Civil Service Commission, 201
Clark, Tom, 41, 122, 124; *Amerasia* case, 102n, 105; Coplon case, 84, 87–88, 89n; FBI wiretapping, 42n, 84, 164–167; House Committee on Un-American Activities, 157
Clarke, Carter, 9, 24, 26
Coe, Frank, 96, 97
Cohen, Benjamin, 102n
Cohen, Morris, 17
Cohn, Roy, 203, 208
COINTELPRO, 143–144
Cole, Lester, 159n
Collins, Eileen, 136–137
COMINFIL, 140, 143–144
Comintern records, 6
Communications Act of 1934, 93, 166
Communist Party (Soviet Union), 5–6
Communist Party (U.S.): Espionage Act, 79–80; espionage activities, 7,

Index

15–18, 28, 29, 31–32, 34–78, 237; FBI bugging, 145; FBI surveillance, 110, 110n, 139–143; FBI wiretapping, 56, 59, 94; Foreign Agents Registration Act, 80; Hollywood, 151–169; records, 6; Smith Act, 80
COMPIC, 58–59, 140, 144, 151–169
COMRAP, 62–78, 94–95, 110n, 237
Condon, Edward, 85
Congress: FBI monitoring members of, 241–244
Congress of Industrial Organizations (CIO), 57; FBI wiretapping, 59
Connally, Thomas, 39, 183
Consumer National Federation, 111
Consumers Union, 111
Contreras, Manuel, 245
Coplon, Judith, 17, 46, 78, 236; case, 81, 84–93, 95; espionage activities, 32, 45, 48–49, 54, 84, 85–86
Corcoran, Thomas, 230; FBI wiretapping, 102, 102n, 105–107, 108, 247n, 268n25
Correa, Mathias, 99
Council for a Democratic Germany, 57
Coyne, Patrick, 123
Cronin, John, 234; covert relations with FBI, 120, 144–151, 197; adviser to Richard Nixon, 272n5
Crum, Bartley: FBI wiretapping, 59, 164–167
Currie, Lauchlin, 24–26

Dallin, David, 50–51
Damon Runyon Cancer Fund, 226
Dawson, Donald, 184
Democratic National Committee, 16, 268n25
Dennis, Eugene, 32
Denver Post: Responsibilities Program, 227–230
Department of Justice: *Amerasia* case, 105–106; Coplon case, 84–89
Devin-Adair: Bentley book, 136–137
Dewey, Thomas, 16; homosexual threat, 173
Dickstein, Samuel, 19, 23, 253n4
Dieterle, William: FBI wiretapping, 69
Dirksen, Everett, 181, 182
Disney, Walt, 144
Dmytryk, Edward, 159, 159n
"Do Not File," 142, 245, 246–247, 250
Dodd, Martha, 19
Dolgov, Vassili, 63, 65, 66, 67
Donegan, Thomas, 42, 127; Brunini's collaboration with Bentley, 137; Hiss grand jury, 115, 117, 128–129, 130; Remington grand jury, 97, 131, 134–135
Donovan, William, 26
Dulles, Allen: Alsop matter, 192–197
Dulles, John Foster, 192
Durr, Clifford, 90

Eastland, James, 217
Eden, Anthony, 190, 191, 194
Edge of Darkness, 153n
Edwards, Albert, 73n
Edwards, Willard, 200
Eisenhower, Dwight: regarding homosexuals, 189, 190–191, 194–196; FBI reporting procedures, 187–189; secrecy of records, 221–223
Eisler, Gerhart, 73n
Eisler, Hanns, 158

Eldridge, Florence, 166
Electrical Communications: FBI wiretapping, 69
Electronic Corporation of America, 27n, 69
Emerson, Thomas, 112–113
Espionage Act, 32, 79, 93
Executive Order 8895, 7

Fahy, Charles, 112
Farmers Union, 111
Fay, George, 167
FBI Executives Conference: minutes, 178–179, 252n8
Federal Bureau of Investigation (FBI): administrative pages, 91–92, 142; Administrative Review Unit, 242–243; *Amerasia* case, 97–109; anonymous letter, 63, 65; appropriations, 11–12; attorney general oversight, 247–250; Bentley case, 42–45, 84, 95–97; blind memoranda, 142, 145–146, 159–160, 162, 162n, 163, 180, 200, 276n39; break-ins, 11, 34, 43, 56, 57–59, 64, 69, 80, 84, 95, 98, 99, 100, 103–104, 105, 112, 131, 154, 155, 163, 245–247; British intelligence, 18n; bugging, 11, 34, 56–58, 64, 70, 74–75, 84, 99, 112, 145, 240, 247–250; Central Records System, 142; civil rights activists, 110, 111, 139, 140, 154; Communist Party, 9, 10–11, 60, 68–77, 237; COMPIC, 140, 144, 151–156; Coplon case, 81, 84–93, 95; Thomas Corcoran, 102, 102n, 105–107, 108, 230, 247n, 268n25; counterintelligence, 9, 11, 17–18, 27n, 28–29, 31–33, 34–78, 94–95, 110, 110n, 235–237, 239; John Cronin, 144–151; "educational campaign," 168; educational institutions, 110, 113, 169, 212, 214–215, 226–230; espionage prosecutions, 79–109; expanded role and authority, 11–12; FBI Executives Conference, 8n, 112–113; Freedom of Information Act, 64–66, 67, 68, 72, 73–74, 73n, 77, 144, 212, 225, 252n8, 253n9, 268n25; Henry Grunewald, 230–234; Hollywood, 57–59; homosexuals, 174, 177–197, 205; House Committee on Un-American Activities, 91, 138, 156–164; Rock Hudson, 197; "intelligence" investigations, 140; June Mail, 92–93, 142; labor unions, 110, 111–112, 139, 145, 151–152, 169; leaking practices, 110, 142, 151, 168, 199–230, 234, 247n; loyalty programs, 11; Joseph McCarthy, 199–210; National Archives, 178–179, 221–222, 243–244, 286n46; Richard Nixon, 120–124, 138; office files, 142, 292n9; personnel, 12; political surveillance, 9, 85, 87, 90, 91, 110–114, 139–142; record destruction, 68n, 112, 178–179, 240–245, 292n8, 293n9; Record Destruction File, 241–244; records restrictions, 8n, 223; Responsibilities Program, 212, 223–230; Rosenberg case, 82–83; SAC Letters, 13; Senate Internal Security Subcommittee, 202, 210–220; separate records procedures, 142, 200–201, 242–243; Sex Deviate program, 177–179; Soviet funding of U.S. Communist Party, 57; Adlai Stevenson, 179–186; "summary

memorandum" procedure re members of Congress, 241–244; Venona Project, 7–8, 8n, 9–10, 89, 89n; White House Security Survey, 101–102; withholding of records, 8n, 12–14. *See also* CINRAD; COINTELPRO; COMINFIL; COMRAP; "Do Not File"; Mail covers; Mail opening (intercepts); Wiretapping.
Federal Employee Loyalty Program, 85, 133, 156, 171, 172
Federal Records Act of 1950, 243, 292n8
Federation of American Scientists (FAS), 113–114
Feuchtwanger, Lion, 58
Fine, John, 226
Fitzgerald, Edward, 45
Flanagan, Francis, 206
Flato, Charles, 77
Fleming, Arthur, 149
Fletcher, Howard, 9
Food, Tobacco, Agricultural & Allied Workers of America (CIO), 112
For Whom the Bell Tolls, 153n
Ford, Peyton, 106; *Amerasia* case, 105–106; Coplon case, 89
Ford Foundation, 205
Foreign Agents Registration Act, 32, 79, 93
Foreign Intelligence Service (Russia), 4, 12
Forrestal, James, 41, 100–101
Foster, William, 32
Franey, Joseph, 74
Frank, Leonhard, 58
Free Germany Committee, 57, 58
Freedom of Information Act (FOIA): FBI records, 8n, 12–14, 56, 64–66, 67, 68, 72, 73–74, 73n, 77, 144, 212, 225, 252n8, 253n9, 268n25
Freeman, Joseph, 73n
Fuchs, Klaus, 17, 18n, 236
Fujii, Shuji, 73n
Fulbright, J. William, 218

Gabrielson, Guy, 172
Gaither Commission, 195
Gale, James, 249
Gardner, Meredith, 2
Garfield, John, 166
Gates, Thomas, 218–219
Gayn, Mark, 99, 100, 103
General Service Administration: Morgenthau diaries, 221–222
George Washington University, 177, 179
Getsov, Eva, 55
Girl from Stalingrad, 153n
Gitlow, Benjamin, 74n
Glasser, Harold, 31n, 55
Gleason, J. Everett, 221
Gold, Harry, 17, 18, 18n, 81, 236
Golos, Jacob, 86
Goodpaster, Andrew, 191
Gouzenko, Igor, 38, 39
Graf, Osker, 58
Granich, Grace, 73n
Granich, Max, 73n
Gray, L. Patrick, III: record destruction, 243–244
Gray, Robert, 196
Green, Ed, 187
Greenglass, David, 17, 18, 31, 46–47, 81, 82, 83, 236
Greenglass, Ruth, 46–47, 83
Gregg, Joseph, 26
Grimes, Charles, 219–220
GRU (Soviet military intelligence), 27, 38; records, 20–21, 30

Grunewald, Henry, 230–234; FBI wiretapping, 232–234, 291n67
Gubitchev, Valentin, 84, 85
Gurnea, Myron, 101

Hall, Gus, 32
Hall, Theodore, 17, 31–32, 78, 81–83, 236
Hammerstein, Oscar, 212
Hand, Learned, 133, 135–136
Hangmen Also Die, 153n
Hanssen, Robert, 10
Harding, Warren, 234n
Harris, Lement, 73n
Hart, Moss, 212
Harvard University, 215, 226
Hayes, Harold, 25, 26
Haynes, John, 5, 6, 18, 23–28, 27n, 35, 41, 138n, 254n16
Hays, Arthur Garfield, 212
Heiman, Julius, 73n
Helms, Richard: destruction of office file, 245
Hemingway, Ernest, 144
Herter, Christian, 195
Hill, Lister, 173
Hill, Milt, 183, 187
Hillenkoetter, Roscoe, 9
Hiskey, Marcia, 73, 73n
Hiss, Alger, 113, 170, 241; Ales code name, 20, 30–31, 31n; alleged espionage activities, 19–21, 29–31, 36–41; FBI wiretapping and mail opening, 39, 241; grand jury investigation, 114–131, 247n; grand jury records, 13
Hochberg, Getzel, 73n
Hoey, Clyde: investigations of homosexuals, 173–177
Hoey Committee, 173–177
Hollywood: blacklist, 167–168, 205
Holmes, Julius, 99
Holtzoff, Alexander, 231
Homosexuals, 170–197
Hood, Richard: Communists in Hollywood, 151, 152, 157–160, 163; wiretapping request, 59
Hoover, J. Edgar: *Amerasia* case, 100, 104–105, 104n, 107–109; American Business Consultants, 149; Elizabeth Bentley, 43; Charles Bohlen, 204–205; break-ins, 112, 245, 250; Tom Clark, 165–167; COMRAP, 50, 62–63, 70, 73; Coplon case, 87–93; *Counterattack*, 149 counterintelligence, 60–61; John Cronin, 146–148, 150–151; “Do Not File,” 245, 250; “educational campaign,” 168; educational institutions, 215, 229–230; FBI records, 223; Henry Grunewald, 230–234; Grunewald wiretap, 232–234, 291n67; Alger Hiss, 37–40; Hollywood, 151–164; House Committee on Un-American Activities, 122–123, 124, 139, 156–164; “intelligence” investigations, 140; labor unions, 111–112; Joseph McCarthy, 199–210; Official and Confidential File, 180–183, 186, 241–242; *Plain Talk*, 149; political surveillance, 111; record destruction, 241, 292n8; Responsibilities Program, 223–230; Roosevelt administration, 60–61, 141–142; Senate Internal Security Subcommittee, 210–220; Sex Deviate program, 177–179; Adlai Stevenson, 179–186; Truman administration, 142, 184–185, 275n28; Arthur Vandenberg, Jr., 186–191; wiretapping, 93–94
Hornbeck, Stanley, 98n

Index

Horne, Lena, 166
Hottel, Guy: Joseph McCarthy, 201; Adlai Stevenson, 183–184
House Committee on Un-American Activities (HUAC), 85, 87, 150, 206, 215, 218, 224, 239, 247n; covert relations with FBI, 59, 120, 156–164; Hiss-Chambers investigation, 114; National Lawyers Guild, 91
Houston, Charles, 166
Hudson, Rock, 197
Hudson, Roy, 145
Hull, Cordell: Kravchenko defection, 52
Humelsine, Carlisle, 175
Hunt, Marsha, 166
Huston, John, 166

Inslerman, Elizabeth, 130–131, 136
Inslerman, Felix, 128–131; FBI wiretapping, 129, 130
Institute of Pacific Relations, 212, 214
International Juridical Association, 118
International Longshoremen's and Warehousemen's Union, 112
Irvine v. California, 248
ITT World Communications, 7
Ivanov, Ivan, 50
Ivens, Joris: FBI wiretapping, 69

Jackson, Robert, 61
Jaffe, Philip, 98–99, 100, 101n, 103–104, 105; FBI wiretapping and break-ins, 98, 99
Jenner, William 234; covert relations with FBI, 212–223
Joint Anti-Fascist Refugee Committee, 73; FBI wiretapping, 69
Joint Committee on Atomic Energy, 205–206
Johnson, Louis, 89
Johnson, Lyndon: FBI reports, 186, 197
June Mail, 92–93, 142

Kahn, Gordon, 169
Kalugin, Oleg, 27
Katz, Joseph, 55
Katzenbach, Nicholas: FBI bugging, 249
Kean, Robert: Grunewald investigation, 231–233
Keeper of the Flame, 153n
Kellogg, William, 227–228
Kelly, John, Jr., 88
Kennedy, John, 144; Alsop file, 196–197; FBI reports, 185–186, 242
Kennedy, Robert: Alsop file, 196–197
Kennon, Robert, 226
Kerr, Jean, 208, 209
KGB, 15, 16, 17; Alsop matter, 191–192; espionage activities, 21–23, 27, 47–55, 56, 82, 96; records, 4–5, 18–23, 76, 86, 235–237
Kheifets, Gregory, 63, 65, 66, 95n
Khruschev, Nikita, 191
King, Bob, 124
King, Cecil, 231
King, Martin Luther, Jr., 143
Kirch, Egon, 58
Klarin, Pavel, 63, 65, 67, 72
Klehr, Harvey, 5, 6, 18, 23–28, 27n, 35, 41, 138n, 254n16
Knauff, Ellen, 212
Knight, Goodwin, 226
Koch, Howard, 166

Kohlberg, Alfred, 149, 149n
Koral, Alexander, 55
Kramer, Charles, 55
Kravchenko, Victor: defection, 50–53, 55
Kuchel, Thomas, 186
Kusman, Felix, 73, 73n
Kvasnikov, Leonid, 47, 48, 63

Labor unions, 110, 111–112, 139, 145, 151–152; FBI wiretapping and bugging, 112
Ladd, D. Milton, 99, 124, 148, 149, 162–163, 169, 180, 233
Lamphere, Robert, 26n
Langer, William, 221
Lardner, Ring, Jr., 159n
Larsen, Emmanuel, 101n; *Amerasia* case, 99–100, 103–105; FBI break-ins and bugging, 99, 103–104, 104n
Lausche, Frank, 226
Lawson, John, 159n, 164, 165, 166; FBI wiretapping, 59, 99n
Leach, Elizabeth, 59
League of American Writers, 111
Lennon, John, 144
"Leo," 22, 23
Letelier, Orlando, 245
Levine, Isaac Don, 37
Levy, Philip, 73n
Lewis, Fulton, Jr., 106, 181
Lichtenstein, Irving, 166
Lodge, Henry Cabot, 242
Lore, Ludwig, 21n, 37–38, 85
Lotus, Richard, 129, 130
Love, C. Robert, 181
Lukianov, Serghei, 64, 65, 66, 72

Maclean, Donald, 17, 236
Mail covers, 64, 69
Mail opening (intercepts), 11, 34, 42–43, 57–58, 64, 69, 70, 80, 84, 131
Mailer, Norman, 144
Maltz, Albert, 159n
Manhattan Project, 15, 31–32, 38, 47, 63, 74, 81, 82, 235, 254n16
Mann, Heinrich, 58
Mann, Thomas, 58
March, Frederick, 85, 166
March of Dimes, 226
Margolis, Benjamin: FBI wiretapping, 59
Maritime Book Shop: FBI wiretapping, 69
Marsh, Henry, 230
Martens, Ludwig, 85
Massachusetts Institute of Technology (MIT), 226
Matthews, Francis, 147
Matthews, J. B., 200, 206–207
May, Allan, 38
May, Gary, 136
McCarran, Pat: covert relations with FBI, 210–212
McCarthy, Joseph, 174, 234; Frank Carr appointment, 208–209; Communist threat, 32–33, 35, 61, 170–171, 239; covert relations with FBI, 199–210, 247n; homosexual threat, 171–172
McCone, John, 197
McCormack, John, 39
McElroy, Neil, 195–196
McGranery, James, 183; *Amerasia* case, 102n, 105; FBI bugging, 247–248
McGrath, J. Howard: National Lawyers Guild, 90; Remington indictment, 137; Senate Internal Security Subcommittee, 210, 212; Venona Project, 89n

Index

McGuire, Matthew, 112
McInerney, James, 106; *Amerasia* case, 100
McKim, Edward, 101
McManus, Jack, 166
Mechem, Edwin, 226
Meet the Press, 133
Melchiore, Gene, 180, 181–182
Meredith, Burgess, 166
Milestone, Lewis, 166
Military Intelligence Division: Venona Project, 7
Miller, James, 69
Miller, Robert, 76
Mironov, Vassili, 63–64, 65, 66
Mission to Moscow, 153, 153n
Mitchell, Kate, 99, 100, 103
Mohr, John, 161–162
Montgomery, Robert, 159
Morgan, E. P., 43
Morgenthau, Henry: diaries, 221–222
Morris, Robert, 106, 213, 214–215
Morros, Boris, 19, 19n, 23, 64; COMRAP investigation, 73, 73n, 75–76; FBI wiretapping, 68
Mundt, Karl, 53, 172, 234; covert relations with FBI, 120, 126n, 218, 220

Nardone v. U.S., 87, 166, 239
National Archives: FBI records, 221–222, 243–244, 286n46; FBI records destruction, 178–179; Morgenthau diaries, 223
National Governors Conference, 224
National Lawyers Guild, 90–91, 111
National Security Agency (NSA), 24; records restrictions, 8; Venona Project, 7–10, 18
National Union of Maritime Cooks & Stewards, 112
Needle Workers Council for Peace and Civil Rights, 111
Nellor, Ed, 200
Nelson, Steve, 62, 77, 93–94, 237; COMRAP investigation, 73, 73n, 74–75; espionage activities, 49–50, 56, 95
New York City Housing Authority, 226
New York University, 177, 179
New York World-Telegram, 44
Newspaper Guild, 111
Nichols, Louis, 90, 188; *Amerasia* case, 105–106; "the cause," 198, 250; Coplon case, 89; John Cronin, 146; House Committee on Un-American Activities, 122–123, 161, 162, 164; Joseph McCarthy, 202–203, 206–209; Richard Nixon, 120, 121–122; Senate Internal Security Subcommittee, 202–203, 210–211, 212, 214–215, 219–220; Adlai Stevenson, 183; Arthur Vandenberg, Jr., 187–188
Niles, David, 85
Nixon, Richard, 215; covert relations with FBI, 120–124, 247n; Hiss-Chambers investigation, 119–120; Hiss grand jury, 119, 123, 124–126, 126n
Noonan, Gregory, 133, 137–138
North Star, 153n

O'Brien, Lawrence, 185, 186
Office of Censorship, 7, 69
Office of Naval Intelligence (ONI), 218–219
Office of Strategic Services (OSS), 15; *Amerasia* break-ins, 98; Soviet code book, 26, 26n

Olney, Warren, 228
Oppenheimer, J. Robert, 54, 69, 205–206, 254n16; FBI wiretapping, 86
Ornitz, Sam, 159n
Orwell, George, 250
Our Russian Front, 153n
Ovakimyan, Gaik, 86
Owen, David, 180, 181–182, 185
Oxnam, G. Bromley, 165

Palmer, Archibald, 88
Parks, Larry, 276n39
Pearson, Drew: FBI wiretapping, 102
Pelovitz, Samuel, 127–128
Pepper, Claude, 165
Perlo, Victor, 29, 54, 86, 96, 131, 132
Permanent Investigative Committee, 209
Persons, Wilton, 196, 215n
Peters, Joszef, 57, 77
Peurifoy, John, 172
Philby, Harold "Kim," 17, 55, 236
Picator, Erwin, 58
Pichel, Irving, 166
Pike Committee, 144
Pinkerton Detective Agency, 182, 185
Pollard, Jonathan, 10
Popper, Martin: FBI wiretapping, 59, 164–167
Powers, Richard Gid, 35–36
Poyntz, Juliette, 85
Pravdin, Vladimir, 48
Prichard, Edward, 112, 112n; FBI wiretapping, 101–102

Quinn, T. Vincent, 164–167

Rauh, Joseph, 90
Rayburn, Sam, 39
RCA Global, 7
Reagan, Ronald, 144, 159
Reeves, Albert, 86–87
Remington, Ann, 134–135, 138n
Remington, William, 42; Bentley allegations, 29, 42n, 44, 131–133; FBI wiretapping, break-ins, and mail opening, 131; grand jury investigation, 80, 133–138; grand jury records, 13
Renn, Ludwig, 58
Responsibilities Program, 212, 223–230
Roach, Ralph, 42, 87–88, 184
Robison, David: FBI wiretapping, 59
Rodgers, Richard, 212
Rogers, Leila, 159
Rogers, William: Alsop matter, 194–196; FBI assistance to Senator McCarthy, 202–203; FBI relations with Senate Internal Security Subcommittee, 213–214, 220; Grunewald wiretap, 233
Roosevelt, Eleanor, 144
Roosevelt, Franklin, 15, 17, 35, 86, 153; apparent "softness toward communism," 32–33, 35–41, 44, 61, 68n, 199, 218–219, 221–223, 239; FBI counterintelligence, 11–12, 13, 60–61, 111; FBI reports, 141–142; Kravchenko defection, 51–52; Office of Censorship, 7
Rose, H. Chapman, 223
Rosenberg, Ethel, 32, 46–47; atomic espionage, 81–82
Rosenberg, Julius, 17, 18, 31–32, 46–47, 78, 236; atomic espionage, 45, 56, 81–82; industrial espionage, 81n
Rosenfeld, Seth, 279n13
Roth, Andrew, 99, 100, 103, 104

Rowlett, Frank, 25, 26
Russell, Louis, 164
Russian American Club: FBI wiretapping, 69
Russian Center for the Preservation and Study of Documents of Recent History, 5
Russian People, 153n
Ryan, Sylvester, 88–89

SAC Letters, 12, 13, 253n9
Sager, E. R., 103
Salant, Alfred, 82
Salisbury, Harrison, 144
Salt, Waldo: FBI wiretapping, 59
Salt Lake Tribune, 218
Sarah Lawrence College, 113, 215
Scheidt, Edward, 180
Schevchenko, Andrei, 64, 65, 67, 73n, 74
Schlesinger, Arthur, Jr., 221
Schuster, Bernard, 55
Schweiker, Richard, 246–247
Scott, Adrian, 159, 159n
Scripps-Howard, 105
Secret Service, 190
Secret Service in Darkest Africa, 153n
Seeger, Pete, 226
Sefa, Leyla, 136–137
Seghers, Anna, 58
Semenov, Semen, 47, 48, 63, 65, 66, 67, 72
Senate Committee on Expenditures in Government, 132, 173
Senate Internal Security Subcommittee (SISS), 218–219, 221–223; and covert relations with FBI, 168, 202, 210–220; Harry Dexter White case, 107–108, 221–222
Service, John S., 99, 101n, 102n, 103, 105
Seventh Cross, 153n
Sex Deviate program, 177–179
Shalyapin, 48
Sharecroppers Union, 111
Shivers, Allen, 226
Signal Intelligence Service, 24–26
Silverman, Abraham George, 96, 97
Silvermaster, Nathan Gregory, 16, 23, 23n, 25, 29, 48, 53–54, 55, 80, 96, 131, 132; FBI counterintelligence, 77
Sinatra, Frank, 144
Smith, Edward, 73n
Smith, H. Allen, 160, 162
Smith Act, 32, 80
Sokolsky, George, 105
Song of Russia, 153n
Sourwine, Jay, 210–211, 222
Southern Christian Leadership Conference, 143
Southern Tenant Farmers Union, 111
Soviet Government Purchasing Commission, 16–17, 27n, 50–51, 64, 71; FBI break-in, 56
Soviet Union: code security, 45–46; espionage activities, 4–5, 7, 8, 15–32, 34–78, 81, 94–95, 235–237; funding of U.S. Communist Party, 57, 237
Spellman, Francis Cardinal, 147, 150
Spencer, Thomas, 39–40
Sputnik, 195
State Department, 98n
Steelman, John, 42, 87–88
Stennis, John, 207
Stern, Alfred, 19, 19n
Stettinius, Edward, 30, 38
Stevenson, Adlai, 144; FBI investigation of homosexual allegations, 179–186, 242

Stone, I. F., 27
Stone, John, 166
Stone, Victoria, 73n
Streitfeld, David, 282n37
Stripling, Robert, 121; covert relations with FBI, 122, 156–158; Hiss-Chambers case, 117–118
Sullivan, William, 201, 246
Summerfield, Arthur, 188
Surine, Don, 200–201; covert relations with FBI, 203

Taft, Robert, 171
Tamm, Edward, 111–112, 162; COMRAP, 94–95; John Cronin, 146, 147–148, 150–151
Tatlock, Jean: FBI wiretapping, 68–69
Taylor, Robert, 159
Temple University, 226
This Land Is Mine, 153n
Thomas, J. Parnell: covert relations with FBI, 156–164
Thornton, Dan, 227, 228, 229, 234
Through Embassy Eyes, 153n
Tolson, Clyde, 122, 162, 200, 201
Transport Workers Union, 111
Truman Harry, 107, 165, 210; *Amerasia* case, 101, 101n, 107–108; apparent "softness toward communism," 32–33, 35, 41–45, 170–171, 199, 215–217, 239; Coplon case, 88, 89n, 90; FBI counterintelligence, 11–12, 13; FBI reports, 142, 184–185; Hoey Committee, 174–176; Venona Project, 9–10, 89n; Harry Dexter White nomination, 41–42, 215–217, 216n; White House Security Survey, 101–102
Trumbo, Dalton, 59n, 165, 166
Twining, Nathan: Alsop matter, 196
Tydings, Millard, 171, 172–173

Uhse, Bode and Alma, 58
United Automobile Workers, 112
United Electrical Radio & Mechanical Workers of America, 112
United Mine Workers, 112
United Nations, 214
United Public Workers of America, 112
United States Chamber of Commerce, 147–148
University of California-Berkeley, 226; Radiation Laboratory, 49–50, 62–63
University of Wisconsin-Madison, 226

Vandenberg, Arthur, Jr.: allegations of homosexuality, 186–191
Vandenberg, Arthur, Sr., 39
Vardaman, James, 101
Vassiliev, Alexander, 4, 5, 12, 18–23, 31n; KGB records, 4–5, 86, 86n
Vaughan, Harry, 101n, 108
Vazzana, Nicholas, 121
Venona Project, 6–10, 15–18, 24–32, 34–35, 45, 47–48, 77–78, 80–83, 81n, 235–237
Vest, H. Grant, 229
Viertel, Berthold, 58
Vincent, John Carter, 31n, 98n
Vinson, Fred, 101
Vitale, Albert, 4
Voice of America, 203
Volodarsky, I. V., 86
Vyshinskij, Andrei, 30

Wahl, David: FBI wiretapping, 59, 164–167
Wallace, Henry, 85, 165–166
War Powers Act of 1941, 7
Warner, Jack, 159
Warner, Michael, 24, 25
Warren, Earl, 227
Washington Committee for Democratic Action, 118; FBI break-in, 112
Washington Post, 148
Waters, George, 200
Watson, Marvin, 186
Wechsler, Herbert, 113
Weigel, Helene, 58
Weinberg, Joseph, 49–50, 56, 62, 73
Weinstein, Allen, 4, 5, 6, 18–23, 28, 31n; KGB records, 4–5, 86, 86n
Weisband, William, 17, 18, 236
Western Union International, 7
Whearty, Raymond: Hiss grand jury, 115–116, 117–118, 127, 129, 130
Wherry, Kenneth, 172–173
White, Harry Dexter, 20n, 31n, 41–42; Brownell allegations, 215–217, 221–222; FBI wiretapping, 97, 240; grand jury testimony, 96–97
White, William Allen, 234n
White House Security Survey, 101–102, 268n25
Whitten, Jamie, 217
Wilder, Billy, 58
Williams, J. P., 218
Williams, Sydney, 228
Williams, Willard, 106
"Willie," 21–23, 56
Wilson, Lyle, 90–91
Winstead, William, 217
Wiretapping, 11, 34, 39, 42, 42n, 49, 54, 56, 57–59, 64, 68–69, 68n, 80, 84, 87, 88–90, 92–94, 95, 97, 98, 100, 101–102, 102n, 105–109, 112, 129, 130, 131, 164–167, 232–234, 239–241
Woetzel, Robert, 186
Wohlforth, Robert, 46
Woltman, Frederick, 105, 106
W. W. Norton, 212

Yalta Conference, 30, 236
Yeltsin, Boris, 5
York, Joseph, 17, 18

Zarubin, Vassili. *See* Zubilin, Vassili.
Zubilin, Elizabeta, 47–48, 63, 65, 75–76
Zubilin, Vassili, 50, 50n, 56, 62, 63, 64, 65–66, 74–75, 77, 93–94, 95, 95n, 237; departure from the United States, 53